THE
LAW FIRM
OF
PSYCHO
&
SATAN

BY

TRACY EDINGFIELD

NOTE: This is a work of fiction. All of the
characters, organizations, and events portrayed in
this novel are either products of the author's
imagination or are used fictitiously.

THE LAW FIRM OF PSYCHO & SATAN

ISBN-13: 978-0-9794215-8-7
ISBN-10: 0-9794215-8-6

Printed in the United States of America
Create Space edition / December 2016

Acknowledgements

I wish to acknowledge the following people, mostly attorneys with whom I worked, who have added to my life and my outlook:

Thomas C. McDowell, Eric Kidwell, Leah Gagne, Cindy Cleous, Ross Alexander, Mark White, Jake Scoby, Larry Maples, Mark Schoenhofer, and Don Lambdin. These are the lawyers I've known for years, the ones with whom I worked shoulder-to-shoulder with my career. I could always count on these people to tell it to me straight, even in the heat of battle. It's important the work we do; every case is crucial. Each one of these attorneys exemplifies the highest excellence which enables them to be the best in this field. For those who unravel problems others create, thank you. Without your honesty, intelligence, creativity, idealism, and strength, the world would be a much poorer place. You are warriors and knight gallants. This book is for you. Keep fighting the good fight.

Other Books by Tracy Edingfield

HIS SUNSHINE GIRL

A GOVERNESS' LOT

PRUDENCE

Chapter 1

Lucifer & Mrs. Cuttlebum

On my first day as a brand, spanking new lawyer, I dressed in my finest suit, which I picked up for half-price at a big box store. My smooth hair caught in a silver clasp my dad had given me for graduating college. Black ballet slippers completed the outfit.

With butterflies in my stomach, I entered Whilts & Hatdiff, P.A.

The lobby held two brown, respectable settees, a Bombay side table with cabriolet legs, and the obligatory office fern, its brown ends drooping as if it had already lost hope. Framed reproductions of the Declaration of Independence and the United States Constitution were displayed in expensive gilded frames, ensuring nobody would read them. A tattered oriental rug lay prostrate on the floor, abandoning ambitions of grandeur. The atmosphere smelled stale. That odor, malevolent for unclear reasons, would linger—somehow I knew that.

"Hi! Cooper, isn't it?" Her white teeth gleamed against her ebony skin, causing me to marvel at the stark contrast.

I approached the rounded, stainless steel console and nodded to the African-American receptionist who sat behind it. She was in her thirties, wearing sleek hair with tendrils plastered into curlicues onto the sides of her cheeks. Her dress was colorful and every bit of "off the rack" as mine.

My chest tightened. I didn't want to cultivate friendships or ties. I'd learned my lessons the hard way; once bitten, twice shy—but three times? I'd be an idiot. Sticking out my hand, I shook hers, keeping my voice cool and distant.

Distance was important.

"Cooper Bach," I said.

The wattage of her smile dimmed, but she said, "Melinda Jackson. Tanny and Sam aren't here yet, so go on to your office. You're to go to court this morning on an Order in Aid. I'll bring you Cuttlebum's file."

I doddered, not having a clue where my office was. "Sure."

Her head jerked up and she flashed a pink palm down the corridor. "First door on the left."

An aisle ran down the center of the rectangular building with smaller offices flanking its sides. Cracker box design, nothing architecturally interesting about the building. The décor wasn't interesting; rather than impress, it chose to baffle the occupants. An art deco console table detracted from the framed historical documents, but boasted a thin stack of outdated magazines. A chunky wooden mirror hung above the art deco table. Walking down the corridor, I came to another secretary's desk. It's a wobbly little thing. Upon closer inspection, one leg is propped with a can of tuna.

"Hello, Charlie," I muttered.

Behind the desk, a photocopier, scanner, and printer hum along, noisy as they devoured electricity. Cables hung from the drop-down ceiling tiles, resembling dead, plucked geese in a Chinese food market.

There's that smell again.

"Oh joy!"

I open the door—"Shit. Shit on a Ritz cracker." My office was gray, gloom and despair in a monochromatic range. Gray walls, carpet, and desk.

"Geezus, it was more welcoming in the morgue."

Recalling my recent visit with Gloria, my fingertips tingled, as if they once again touched her cold body. The sound of blood dripping onto the floor echoed in my ears; I smelled stainless steel, lavender perfume, and white wine. That's the scent of Death, all right. Separate smells which don't mingle together.

"Focus." With a shaky breath, I plunked into my chair, the seat cushion so rigid, it jarred my back. I tried to adjust the seat's height, but the lever didn't work.

"Shit again."

It didn't take long to inventory my office. One client chair, one desk, this shitty chair. My office was void of accoutrements, garbed in a sullen veil of resentment. "Well, fucking la-de-dah fantastic."

Melinda leaned against the door jamb, holding an inch-thick folder in one hand and a vase of bright Gerber daisies in the other. She blinked several times, her face a careful study in blankness.

"Oh, I'm sorry. I didn't mean to…" What could I say? That I didn't mean to accurately describe this shithole of an office? That I hadn't meant to speak out loud? That it had become a habit of mine lately?

She offered me the vase of flowers. "These are for you. I meant to have them on your desk before you got here, but I didn't make it. Sorry."

"Oh. Thanks."

"Never mind." Melinda set the vase on my desk.

"Thanks. Much better than peace lilies."

"Yeah."

"You mentioned a Cuddleson case?"

"Cuttlebum," Melinda corrected. With a frown, she handed me a folder.

"Docket's at nine o'clock?"

"Yes." She opened the file, showed me a questionnaire then explained Mrs. Cuttlebum should fill it out. "We have a judgment for $1,428 against her. Have her tell you where she banks, what money she has, furs, jewelry—anything we can attach and apply to the judgment. Bring the questionnaire back. I'll do the rest—you just sign the garnishment order."

I closed the folder. "Okay, that sounds easy enough."

Between Melinda's finely-plucked brows, a fret formed.

"What?"

Hearing the irritation in my voice, Melinda shook her head, said, "Nothing."

"I'm sorry." To my embarrassment, that lame apology of mine hung in the stale air. The receptionist had already left.

Melinda drove me to the courthouse, pulling near the concrete steps then sent me off with a cheery salute, showing she wasn't the kind of person to harbor a grudge.

Like some skittering virgin, I sat in the peanut gallery waiting for Court. Sitting on the interior side of the pony wall, or bar, I took pride in knowing I'd earned the right to cross it. For seven years I sacrificed, living off generic brand foods while racking up staggering loan amounts. I sweated through three days of cumulative testing for the grueling finish. Now I'd been launched into the strata of the elite, well-educated, and debt-ridden.

Nine suits milled about the pit. All men. No women. Eight of the nine suits were white, middle-aged men with shiny pates. The ninth man was also white, but he was trim, attractive, and youngish. An Italian leather belt cinched his slim waist. Either he was an avid runner or did cocaine. Blithely, I skipped over the threshold of Dante's Inferno, catapulting myself into hell.

As I sat, watching the Suits and running my hands over the hem of my skirt, I sensed their curiosity, but nobody said 'hello.' They'd glance in my direction, but never spoke.

"All rise!" The bailiff called.

Scurrying sounds filled the courtroom. Everyone stood for His Honor. Judge Powers and his ego entered from the side door nearly simultaneously. The corpulent judge took the bench and adjusted his five hundred dollar designer eyeglasses. He took his time settling into his leather chair then adjusted some pens, papers, and Post-It notes on his desktop.

The writing instruments were placed in right angles to the paper products. Those anal retentive tendencies would have delighted Dr. Freud. Here sat a veritable treasure trove of repression.

Judge Powers leaned back, his robe draping his rotund body. He shook his sleeves, embellished with velvet Order of the Coif stripes, meant to impress. It did. He cast his supercilious gaze upon his fiefdom then nodded to the bailiff, finally prepared to pass judgment on lesser mortals.

Pulsating waves of boredom flooded the courtroom as Judge Powers read the case names from the docket. There were other things he'd rather do. I knew he felt disdain for this array of unwashed citizenry. Did any of them appreciate what a pain in the ass they were? As he called off the docket, his lips puckered in disapproval. Sometimes, he'd lowered his glasses to stab a litigant with an angry stare. Once, he harrumphed then scribbled a note and slapped the Post-It into the official court file. A lawyer involved in that case, one of the nine, shuddered.

I didn't blame him.

He barked, "Law Firm of Whilts and Hatdiff versus James Cuttlebum and Eileen Cuttlebum."

I rose, praying the starch in my knees would hold me upright. Craning my neck, I looked for the defendants, Jimmy and Eileen Cuttlebum. Clutching the legal file close to my bosom, the feel of the manila folder calmed me. I breathed in and exhaled, hoping I wouldn't irritate Judge Powers.

Neatly printed at the top of the folder was the defendants' surname, then first name, followed by the case number and the words, 'Debt Collection.' I opened the file, searching for the Postal Service's green card, which showed Return of Service.

From the corner of my eye, I caught a small, labored movement. An old woman rose from the pew, her bones creaking in protest. Mrs. Cuttlebum's joints crackled like cereal drowned in milk. She straightened her hunched shoulders, but they sagged in the next heartbeat. Her cheeks were hollowed, her eye sockets sunken. Atop her steel-colored curls perched a knitted toilet paper cozy. I recognized it from having seen one as a child in a church bazaar. The lenses in her glasses were thick and so heavy they left red indentations where the bridge rested on her nose. Scores of bruises ranging from purple to lime trailed her arms. Her legs were clad in heavy nylon stockings, molecularly similar to the structure of some petroleum by-product.

"Here." Her frail, uneven voice broke the stunned silence of the courtroom as her liver-spotted hands clutched a brown, worn satchel.

"Double Doodoo Dog Shit." I muttered the longtime phrase my sister and I bantered around, having been struck with the epiphany that my employers had smoked me.

Collectively, the nine lawyers stared at me as if I were a monster. Quickly, they glanced away, as if their retinas stung from the sight of my gorgonesque existence. If I ever thought I'd be welcome amongst this group, I could forget those delusions.

"Geezus, does Tanny want me to mug her?" My hand trembled as I wiped lines of tension from my face.

Law school didn't prepare me for this.

Judge Powers' gaze stabbed me, piercing my shroud of unreality. He lowered his glasses a fraction, just enough to convey his disdain. "And you are?"

"Cooper Bach. New associate with Whilts & Hatdiff."

That announcement injected another megavolt into the already-electrified atmosphere of the courtroom. Tension spun out as *tut, tuts* murmured and despairing heads shook. The Judge wrinkled his nose, the only part of his fleshy face which moved, like he'd discovered a turd wrapped in a silk ribbon on his clearly compensating-for-something-desk.

The khaki-covered bailiff offered a small cough, a tiny island of neutrality.

With a heavy sigh of disgust directed toward me, the judge asked the defendant, "Are you ready for the examination, Mrs. Cuttlebum?"

"Could... could I have a minute, please, Your Honor?" I asked, raising my hand, as if I were still some geeky 1-L.

Judge Powers pressed his double chins against his throat. A pale mound of flesh between lip and chest quivered with gelatinous movements, but he stated the matter would be placed on second call then continued reading the remainder of the docket.

"Ma'am, can you follow me, please? Let's find somewhere a little more private," I invited the old woman.

I led her from the high-ceiling courtroom down a dim hallway, peeking into doors along the way. We came to a suitable room for a conference. I squeezed my slim frame past a stack of cardboard boxes and motioned for Mrs. Cuttlebum to take the chair. Carefully, I set the collections file on the boxes, using it as a temporary desk.

"Jimmy paid Mrs. Whilts. He told me he did. I have receipts." She opened her satchel with gnarled hands and scooped some slips of paper, offering them to me with her claw-like fingers.

"Where's Jimmy?"

"What's that you say?" She touched the corner of her ear, palm outward.

"WHERE'S JIMMY?"

Her aged voice vibrated. "Who's Jimmy? Why, he's my grandson. Got the divorce when his wife left him with the little one, Brandon."

"Oh." I scratched my head, hoping to find a way to handle this. I got nothing. Gloria must have taken Jesus out for lunch because no heavenly aid rained down like manna, either.

I studied Mrs. Cuttlebum's receipts; they were for money orders. Some paid the gas bill, some the water or trash. Four receipts for $75 had no name on the stub, but those payments didn't match the firm's ledger of accounts receivable, so I couldn't credit them.

"Were these payments made to Whilts & Hatdiff?" I asked, trying to justify giving her the benefit, nevertheless.

"What?"

I took a deep breath then said louder, "WERE THESE PAID TO TANNY WHILTS?"

"What?" She looked at the receipts in my hand, as if she were surprised to see them.

"WERE THESE PAID TO MRS. WHILTS?"

"I don't know." She dabbed a tissue against her upper lip. Her liver-spotted hands shook, but the trembling was due to agedness, not nerves.

"WHERE IS JIMMY?"

"Dead."

For the first time, I looked into her eyes. Her watery, clouded-by-cataract eyes.

"Dead," she said. "Died last June. Motorcycle crash."

She fished through the papers, extracted a crinkled newspaper clipping.

Her grandson Jimmy's obituary.

I groaned.

Words of condolences half-formed, but I couldn't get them past my lips. Swallowing freed the constriction in my throat, but it took me three gulps before I could mumble I was sorry for her loss. I needed to end this and leave. Gathering the receipts, I returned them to her satchel and handed it to the old woman. "WE'RE DONE."

She rested her bony, freckled hand on top of mine and murmured, "Jimmy was a good boy, said he paid Mrs. Whilts."

"I'm sure, Mrs. Cuttlebum," I said, hating myself for getting sucked into this uncomfortable situation.

She left and I sat for a long while, staring at the cinderblock wall. Flipping through the file, I found the original fee agreement with Jimmy's signature and his grandma's as a guarantor. I puffed out some air, scrubbed my face, and inwardly cursed that the solution was so clear. Life's like that, I suppose—distinguishing right from wrong isn't hard. It's the doing part that's tough. I un-pegged the papers and tore up the fee agreement then dumped the shreds into the wastebasket. For good measure, I ferreted out a can of soda pop, poured its remainder over the pieces then let it drop back into the wastebasket.

Once I returned to the courtroom, a smarmy judge informed me I'd missed second call.

"No problem. If I can't find a written fee agreement, do I have to vacate the judgment or dismiss the case?"

"I'd dismiss," he said. "That's not like Tanny—taking judgment against the guarantor without a written fee agreement."

"Is that so?" I threw the question out there as I inspected my nails.

"Probably can't collect against Jimmy's estate, if he even had one, eh?" Judge Powers tapped his gavel three times. "Case dismissed—how's that for you?"

I shrugged, not caring. "Pretty crappy, I guess."

Back at the office, Tanny was pissed when I told her Powers had dismissed the case.

"Why?"

"Couldn't find the fee agreement and he set aside the judgment to the guarantor."

"No fee agreement? Are you sure?" She frowned. "I almost always have a guarantor sign."

"Is that so?" I asked, repeating myself. I didn't appreciate being sent to rough up an AARP member, but I also didn't feel comfortable lying to my boss. Like my office, it was a shitty spot. On the whole, I figured her sin was worse than mine so managed to squelch those pestering niggles of guilt.

Tanny tilted her head, staring at me for long minutes.

I remained mum, now understanding why Melinda had been so hesitant in sending me off to the docket this morning. It wouldn't make any difference if I told Tanny how pathetic Jimmy's grandma looked in her lopsided, toilet paper cozy.

"Judge Powers has it in for me," Tanny spat out. "Screws me over on fees whenever he can.

"Well, there you go," I said, playing into her paranoia.

Throughout that day, I'd catch my boss staring at me. That suspicious glint in her eyes didn't bode well for my future as their associate. Ignoring those stony glares, I promised not to do a decent thing for the rest of the month. I had too much to lose to cross swords with Lucifer. She'd hired me as her associate. The least I could do was pay her lip service.

Chapter 2

Ted Danveldt, Barkeeper

Thank God I found a bar in this town!

I launched out of my beat-up Ford Festiva and dashed through the rain, needing to outrun my horrible day. The bar's neon sign beckoned me. I wrenched the door open and burst through it. As I tumbled over the threshold, laughter bubbled from the depths of my belly—well, whadyaknow? I could have sworn I'd forgotten how to laugh.

'Good' was too mild to describe how I felt to be away from my crappy office and out of my crowded apartment. Both were depressing for different reasons. At home, boxes waited to be sorted, but I couldn't face that. All that stuff weighed me down and I wasn't going to deal with it this week. Maybe next week, maybe not—who knew?

I smoothed blonde, stray hairs back into my ponytail then tightened the belt of my designer brand knock-off trench coat. The coat wasn't lined and the rain chilled me. I rubbed my palms together, trying to get warm. As I did so, I noticed my nails were shot. I really needed to do something about that. God only knows where my clippers and file were…

"Focus, Coop." I shook off those trivial concerns and forced myself to pay attention to my surroundings. A single girl, entering an unfamiliar establishment, couldn't afford to be lackadaisical. I had to pull my head out of my ass.

The bar, "Tipping Cows," was painted in black and white splotches with hunter green accents. I wondered if the decorator hadn't been infected with Mad Cow's disease, but the tables and floors were clean. The place smelled of hops and welcome and, by God, that was good enough for me. It sure as hell beat that odor of the law office, which I'd finally pinned as fragrant, dead dreams.

"Hey."

I turned to see who greeted me. It was the bartender. With brown hair, brown eyes which sparkled with humor, he was one deliciously-wrapped package. It didn't hurt, either, that his t-shirt stretched across a broad chest and the sleeves bulged from muscular shoulders. Man, he was hot.

And leaning against the counter, smiling and not too concerned that I'd been checking him out.

My face heated from embarrassment. It'd been a while since I'd felt any sexual interest. Longer than that when I'd last had sex. Nervous, I stammered out a hello before realizing that he was so busy checking *me* out, he hadn't heard my lame-ass greeting.

Suddenly and for reasons I didn't understand, I was pissed off. "Cheese and rice!"

"What?"

I shook my head, unable to respond without wanting to smack the bartender. Which is absurd, really. Wasn't it? Slug a guy who checked you out after you gave him the look-over? What the hell was wrong with me?

"Hey, I don't recognize your face and I'm pretty sure I'd remember it."

I stared at him before muttering, "Unbelievable. Un-fucking-believable."

"What?" he asked for the second time, clearly flummoxed.

I pinched the bridge of my nose and closed my eyes as I explained, "Look, I know your type. You're a player. And I hate players so just don't talk to me, all right?"

I glanced out the window. Rain poured down.

The silence stretched uncomfortably until he said, "Relax. Watch TV, if you want—I won't bother you."

"Great. Fine by me."

He said. "Fine."

"Fine." I nodded, just to prove I meant it.

Taking a deep breath, I found a small table beneath the TV and went to it. As I removed my wet, chilly coat, I sent him a sideways look. His gaze hadn't missed one of my movements. Did he not get it?

"Don't come on to me."

He chuckled. "I won't. Not until you ask. Nicely."

"Look, I don't mean to come across as…"

"Pissy? Bitchy? Hard-ass?"

I glared at him, trying not to grin as I spoke as sternly as I could. "Aggravating, but I really don't need the hassle tonight. I've had the worse beginning day of a career."

The smile slipped from his face. "I'm sorry to hear that. How about a beer on the house?"

"That'd be great. Thanks."

He poured a draft and brought it to my table, setting it down and backing away with his palms held up in a decidedly defensive posture.

"Ha ha," I said. "Very funny."

His mouth twitched, but he turned back to the bar. I stayed him by touching his forearm briefly. "So…you're not going to bug me, right?"

He looked at my hand until I withdrew it and said, "You, lady, are one large inconsistency."

"Promise me," I said, refusing to be swayed.

He held three fingers in scout formation. "I promise."

Seeing the familiar salute, I snorted then scoffed, "Like you're a frickin' Boy Scout."

"I was!" he protested, returning to his post behind the bar.

"What if I didn't want a beer?"

He sent me a warning look. "Stop being a pain in the ass. Now, do you really want a glass of wine or something else?"

"No." I lowered my gaze, embarrassed at my bad manners. "Thanks."

His warm chuckle sounded lovely after the day I'd had. "You really ARE contrary! So, tell me—I'm Ted Danveldt, by the way, owner of this establishment— what made your day so lousy?"

"I practiced law."

"Ah." The brow lowered, as if he comprehended a multitude of facts in those three simple words. The recognition could have been insulting if it weren't so tragically true.

He turned on the television and flipped through the channels until I waved him to stop. The program was some cooking show. I don't know the first thing about boiling water, so again my mood mystified me.

"What's your name?"

"Noneofyourbizwax."

He roared with laughter, shook his head then greeted other patrons who'd just arrived.

I dug into the small stainless steel pail of peanuts, snarfing them up as if I were half-starved. Maybe I was.

There comes a point, however, when you start to relax that you can feel the tenuous hold on your emotions slipping away. Right here in the Tipping Cows bar, sipping a cold beer, it occurred to me that I shouldn't relax. Lowering my guard might not be for the best, so I searched for shelter. I found that hazy fog had filtered my brain these past few weeks. I wrapped it around me like a pillow and all the hard edges of life softened to a murky, surreal plane.

Without attending, my eyes watched the cooking show and a distant part of my brain wondered how I could stare at a screen and not see anything. This detachment happened all the time anymore. Tonight, I embraced it and sank inside the insulating layers of oblivion, glad to be numb.

Picking up a double peanut, I tossed it into my mouth. My tongue played with it then I spit it out and cracked it open. One peanut inside a shell meant for two. Apparently, Mother Nature was a sneaky little trickster who enjoyed gypping me.

"Little bitch."

Tears came, which I blinked away. The television cook nattered in her cheerful tone, reminding her viewers not to make the fundamental mistake of scorching the butter. I wanted to grip her by the throat and yell, 'Shut the fuck up!'

Maybe I was being pissy.

Some suits entered the bar, which I recognized from earlier in the day. These were the lawyers from Judge Powers' courtroom, the ones who looked at me like I was Typhoid Mary. "Great."

"Hey."

Startled, I looked up, unaware the youngest male had approached my table. "Hi."

"I'm Matt Bearus. Can we join you?" He gestured the others to come sit down. As his hand moved, I caught a flash of a gold band. His wedding ring.

"Le-de-dah fantastic," I mumbled.

"What?" His blond head bent toward mine.

Speaking louder, I lied, "Sure, that'd be great."

The other lawyers sat and removed their jackets, loosened their ties. One pulled out a pack of cigarettes.

"I started early." Raising my beer, I made a salute.

Two laughed, as if I'd made a joke.

They were trying too hard and I wasn't trying at all. Matt asked, "Is that your first beer?"

Figuring this wasn't any of his business, I lied again. "Nope, it's my fourth."

Frowning into my mug, I wondered when I'd developed this habit of lying. First about the Cuttlebum fee agreement, now about beer intake? What the fuck was going on in my head? Maybe later, I'd figure it out. Maybe not.

"Fourth? Impressive." Matt whistled for the bartender, who'd overheard my remark and scowled at me. "Ted, bring us three pitchers."

"So, you're Cooper Bach, eh? Work for Tanny Whilts and Sam Hatdiff?"

"Yeah. Today was my first day."

"And they sent you to an Order in Aid docket to shake down my old Sunday school teacher." He whistled. "I'm Luke. Luke Winston."

"Yeah. Nice to meet you, Luke."

The smoker was named Gary, who had a weak handshake. Nicotine stained his fingers yellow, but his teeth were an impossible shade of white, advertising they were either caps or bleached or both. But compared to James, who was middle aged and balding, Gary didn't look half bad.

Matt steered the conversation. We all talked about law school. They talked about cases and judges. Soon the discussion descended into some plain, old-fashioned gossip. Rather astonished to discover men talked like a gaggle of hens, I learned who was getting a divorce, who cheated with his secretary, who was sleeping with the judge, and who filed bankruptcy in another town to avoid the embarrassment. It wasn't a big town; eventually, I'd meet some of these characters. I wasn't sure if I'd be glad or not, after hearing such details about their personal lives.

"So, you'll be specializing in divorce law, eh?" Luke asked when a lull occurred.

"I guess."

"Funny thing about divorces. Ask a client why he got married and why he's divorcing, you'll find a lot of overlap."

"Who said that?" Gary flicked the ash from his cigarette.

"I did, you idiot."

"No." He made an irritated gesture and spread ashes across the table. Mechanically, he brushed them to the floor and continued without missing a beat. "I mean, who said it originally?"

Luke rolled his eyes. "You want me to cite my source? For fuck's sake, Gary."

The men glared at each other until Luke chuckled. "All right, you asshole. Probably Mignon McLaughlin."

"Who's that?"

"How the fuck should I know? You asked, I told you. Now shut up about it."

Gary refilled everyone's mug, pouring from the pitcher as he considered this advice. "Probably Mignon McLaughlin? Then you're not sure? Can't be a direct quote then."

"I paraphrased, okay? Now quit busting my chops." Luke snapped.

"They're always doing that—squabbling," Matt explained. "Like an old married couple."

James thumped the table, signaling silence. "Enough. I propose a toast."

"Okay. What to?" I asked.

"To our clients, magnificent bastards that they are."

Several agreed. "Hear, hear."

A silence broken by sounds of slurping followed.

Turning to Luke, I asked him to explain what he'd meant by the two lists.

"Take the guy who wants to marry a stay-at-home wife. Very traditional, conservative. He likes having her at home until he decides to scratch his itch with the young thing at the office. Now he wants to ditch the wife, who's suddenly a lazy bum, sucking him dry. He doesn't want to pay alimony—"

"Who does?" Gary asked.

Matt nodded. "Sure, but the wife's been out of the workforce for ten or fifteen years. Who's going to hire her? She's got no game, no skills. Can't compete in the work force."

"Or against the pretty, young girls who will screw her husband's brains out, wedding vows notwithstanding." Luke shook his head.

"Ouch. She's screwed," I popped a peanut into my mouth.

"Course she is." Gary dusted the table top, brushing off the peanut shells. "Works both ways, you know. The girl marries her high school sweetheart who was such a great partier then gets surprised when he cheats on her. Christ, what did she think was going to happen?"

"Marriage is the leading cause of divorce," Matt said with mock severity.

"In both instances you've cited, the guy can't keep his zipper shut," I said.

Gary and James looked at each other then gave me a pitying glance.

"Most guys can't," James explained gently.

Luke grinned then waved off Gary and James' phony solicitude. "But the point is if you're looking for grounds for divorce, they're pretty easy to find. The trick to avoiding divorce court is to look for the grounds for marriage." He glared at Gary and acknowledged, "Robert Anderson."

"Don't know him." Bored, Gary drank his beer. After a few swallows, he frowned at Luke and said, "Why can't you just quote Shakespeare? Somebody everybody knows?"

Exasperated, he muttered, "You're an idiot. Not everyone knows Shakespeare."

"I may be an idiot, but I know Shakespeare."

I glanced at Matt, who was smiling as if to ask, 'See? What did I say? Old married couple.'

"Still, Coop," James said, "Practicing divorce law sucks. It's watching a train wreck every day and not being able to stop it."

"Just when you think nobody can be this stupid, in walks your next client and proves you wrong."

Around 10:00 o'clock, Gary stood up and said he needed to get home. He made his goodbyes and left a twenty dollar tip for Ted.

Twenty dollar tips weren't in my budget.

Matt, James, and Luke left generous tips, too.

James asked if I was okay to drive myself home and I said, yeah. Watching me, he guessed the cause of my embarrassment and slipped another twenty beneath the pitcher. "I'll cover your tip. I remember what it's like to be fresh out of law school, broke as hell."

"Oh, no, that's all right—"

"Forget it," he said.

"Thanks," I mumbled.

"Nice to meet you, Coop. See you around." James whistled as he trailed Matt, who waved goodbye from the door.

Luke hovered, standing at the table and giving me a considering look, as if he were trying to decide whether to tell me something.

"Yes, Luke?"

He shook off the brown study he'd fallen into and said, "You seem like a nice person, Cooper. Watch yourself, okay?"

"Watch for what?"

"Watch out for Tanny. She's a real bitch. Part-psycho." He shrugged. "It's no secret. If you need to talk, call me."

He handed me his business card then scribbled his cell number on the back.

"Okay," I said, thanking him.

"Goodnight."

"Goodnight." I watched him leave, feeling less lonely than I had when I'd entered the bar. Being around the other lawyers made me feel...like somebody had my back.

Taking my purse, I went to the ladies' room and studied my reflection for the first time in weeks. My cheek bones protruded so that my face was pale and gaunt. Mentally, I promised myself I'd start wearing make-up.

And stop being pissy to bartenders.

I had to apologize to Ted. Just because I'd had a rough day—a rough year—I'd been rude to the guy. From the amount of tips he received, the Suits held Ted in high regard. It was a small community; it'd be better if I patched things up.

"Here goes nothing, Cooper Bach." Bracing myself for the confrontation, I squared my shoulders and marched from the bathroom—walking straight into the bartender.

"Geezus!" In the crash I dropped my purse.

"Sorry," he said.

"Were you lurking out here?"

A single brow lifted as he asked, "Lurking?"

I shrugged his hands off my shoulders.

His brown eyes narrowed at the rebuff.

"Sorry." I sighed then slumped. "I meant to come out and apologize for my earlier rudeness."

He folded his arms across his body, just as frustrated with me as I was with him. "So?"

"So?"

"So, I'm waiting for my apology."

I snapped, "Fine. I apologize."

"Want to give it another go?"

The absurdity of the situation struck me and the corners of my mouth twitched. Glancing at his face, his irritation had left, but the expression which replaced it scared me to death.

"Bye." Without breaking stride, I snatched my coat off the back of my chair and headed for the door, flinging it over my head. Outside the bar I dashed through the pouring rain to my car, stepping into a puddle and sliding across the pavement. "Fucking fantastic." My black ballet slippers were completely soaked.

At my car, I paused, searching for my keys, only to discover I had no purse. "Shit!"

For the second time in as many minutes, I turned and collided with Ted.

He thrust my purse at me. "You forgot this, Miss Pissy."

He held an umbrella over my head, protecting me from the worse of the downpour.

"Oh." I shuffled aside and he stepped into the space as we shared the umbrella.

His eyes were warm, the color of caramel. That single brow lifted again, reminding me that I'd been staring. Giving myself a mental shake, I searched through my purse trying to find my car keys. My breaths came in gulps and I wiped my wet cheeks.

"Are you all right?"

"I'm not crying."

"Of course not." His tone belied his words.

"I'm just exhausted." I jostled my purse. "Where the hell are my keys?"

He handed the umbrella to me and without arguing, I handed him my purse.

Deftly, he found the keys and unlocked my car door. He opened it, gently moving me out of the way to do so then helped me sit down.

"You're okay to drive, aren't you? I could swear you didn't drink that much." One of his hands rested on the door frame, the other held the umbrella. His body blocked the wind and rain and it felt nice to pretend I existed in this small, protected pocket.

"Yeah. Yeah, I'm okay." I'd spoken the refrain so many times before, it'd become second nature.

Yes, those eyes were definitely caramel-colored.

He leaned down and kissed me. His mouth brushed mine twice, maybe three times, as soft as a butterfly's wings.

My fingertips flew to my lips where tiny flames had erupted.

"Go," he said. Without another word, he jogged back to the bar, dodging puddles. I watched the red dot of his umbrella jounce his progress.

Staring into nothing, I sat there momentarily. Something big had just happened. Something shifted inside me, like that tight little ball in the pit of my stomach had begun to roll and gather momentum. I had a sudden flash of insight where my anger was coming from—that ball, which had been set into motion, dripped rage in its trail. The pieces of my broken heart were reforming, coalescing into a new pattern.

It frightened me. That's why I ran from Ted, why I was—what had he called it? Miss Pissy. In the early days following Gloria's death, I sought out the numbness of the fog. Perhaps, like some opiate addict, I'd clung too tightly to it.

As I drove home, I mourned another loss. Without being told, I knew the brain fog had been a blessing and that life was very much going to suck without it there to blunt the pain of losing my sister, Gloria. Now that brain fog was leaving me, too, and I mourned its loss. Was that why I cried as I drove home in the rain?

Chapter 3

Mr. Flotaki Abrams

Tanny was still annoyed with me. She'd said 'Good morning' but not in any way that could be interpreted as cheerful. She wore high heels and a purple shantung silk dress. Even the clang of her golden bracelets sounded irritated. Looking like she'd stepped out of an exclusive clothing line catalog, Tanny could have been a model. Already tall, she insisted heels gave her an edge and she exploited it to intimidate others during sticky negotiation sessions. She laughed at my ballet slippers, still damp from last evening's foray across the flooded parking lot.

Sitting with one hip propped on Melinda's desk, Tanny cast an assessing gaze over my linen dress, another outfit purchased on clearance in a department store. Tutting, she rolled her eyes, then gave a conspiratorial look to the receptionist. "What's to be done with that one?"

"She'll learn," Melinda replied.

I clamped my lips shut, determined to purchase a designer suit and rub her nose in it. Then I recalled my strict, anemic budget. That designer suit wouldn't be happening anytime in the near future. Maybe not for another year or two.

"I'm meeting Mr. Abrams. Come sit in on the appointment," Lucifer ordered, unwinding her long legs and rising from Melinda's desk.

"Now?"

She didn't answer. My question, I think, was too stupid to merit a reply. "This custody battle could be worth ten grand if we play our cards right. Abrams is good at paying his bill. Gotta love clients like that, don't we, Mel?"

"You bet, boss." Without looking up, the woman continued typing on her keyboard.

"Whatcha working on?" I whispered to Melinda, forgetting my earlier resolutions to try not to befriend anybody.

"Billings," she whispered back. Then she gave me a wink.

That made me grin.

I turned, following the silken-clad devil to her office. "What do you want me to do?"

She used an envelope opener to rip into her mail. Waving it around the room, she replied, "Take notes. Research topics. Flesh out arguments."

"Take notes, look for topics to research, flesh out the issues." I nodded, then referred to yesterday's assignment from her husband/partner. "What about the *Bronski* motion Sam wanted me to draft?"

"Sure, you should do that, but *after* we meet with Ed. If you run out of time, work through lunch," she offered.

Lucifer's pet client, Mr. Abrams, was a meaty businessman covered in body hair and wearing a torn t-shirt that was too-tight. He topped it off with a navy windbreaker. His dark eyes, closely set, lent him a villainous look. Stubble dotted his jawline. More than a days' worth. When he removed the windbreaker, he belched, and the hair on his forearms spiked. It moved, swaying in the wind, like a flotaki rug hoisted on a flag pole. His hello was a clammy, painful handshake, the whiff of the last thing he ate still lingering near.

I didn't like him. And I didn't know anyone who would. He was that kind of a guy. A real asshole.

My role was more stenographer than anything else. The attorney/client interview between Psycho and Flotaki could have been scripted for a play. Only thing, I couldn't figure out if this was supposed to be a comedy or a tragedy.

"Me and Louisa—you remember her—you did the divorce—what was that? One? Two years ago?"

Tanny corrected him, "Eight months ago. Joint custody. Property division weighed heavily in your favor. Short-term marriage. Nasty child support obligation per the state guidelines."

"Yeah," Flotaki spat. "Four Hundred Fifty frickin' dollars a month!"

"On the income you DID report. They totally missed your unreported income, which is pretty substantial. Her attorney should have been more aggressive on that issue, but it was a lucky break for us."

"Yeah, that Louisa is always asking for more money."

"For what?" Tanny boggled.

If you've never seen the devil affronted, it's hilarious. Despite my initial dislike for Flotaki, the man was amusing. I had to bite the insides of my cheeks to keep from smiling.

"Oh, you know." He waved his hand. "School lunches, field trips, Traylor's dance costumes—stuff like that."

"You don't give it to her, do you?"

"Sometimes it's hard to say no." He shrugged.

"I can't believe she does that. How low can you get? I mean, really! That's what child support is for. Don't let her hassle you," she scolded.

If Flotaki paid the actual amount he owed, based on his real income, perhaps his ex wouldn't hassle him for more dough? Just a thought. I glanced at Tanny. What a windbag.

Flotaki handed her a few sheets of paper. Tanny rifled through them, scanning them quickly before handing them to me.

Looking up from them, her gaze narrowed on him and her lips tightened. "So why does she want supervised visitation now?"

He wiped his shiny upper lip.

After a beat of staring at her non-responsive client, she says, "You're still screwing her, aren't you?"

His tubby gut lifted with his heavy sigh. "Yeah."

"Does Caroline know?"

Frowning, I ask, "Who's Caroline?"

Flotaki glares me into silence.

Her lips curving in displeasure, Tanny tells Mr. Abrams, "Don't mind her. She's only my associate. She won't bother us anymore."

"Oh. I get it. I'm supposed to be quiet."

Together, they craned their heads toward me, blistering me with contemptuous looks.

I gulp. "Sorry."

"Louisa's still a sweet tail. You know how she is. Those big titties…" His eyes half-closed as he lost himself in reminisces. His hands spread as if he were cupping his ex-wife's boobs.

I shifted in my seat, more than a little creeped out.

"For God's sake! Does Caroline know? About you and Louisa?"

"God, no!"

Tanny chuckled. "If Caroline finds out, you'll be headed for divorce number two, though, am I right?"

"Yeah, and Caroline's gonna cost me shitloads more than Louisa ever dreamed about."

"So what's the problem?"

"Louisa's threatening to tell Caroline about me and her."

Well, maybe Louisa wasn't such a dummy, after all.

Meanwhile, this little pearl landed with the force of napalm, destroying a forest. "That witch!" Tanny said.

"I know."

"So Louisa is essentially blackmailing you? Wanting more child support so she doesn't spill the beans to Carolina, eh?"

"Yeah, that skanky little bitch." Hearing his attorney summarize it added a couple of notches to Flotaki's Indignation Register.

Tanny grabbed the documents back from me, flipping to the second page. "Right here. See?" Flashing the paragraph at me, as if I could read it, she nodded. "Louisa says the children's aren't safe when they're with you in the shop. That you're leaving them alone for a long time around dangerous machinery. Yada, yada."

"I know." His shoulders dropped in relief as he discovered his attorney understood the nasty plight he'd found himself in. "Well, she ain't gonna blackmail me. If she can't afford the kids, then I'll just take them and raise them."

He followed up with that threat by cracking his knuckles.

I flipped back through the original filing papers, trying to find the names and ages of the kids.

Tanny clucked sympathetically for poor Mr. Abrams. "You were wise to come to me. Louisa could have played you, taken advantage of your generous nature. But you didn't let that happen. You were smart." She stood, walked around her desk, and sat behind it. She moved the keyboard closer to her, pounded out another fee agreement and spoke. "We have to fight fire with fire. She drew first blood by filing that motion, opening everything up again. Has to go in to mediation—you know the drill. Just don't agree to anything you don't want. Tell her you'll take the kids, she can see them a couple evenings during the week and every other weekend. That oughta convince her not to fuck with you anymore."

Mr. Abrams glowed with happiness—or that was the perspiration causing his face to shine?

"Um...sorry to interrupt," I said, "but what were the names and ages of the children? I can't find it in the original file."

Rising from his chair, Flotaki ignored my question and addressed Tanny. "How much for the retainer?"

"Three thousand."

He didn't blink. Just pulled out a wad of cash, counted out the sum then pocketed the rest.

With his hand on the doorknob, he told me, "Curtis is six, Traylor's three—maybe four. Hell, I can't remember."

Tanny accompanied him out of her office and to the front door. "Don't worry. We'll have their birthdates on the original filings. Ms. Bach's fresh out of law school, but she does know how to read."

I blinked.

Flotaki rolled his eyes at me then gave Tanny a look of condolence, as if he felt sorry she had to work with a newbie.

He left, but his musky scent lingered in the lobby. I stared at the closed door, wondering what he did to lay his hands on that kind of cash. Some questions I really didn't want to know the answer to, so instead of following that line of thought, I glanced down at his ex-wife's custody motion for supervised visitation. "I don't get this."

"Get what?" Tanny asked, re-entering the office and stretching her back.

"Why did Ms. Abrams file for supervised visitation if all she's wanting is more child support?"

"Because in the fourth paragraph of her motion, she states this is not about finances."

"So?"

Tanny gave a mirthless laugh, thumbing through her stack of phone messages. Then she taught me a lesson that I'd never forget for the rest of my legal career. "So, when anyone tells you, 'It's not about the money,' don't believe him. It's ALWAYS about the money."

"Wow."

She dismissed me with a flick of her hand, like she was royalty or something, but I pondered those words as I returned to my drab office.

On impulse, I dialed Gloria's cell number and listened to her greeting. Her voice was vibrant, perky, saying she's sorry she missed my call, but go ahead and leave a message.

Forgetting the *Bronski* motion for a minute, I re-dialed and listened again. My chest ached as I stared at the chair opposite my desk, indiscernible in the gray surroundings. It took several minutes of deep breathing to clear the mist from my eyes.

Focus.

Gloria had been gone for two months, two weeks, and three days. I could even tell you the exact hours, but that seemed maudlin. But I knew. I knew down to the minute. Someone plunged a knife into my gut and twisted. Then jerked up and stabbed me for a second time. This wasn't the first time I'd experienced physical pain in grieving. The episodes were intense and lonely and I wondered if anybody but the ones who'd lost a loved one could ever understand how I felt, awashed in grief.

An image of Ted's face sprang to mind, haloed by that red umbrella. A tingling sensation crossed my lips as if sparking again under those light kisses.

Focus, Coop and quit being a damned idiot.

That mantra was now my lifeline. I cracked open the *Bronski* file and got to work.

Chapter 4

Look Who's Got a Boyfriend

It was hard waking up the next morning, so I rambled on to Gloria about my first two days while I got ready for work. Thank God Gloria's not a prig about talking while I'm peeing. We have some of our best conversations when I'm on the pot.

"Tanny had me drafting motions and sitting in on client interviews. It was pathetic, really. She bragged herself up and boasted how she was the best attorney in town. She insisted I accompany her and Sam to lunch yesterday. It would have been flattering, if they hadn't made me buy my own lunch."

I smeared foundation on my face, trying to mask the paleness. "On what they're paying me? Are you kidding me! And my office is a shithole. They didn't even paint it before I got there. How long have they known I was coming?"

Applying taupe eyeshadow and navy eyeliner, I paused while my mouth stretched into an 'O' formation. With my ring finger, I swiped the corner of the eye and said aloud, "Real classy."

Gloria would have agreed. I felt sure of it.

"Anyway, she blabbed on during the whole lunch of how frickin' lucky I was to be working with such a prestigious husband/wife lawyering team. I think Tanny'd hoped for a little more enthusiasm on my part, but I used to beat up the cheerleaders in high school. Remember?"

I caressed a picture of Gloria, one of precious few things displayed on my bureau. She smiled back at me. My sister really does have a lovely smile. I don't know how many times I told her she should model toothpaste advertisements.

Topping off the lashes with a bit of my beloved waterproof mascara, I whistled. "I'm tellin' ya, sis, the more I get to know her, the creepier she gets."

I spritzed body spray then tossed it on the dusty dresser on top a pile of bottles, jars, and three cans of peaches.

"Oh! And that Sam! Why, he's a pig—fat, white and bald. You might as well slap a billboard on his ass that says, 'Low Testosterone.' No way is that guy having erections. Still, with Tanny as his wife…"

I shuddered, trying to block out the image of their two naked bodies entwined in copulation. I moved two boxes from the left side of the bed to the foot.

"I'm looking for my brown boots. Any help, sis?"

I climbed over a small mountain of clothes and boxes that lay strewn between me and my closet. Huffing a little, I reached in and pulled out a brown boot then mumbled, "Where's the other one?" I scanned the floor, unable to see the carpet as it was littered with bins full of belts, scarves and other shoes, but found no mate.

"Dammit! I'm gonna be late for work!"

I picked up a carton of Gloria's curlers and hurled them across the room.

With an agonized pain across my gut, I realized I had just trashed my dead sister's stuff. And somehow, I knew she'd seen that. There's nothing I hate more than hurting Gloria. She was, after all, my only sibling. In two furious seconds, I had messed up my entire day.

"I'm sorry, sis," I scrambled over the small mountain of crap, gathered her curlers and picked them up. I put each back into the carton with reverential care. "I'm sorry." I said while I teetered on the mound of baskets, boxes, and piles of clothing. There, in the middle of all the stuff, sat a blender.

I could feel Gloria's anger from the Great Beyond. It burned. "I'm sorry. I won't do it again."

I cried now. Long, deep sobs which wracked my body. My tears made the curlers go fuzzy. Everything blurred. I crawled across the piles of junk, hunting for the last curler. "Please help me find it, Gloria!"

Nothing but silence.

"Geezus! It's just a curler, Gloria."

I clawed through the rubble of my room, searching for the lost item, pushing the blender aside, only to uncover a cutting board, a circular saw, an iron, and a colander. Gloria wasn't going to talk to me until I had found the lost curler. That was clear enough. Work be damned. I couldn't leave until the prodigal curler was returned to its nest. For twenty minutes I searched my bedroom, moving laundry baskets out of the way, lifting clothes here and there and peering underneath.

Eventually, I sat down, defeated. Defeated by a lousy, purple plastic curler.

There was sound of wild laughter in my apartment. It reverberated. My knees clamped to my chest and I rocked, trying to remember how to breathe. Huddled in that fetal position, I damned the lost curler. That welcomed feeling of blissful detachment rolled over, taking me to a peaceful abyss, toward Oblivion. From my throne in the Land of Fog and Disconnections, I looked upon that pitiful, blonde woman stranded on top of debris and surrounded by sloppy towers of boxes.

***

With a sharp rebuke, Tanny welcomed me. "You're late. An hour and a half late!"

I didn't look at her, afraid to reveal my red-rimmed eyes. "I… ah… ah… dental appointment, remember?"

Silently, my eyes searched for Melinda's, hoping the intensity of my desperation transmitted to her, lending her the ability to read my thoughts.

"Oh, that's right, Mrs. Whilts. It's on her calendar." Melinda lied like silk—it was so smooth.

My knees nearly buckled in relief.

Our receptionist continued, "I must have forgotten to enter it into your calendar. Which reminds me, do you wish to have Cooper's appointments noted on yours? If so, should I highlight them? You know, to keep them separate?"

Tanny blinked, unsure how close to keep tabs on me.

"No, no, I don't think so, Mel."

Tanny turned to me. "You're not being paid for this past hour and a half."

"Of course not," I gave a small smile. Unfortunate, but reasonable.

"Melinda's pay will be docked by fifty dollars, too." Tanny said in a cold voice, spinning on her Jimmy Choo heel and walking away.

"That's not fair!" I protested.

Tanny's smirk smeared across her face. She slammed her office door shut with a smug look which infuriated me.

Unable to think of anything to say, I spluttered, "Melinda! I'm so sorry!"

"Forget it," she said, smiling, as she drew a deep sip from her coffee.

"I'll pay you the fifty dollars. This was my fault."

Melinda rested her coffee cup on the desk before she gave a short laugh. "From what you make? Don't worry about it. I'm not deducting fifty bucks from my own paycheck. I do the payroll. By Friday, she'll have forgotten this. She's always threatening to dock my pay."

The incident unnerved me. My father warned me that working with lawyers would be difficult, but I never dreamed they'd be such asses. With Tanny, it seemed like she didn't have an ounce of empathy. That didn't just make her hard, cold, and calculating—it made her inhuman. More and more, I liked her less and less.

By the end of the morning I put the finishing touches on the *Bronski* supporting memorandum. After re-reading it for the final time, I resisted the urge to pat myself on the back. It was good—damn good. There are plenty of things I can't do, but I can out-write and out-research most everybody. In fact, I kick ass. False modesty's never become me.

For lunch I crammed a sandwich down my gullet, then met a new client, David Seltzer, housing temporarily in the county jail. Sam had signed me up for the indigent system, being appointed to represent criminal defendants. The public defender system paid me a third of my hourly rate, so I'd be looking to plead him out as soon as indecently possible. Tanny stressed the firm could not take on *pro bono* cases. She was very concerned about not getting paid the full hourly rate and bitched about the firm's high overhead. But Sam assured us this would be an excellent way to bring in new business. I'm not sure what my opinion was on taking criminal cases; neither Sam nor Tanny sought it.

My client, David, found very little success in selling drugs, probably because he snorted his profits. And if he was bad at marginalizing revenue, he was even worse at making an undercover cop. The Chenowith County Sheriff's Department devoted four full-time detectives to selling eight balls to David over the span of nine months. You may wonder how many times they stung David before they finally lowered the boom and arrested this menace to society. Thirty-eight times. Thirty-eight video and audio taped surveillances, at all hours of the day, in several remote locations, with four different undercover cops over the same amount of time it takes for human gestation to occur. This sting operation overloaded the Sheriff's budget, but the Sheriff was up for re-election that year, and he wanted to prove he could be tough on crime. Of course, that's another reason David Seltzer wasn't making any money selling drugs. The stupid sonuvabitch's only clients were undercover cops. And don't think for one minute they didn't sit down with him occasionally, pop a cold one and snort an eight ball—you know they did.

Anyway, we waived the reading of the charges at the arraignment because otherwise it would have taken longer than the Queen's coronation. We went back to the jail's conference hole, entering one of several private rooms. Better equipped than the makeshift office I'd shared with Mrs. Cuttlebum, but nowhere near as clean. Gouges dominated the length of the walls.

"Thanks, Mrs. Bach, for your help. I'm glad I got a real lawyer, instead of one of 'em public defenders." David waved me to use the room's only chair.

An image popped into my head: a gaggle of public defenders in cheap suits riding unicorns while leprechauns pranced about in fields, searching out pots of gold or parcels of Monopoly money so the unicorn-riders could pay their student loans.

"David, where do you think you're going to be living for the next four years?"

He winced.

"I'm going down for four years?" The unfairness of his situation showed.

"Hell, yes, you're going down. You'll be lucky if you only go down for four years. You know there's no flexibility in the sentencing guidelines."

David squatted down, leaving me without the option of remaining standing. I surveyed the vinyl chair.

Styrofoam padding was torn from its arms and a spot near the front of the seat. Testing the upholstery with a tentative touch, I jerked my hand back from its sticky surface.

Could be soda pop.

Refusing to dwell on the other possibilities, I shut my imagination off and very, very gingerly sat on the tip-most edge of the chair, praying my skirt served as sufficient barrier. I'd have to burn it at the end of the workday. The faint sound of scurrying alerted us to a cockroach crawling across the floor. Without speaking, David and I watched the creature in mesmerized fascination. It scraped its antenna against the wall, six inches from my shoe before David batted it away.

He swore softly.

"They got you on video and audio tape thirty-eight times. What were you thinking?"

David grinned. "You sound like my mama."

"Is your mama still here?"

"Yeah, lives over on Millhorn Road."

"Why didn't you check these guys out?"

"I went to elementary school with Roland," he said, referring to one of the undercovers. "Dirty sonuvabitch. How was I to know in third grade that snot-nosed little shit would grow up and snitch on me?"

"That was a lousy break," I acknowledged. There really should be a mulligan for all the bad decisions we make under the influence of impressing childhood friends.

"He led them right to me," he muttered. With his finger, he scored in the dusty linoleum, writing out F-I-N-K. Then he scribbled out the 'I' and the 'N' and replaced the letters with a 'U' and a 'C.' He grinned, shaking his head.

"Look, you need to consider whether you're going to give up your suppliers in exchange for a lighter jail sentence."

He laughed without a trace of humor. "On thirty-eight counts? I'm gonna have to give up somebody."

"Probably."

He drew a circle around the letters written on the floor. I stayed silent.

"I don't know." He shifted his weight, still on his haunches, and rubbed the back of his neck.

"Think about it. That's all I'm asking. How long have you lived here, David?"

"All my life."

"You got any family besides your mom?"

"Yeah, I got eight brothers and sisters."

"Are you on good terms with any of them?"

"Not really. They none of them turned out to be potheads."

I nodded.

"So they want nothing to do with you."

"Uh-huh."

"You ever tried to get clean?"

He laughed. "You mean go to one of them rehab places? Yeah, I've been to the fricking Betty Ford clinic about a zillion times."

"Sure you have." I met his bid for sarcasm and raised him one more. "I'll let you know what the prosecutor's willing to do."

I gathered my briefcase and shook his hand as David stretched to a standing position once more. "Oh and thanks."

"Thanks for what?"

"For leaving me the chair."

He seemed surprised, but his smile was genuine and his eyes lit up.

The illumination in David's eyes sparked a connection between us, forging something tenuous; feelings of gratitude and appreciation overwhelmed me. I felt as though I'd ventured outside after a blizzard, only to discover a fragile, precious flower miraculously sprouting on my front porch.

"You know what, Mrs. Bach?"

"What?"

"You all right."

I smiled as I knocked for the guard to let me out. Without a doorknob, we relied on the good nature of the guard to open the door.

Unnerving, that.

"Can you do me a favor, Mrs. Bach?"

"Depends," I said cautiously. "What?"

"Get me some decent paper? I like to draw and it'll give me something to do to pass the time."

"You got anything to draw with?"

"Oh yeah, I can get pencils from Carnahan—he knows me." David spoke of one of the guards.

I came back to the office, a little after five-thirty, wanting to draft a quick motion for David's bond reduction. I figured I'd give his mom a call, just to sound her out on what, if any, help she'd be willing to give him.

Crossing the lobby's antique, tattered rug, I was about to head to my office when I heard a crash coming from behind Tanny's mahogany door. Sounded like a lamp had been knocked over.

Burglars!

I ran and flung her door wide open. I didn't know what I would do if there were burglars on the other side, but I didn't have to deal with that situation. Instead, it was much, much worse.

Tanny was there, completely naked except for her Jimmy Choo stilettos. Bent forward over her desk, her bare ass presented to the guy whose hands were clamped on either side of her buttocks. His pants puddled around his ankles, his thighs ramming Tanny against her desk. A broken lamp, tossed clothes littered the floor. The groaning ceased when I banged the door into the wall. Now the couple was frozen, staring at me. Tanny's torso swiveled around and she flashed me her flat, brown-tipped boobs.

Oh hell.

Wishing I'd lived my whole life without having seen that, I snapped the door shut and beat the hell out of there.

***

Back at my apartment, I shoved a basket off the couch and settled in with a frozen entrée. My fork chased the refried beans over the plastic ridge, into the corn, which was still cool in the middle. The enchilada sauce was so tame, a true connoisseur of Mexican cuisine would have mistaken it for water. But it wasn't worth my while to nuke it for even thirty more seconds.

It was a crappy dinner, and would always be a crappy dinner. Nothing would change that.

So I cried. Steadily. For hours.

Some time after night fell, I emerged from my lumpy sofa with a running nose and a blotchy face. I stumbled to the bathroom, climbing around boxes and laundry baskets. I stood before the sink and splashed cold water on my face. The hand towel smelled of mildew, but I couldn't find another, so I used it anyway. I wiped my eyes, trying not to breathe in its dank odor.

"I cannot believe I saw Tanny getting screwed," I mumbled, lifting my head up. I no longer smelled the hand towel. Instead, I sniffed the air and discovered Gloria had returned.

I smiled. Granted, she had no words for me, but she could listen. I frowned. "I'm sorry about your curlers, sis. I don't know what's gotten into me."

I high-stepped into my bedroom like walking through a mine field. Sensing my big sister's disapproval from the Great Beyond, I muttered, "Yeah, yeah. I know. I gotta get a handle on this. And I will, Gloria."

But my crying jag threatened to rev back into high gear. I shoved stuff off my bed, trying to create enough space to lie down. Junk slithered off the bedspread and landed in another pile at the foot. I wrapped the covers over me, snuggling in deep.

"I missed you today," I whispered, imagining Gloria stroking my hair, hungry for another person's physical touch.

I remembered other times when I laid prostrate on my bed, Gloria comforting me. Her gentle fingers would glide through my hair as she murmured something soothing, like when I found Michael the Turd kissing another girl, whenever there were fireworks, after Mom died. "I love you, Gloria."

Maybe I was delusional, or just engaging in a strong bout of wishful thinking, but I could have sworn I heard my sister say, "I love you, too, Coop."

My breathing steadied, became regular—not normal.

Nothing will ever be normal. Not with my big sister.

Chapter 5

Ted & Michael

The next evening found me at the local grocery store, the location new. It took a while to learn how it was laid out, but I didn't mind. I had time to kill; it was better than being in my overstuffed apartment, which looked like hell on roller skates.

I strolled through the seasonal display section. Since it was early summer, there were lots of potato chips, ketchup and hotdog buns for sale. Peaches were on sale, six for two dollars; I was figuring out the price per unit—thirty something cents and then a high-pitched scream pierced the air.

"Good grief! Was somebody murdered on Aisle 3?" I muttered, turning toward Produce, only a few yards from me.

"Calm down, Michael," a familiar male voice said.

"No! I want it! I want it!"

"You don't need a stocking hat. It's the middle of June, buddy." The attempt at humor fell on deaf ears.

"But I *want* it!"

Something about the man's voice resonated, but I couldn't place it. I peeked over the display of peaches then grinned. "Well, lookie here. Barkeeper's trying to reason with a two-year old!"

The guy had ignored his high school guidance counselor's warnings and procreated. I watched the dynamic duo for a bit, relishing his growing frustration at the unruly tyke. His smooth, player image was blown.

Michael forgot about the stocking hat and darted off to the apple bins. "I want!"

Ted shook his head, warning, "Don't throw those, Michael."

I flinched. His strategy was so bad, it was painful to witness. But highly amusing. I crouched down, waiting for the tantrum to unfold to full majesty.

As expected, Michael's face lit up, having just conjured up a brilliant idea. Even at my distance, I could feel the heat of his orneriness emanating from him. The little boogar was pleased with himself. His wicked genius tempted Ted to tear his hair out, which would have been a shame. The bartender did have nice hair. And that exact crooked grin.

At that moment, Ted pumped his arms, discouraging Michael from throwing the apples, but it was too late. From the maniacal gleam in the toddler's eye, he had big plans for those apples.

Slowly, so slowly it felt like time regressed, Michael eased his chubby fist, shoulder-high. He reached into the bin and grabbed a Jonathan apple by its stem.

"Put it back."

No response.

Cool Hand Luke's line, 'What we have here is a failure to communicate' intersected with Dirty Harry's

'Make my day.' The collision resulted in 'Put it back' being translated to mean 'Dash it to the ground.'

Michael flung the apple, his eyes never leaving his father's face.

Under my breath, I congratulated the kid. "Bold move, grasshopper." My gaze swiveled to the dad, to see how this would play out. A muscle vibrated along Ted's jaw. Ouch. The grown man struggled to keep his composure.

Seeing the tight leash on that temper encouraged Michael to push his luck a little farther. The toddler stuck out his hand, found another apple then hurled it to the floor.

"Cut that out!"

This was too much fun. Michael was certainly enjoying himself and truth be told, so was I. Silently, I cheered him on. The little grasshopper picked another apple and chucked it. Its short ride fascinated the tyke.

Throwing his head back, Michael laughed, enjoying himself until he caught his dad's 'Look.' Every parent has it. It's that expression which tells a kid when that last nerve snaps and right now Ted had the 'Look.' He didn't just possess it—he owned it and rented it out for Bar Mitzvahs.

Michael panicked. Evasive maneuvers were in order.

"That's right. You'd better run grasshopper," I advised *sotto voce*.

Michael levitated for a short space of time, his knees bent and locked in mid-air, dangling at the end of his daddy's long arm. Barkeep scooped him into his arms, gave him a quick kiss then asked, "Do you behave like this with your mom or am I special?"

Michael's squeals of delight ended with a trail of chuckles. Pressing his palms against his daddy's cheeks, he squished them and mimicked, "Pec-shall."

The man harnessed the kid into the shopping cart, deftly ignoring his struggles. "Now cut it out." Even I was impressed with the amount of patience the bartender showed. Most people would have throttled the kid, but Ted seemed pretty cool.

Shaking my head, I couldn't lose the smile.

"Help me, Michael. We've got to get everything on this list." Ted handed the slip of paper to the toddler, who pretended to read it. Then they wandered off, leaving the produce section.

Why I was holding my breath, I don't know, but I watched them leave feeling equal parts sad and relieved. I was sorry to see Michael go, but I sure as check didn't want his dad to stick around. He really was a piece of work, all right. What the hell did he think he was doing kissing me when he was married with a kid?

What a creep.

What a jerk.

What a *player*.

"I had you nailed for a player in the first ten seconds I laid eyes on you."

Deciding that it was time to get on with my shopping, I picked up a bag of lettuce, some potatoes for baking, a couple of oranges and a bunch of bananas. Some sour cream and bacon would be good toppings for the baked potato, so I headed to Dairy. I didn't worry about the calories because I'd already lost a ton of weight this spring. I should add a few pounds or buy new clothes, which I couldn't imagine affording.

Remembering I needed Kleenex, I headed toward the paper products aisle. My crying bouts from the past few days had wiped out my stock, so I grabbed a couple three-tissue packs. I tossed them into my cart. That's when I discovered Ted and Michael on the same aisle, searching for feminine hygiene products.

"See Michael? Right here it says, 'big-ass' maxi pads. That's what we're looking for."

Michael giggled. "Big-ass."

Ted groaned. "Your mom's gonna kill me for teaching you that."

He stood there looking at the wide array of maxi pads, clearly stumped. "Did you know these things come with wings? What the…will women just buy *anything*?" He picked two packages, turning them over to compare diagrams, and scowled at them, as if blaming them for making the purchases so convoluted.

"Promise me, Michael, you will never let a woman wussify you the way your mom has me." He shook his head in confusion as he put both packages back then selected a different brand, which coincidentally, happened to be the biggest package on the shelf.

"Wuss-a-why!"

"Shhhh, Michael!" he tried to sound stern, but a smile quirked at the edge of his lips.

In full stealth mode, I tiptoed backward down the aisle, wishing for an invisibility cloak. Too late. He spotted me. Mortified to be caught mid-backstep, I cursed myself for not being more adult about the situation. I could have passed him by, said 'hey' or something. Hit him with the Expelliarmus curse—something. Instead, he caught me pulling my cart backward as if I were walking through treacle at Hogwarts. Lovely.

"Hi!" Ted flung the jumbo package into his shopping cart, grabbed the handle and with a decent kickoff, sped toward me. Closing the distance, he jumped on the bottom rails and rode the cart, tot still in it, to a gliding stop next to me.

I beat a retreat, turning the cart and trotting out that aisle and down the next.

"No. Don't go. Hey, wait a second. I just want to talk to you."

"Forget it." I threw over my shoulder.

"Come on. Give me your name." He was kick-surfing with the cart, sailing alongside me.

"No." I slammed to a halt.

Almost he touched my shoulder. As his hand reached toward me, I slapped it away. The sound of smarting flesh cracked. His head jerked back, caught by surprise.

He began to say something, but I screamed, "Get away from me, you JERK!"

That hand fell to his side and he blinked. Then Michael wailed and his attention was diverted to his son.

"Hey, hey now. Easy there," Ted soothed Michael, but glared at me over the kid's head.

Ted lifted a palm in classic surrender, indicating he'd now leave me alone.

Now satisfied my point was crystal clear, I gave him a cool, condescending nod. "May I?" I asked, my gaze flickering past him.

Ted pivoted out of my way, waving me forward with a gentleman's mockery. As I stalked by, he shuffled farther away, pressing himself against the shelving to grant me wide berth. Sure, it was sarcastic, but since his act accomplished what I most desired—distance between us—who was I to complain?

"That's all right, buddy. Hang on. We're almost finished here." Ted spoke in quiet tones, but his eyes were hard as they followed me down the aisle. Two holes burned in my back; my flimsy coat was singed.

I shrugged it off. He was headed for a divorce. That wasn't hard to foresee. Out with his kid to buy Kotex for his wife and tried to hit on the new girl in town. Already kissed her, taking that as payment, I suppose, for getting wet when he brought my purse to me.

It didn't take long to finish shopping, but my luck, which had been horrible of late, wasn't turning around tonight.

The bartender was in the check-out line in front of me. There was only one person working the cashier, so I resigned myself and thumbed through a tabloid to better ignore him.

Curious, I peeked at him. Even in anger, Ted had a classic profile. His nose straight as a blade, his jawline firm—he could have been a throwback from Roman days.

The female cashier was cute, brunette, and if body language was correct, horny as hell. The check-out girl was aptly labeled because her warm eyes roved over Barkeeper like a wolf ogles a lonely lamb. Her lips formed a seductive smile as her curvaceous hips splayed towards him. In honeyed tones, she purred, "How you doing, Ted? Looking good, as always."

I rattled the tabloid pages to cover my sounds of gagging.

That muscle jerked on the side of Ted's face, but he ignored me and spoke to the cashier instead. "Fine. Hey, do you know? Is this the right kind? Karen asked me to get them for her."

The clerk snorted, inspecting the Kotex box. She tossed them into the sack and said, "Yeah, the overnighters go from butt crack to navel."

"More information than I need," he mumbled, shaking his head like he wanted to empty the words from his ears.

"You're a good brother, Ted." The clerk smiled, packing his purchases into a recyclable bag.

I nearly dropped the tabloid, which was no less than I deserved.

"Well, you know, it's still hard for Karen to get around. It's only been three days."

"Yeah, well, God doesn't give you a period for nine months then He makes up for it all in the next one. I remember I ran…" The brunette babbled on.

Ted held his palm in the 'stop' position. "That is WAY more information than I'll *ever* need."

She snorted again then ran her hand through her hair, smoothing it.

"You're so funny!"

He swiped his debit card.

As she handed him his receipt, her fingers lingered, gripping the paper. "Any time you want to go out, sugar, you just let me know."

"Ah… thanks, Bella. You're a real sweetheart." He left the check-out line.

I approached the conveyor belt and loaded it with my meager selections. The flirty brunette watched Ted and Michael make their way out of the store, blindly reaching for my groceries, scanning them and tossing them into a plastic bag.

"Could you put the eggs in a separate bag, please?"

The cashier's head whipped around, noticing me for the first time. "Huh?"

I pointed at the eggs, which she had shoved into a bag, along with the baked potatoes. "Eggs. Separate bag. Please."

Her heavy sigh moved her bangs, fluffing them, but she rang up my sale without further words being exchanged.

Walking away from the registers, the sick realization struck me that I'd been pissy to the bartender and needed to apologize. Again.

At the exit Ted had stopped to talk with a tall, lanky fellow. Michael was still strapped in the seat of the shopping cart. Stalling so that I could have another abject word with him, I pretended to scan the business cards on the ice machine. When he'd wrapped up his conversation, he turned toward me. The wary looks on nephew and uncle would have been funny if I hadn't scared a kid. That was a new low for me. I really had to get over this pissy attitude.

"Hey," I said, swallowing hard, afraid to go on, unsure how to fix this. "I shouldn't have screamed at you. Or called you a name. I'm sorry."

"Okay."

Parked in front of him, he couldn't move around me without acknowledging my presence. It hadn't been intentional on my part, but it certainly wasn't appreciated. Belatedly, I realized my new mistake and swiveled out of his path.

He didn't move past; rather, he leveled a hard stare on me.

I attempted to explain. "I… ah… um…"

He raised one eyebrow, waiting for coherence to come to my speech. I waited, too. We were both doomed to disappointment.

"I thought you were hitting on me!"

After blurting that out, I wished every one of my law professors would form a line and kick my ass. For someone whose professional rate is a hundred seventy-five bucks an hour, that last sentence wasn't worth a buck forty-six. Where was my $84,338 education now?

"I might have been," he said. The cool delivery indicated that was ancient history now.

For some reason, I persisted, pointed to Michael. "I thought you were married…with grasshopper here."

He frowned; scowled, more like.

Then a horrible idea struck me. I'd just assumed this was his nephew, but there was no evidence for that. This really could be his kid, which made my apology lame in the extreme. So I rushed to make a bad situation worse.

"He isn't your kid, is he? I mean, you're not married, are you? Not that you have to be married to have a kid, I guess. Oh, gosh. I'm really screwing this up, aren't I?"

His eyes narrowed to such slits, I wondered if Ted could see anything. His face tightened so that it appeared stone-like.

Beneath my breath, I mumbled, "Man, did I screw up." The sound of a wounded Cessna engine, nose-diving to earth, went off in my head and I pictured myself scrambling in the cockpit, lurching for the joystick, trying to pull up and avert disaster.

"Not that you're that kind of guy, I'm sure."

His upper lip curled in an unattractive sneer.

That look sent a couple of messages. The first message was that I suck at apologies. Fair enough. The second one was that metaphorical plane had crashed and burned. Nothing left for me to do now except hobble from the wreckage.

Ted turned his head to pick an imaginary fluff of lint from his sleeve, taking his time to deliver a cut-down of epic proportions. Instead, he said nothing. His gaze returned to me, but it was devoid of all feeling. It cut me to the quick.

"Come on, buddy." He pushed the cart, leaving me standing in the grocery store's entrance.

The taste of regret welled up like bile in my mouth. Closing my eyes, I tried to push aside that moment where my chest constricted. Barbed wire squeezing me tight. That was my body's reaction to nervousness, to loneliness, to a host of emotions—every one of them negative.

Galvanized into action, I hustled after them. "I'm Cooper Bach. You know, if you need my name to fill in the restraining order."

His foot paused in mid-air and he came to an abrupt stop next to a silver truck.

Interpreting that as an opening, I set down both my grocery sacks and extended my hand.

Ted removed Michael from the cart and settled him into his car seat and fastened him.

My hand dangled before I realized I was being ignored. My cheeks burned as I picked up the plastic bags and shuffled off toward my Fiesta. That burning pressure closed over my lungs again, making it hard to breathe.

"Hey, Cooper!" He called out to me as I placed my groceries in the back seat.

Not sure I wanted to look at him anymore, I partly faced him, pinning my gaze above his shoulder.

Pausing at his tailgate, he jabbed a finger at me. "If you go around thinking every guy's an asshole, you won't be disappointed."

With a curt salute, he turned, smoothly slid into the driver's seat and drove off without a backwards glance.

The flames from the plane crash burned the last of the fog.

***

I nuked the potato, slathered butter and sour cream on it. Maneuvering in the kitchen was difficult with all the clutter. If something needed to be set down, that necessitated moving something else out of the way. Several things had to be relocated to make room for something else, like clearing debris out of a neighborhood ravaged by tornado. And if that wasn't an apt description of my life, I didn't know what was. This apartment looked like a cyclone had come through it. Hell, a tornado might have improved matters, it was so bad.

I would have liked to have had bacon to top off my potato, but I couldn't find a skillet and the stove was buried under a mountain of stuff. My nerves were fried. I had to eat even if I didn't have an appetite. Carrying my plate to the sofa, I scooted my dad's toolbox over to give me space to sit. Another foray into the kitchen to find a drinking glass was beyond my energy levels. I could drink from the bathroom faucet later.

I could almost hear my sister groan in annoyance with me. Drinking from the faucet?

Sighing, I carefully balanced my plate on Gloria's volleyball trophies then journeyed to the kitchen, climbing the boxes and stepping on the uneven piles. After several minutes of hunting through the cupboards, I located a six-pack of soda near the toaster, on top of the refrigerator. Since that search yielded results so quickly, I became foolhardy and decided to look for a drinking glass. I wasn't an idiot. I wasn't going to find ice cubes, so I didn't push my luck. Lord only knows where my ice trays were, but at least I'd sip my soda from a glass.

Opening some cupboards, I found them crammed with spices, box dinners, canned goods and Dad's tackle box.

"This is ridiculous." I hitched up a knee, climbed onto another pile of stuff and stumbled across the heap, searching for anything that could be used for a damned drinking glass. I spied one on the shelf over the sink. It had been used as a vase, holding the shriveled remains of a Philodendra start.

I scooped out the black, organic debris then scrubbed the inside with hot water. I wasn't able to find soap. Relying upon Nietzsche's credo that whatever doesn't kill me makes me stronger, I poured soda into the glass, re-trekked back to my now-cold baked potato.

Nothing was on TV and I was too broke for cable, so I turned it off. I ate the cold potato, drank the warm soda and wondered how civilians spend an evening. Law school took up so much of my time, I didn't know what else to do besides study.

Leaning my head against the back of the sofa, I sighed. "Time to clean the kitchen," I announced to nobody.

My eyes lifted to the mountains of belongings and the sea of crap—the territory I had to cross to return to the kitchen. Weary, but determined, I began the journey. Starting with the basics, I washed my plate and glass then balanced them on piles of magazines to dry. Congratulating myself on that feat, I took a fortifying breath before diving into the first cupboard. I removed everything inside and piled the contents in the sink.

Surveying expiration dates, consolidating containers, and ditching the empties took several hours. When my hand found the bottle of dishwashing soap, an orgasmic thrill pulsed through me. It had been way too long since I'd had sex, I thought wryly, ignoring the burst of satisfaction. It would have been nice to lay the shelves with liner, but my budget wouldn't cover non-essential items. Re-stocking the cupboard, I turned the labels forward to easily see the inventory. Delighted with the result, I opened the cupboards several times, reveling in the view. This evening I discovered food stuffs without requiring satellite assistance.

"Okay, that's two down." I counted the remaining cupboards. "Six to go." Doing the math in my head, I figured I might be able to organize the kitchen if I hit it hard again on Saturday and spent the whole day at it.

"Wonder what color the countertop is?"

To be honest, I didn't know. I barely remember moving into the apartment. That had been a couple of weeks afterward and in the early days my fog was miles thick. Frowning, I reasoned I must have spoken with a property manager, but I couldn't remember if that person had been male or female.

A box of heavy duty garbage bags had been tossed, landing by the couch in the living room. I filled three bags with expired goods and most of the magazines then hauled them downstairs to the dumpster. When I returned, trying to judge the kitchen with an assessing eye, very little difference could be detected after my evening's work.

"Damn, this is gonna be tougher than I thought."

I had too much shit.

Bottles and boxes of duplicates or things I didn't like. What the hell was Gloria doing with three bottles of balsamic vinaigrette, anyway? And who knew Dad bought shaving cream and Worcestershire sauce in bulk? I re-loaded a cardboard box and filled it with the vinaigrette bottles, shaving cream, and Worcestershire sauce. For good measure, I put other cans of green beans and yams and asparagus. I hated those things. I carried the box and another trash bag filled with stuff to the Festiva, planning to deliver them to the local food pantry.

Bedtime. The clock read eleven thirty. Sleep was still a long way away and resting on the bed didn't seem very attractive. Almost with a feeling of doom, I entered my crowded bathroom and stared at myself in the mirror. I picked up a hairbrush, running it through my blonde tresses, liking the sensuous tugging on my roots.

Speaking aloud relieved an empty room of its lonely silence. "After I organize the kitchen, I'm gonna work on this room. It'd be nice to take a shower, not a sponge bath. What I wouldn't give to have a fresh towel to smell." I re-folded the dank one, reconsidered and carried it to the kitchen. I poured dishwasher soap in it then rinsed it and draped it over the sink's edge to dry. Maybe with a little luck, it'd be dry by morning.

I smiled as I looked at the hand towel.

The sight of it looked…I searched for the word. Homey? Reassuring? Normal. Yeah, that was it. It appeared normal, like part of an everyday routine with nothing disastrous or devastating behind it. Just a normal towel, drying out.

Ages ago, my life was normal and so was I.

Brushing the tears from my eye, it felt like some monster pounced on me, attacking and chewing me up like a ragdoll. The greedy monster sucked the joy from my life, devouring my happiness, my sanity, my way of life. Gulping, I struggled to traverse the distance back to the bathroom.

I made it just in time. Then threw up.

Afterward, as I stared into the mirror above my bathroom sink, lost, sunken eyes stared back at me. It was a shocking sight. I looked at myself, really looked. My fingertips traced my cheek bones, feeling the difference in their contours in what grief had gnawed away. My reflection depressed me further. Quickly folding down the toilet seat, I collapsed on it moments before my knees buckled. Cradling my head in my hands, I struggled to breathe.

In and out, in and out. Come on, Coop.

Listening to my ragged breathing, I dimly wondered if this is how asthmatics suffered. If I'd been able to pray, I would have prayed for my last breath.

No more struggle. No more pain. No more anything.

That was fine by me. What was the point in praying? God didn't care. He'd left me long ago. Maybe He was still out to a celestial lunch.

Chapter 6

Mr. and Mrs. Abrams

With effort, I schooled my expression to hide my disgust of Tanny's client, Ed Abrams—Flotaki to me. His lower jaw jutted forward, lending him an 'ape-like' appearance; coupled with the hairy forearms revealed in his t-shirt, he was everything I imagined a silverback gorilla would be.

Tanny had delegated the negotiations to me, so Flotaki and I sat in Matt Bearus's conference room, meeting his ex-wife, Louisa, the mother of his children to whom he referred as "a grubby little skank." The female who walked through Matt's law office, however, bore no resemblance to any PTA mother that I ever knew.

Louisa Abrams—yes, she kept his surname after he divorced her, wore something low-cut. It was a leopard-print body suit made of spandex, which hugged her curves. Marrying the outfit with cherry-red platform shoes showed her instinct for 'trailer trash ensembles' was infallible. Her chest strained against her bodice and her bottom had support from some kind of NASA-designed, gravity-defying material.

Flotaki boggled, but showed signs of confusion in not knowing where to look first. His gaze seared her fleshy breasts, but zoomed in on her ass when she bent over to pick up her purse. Dropping it had been deliberate on her part, but I applauded her. Her strategy paid off. Ever since she entered the conference room, she had her ex-husband's attention. Flotaki fixated on her and if I wasn't mistaken, sported an erection.

Shaking my head, I gave Matt a look of censure, which he blandly turned away.

"I don't want you taking the kids down to your shop, Ed, honey." Louisa's pout accompanied long, talon-like nails trailing over Flotaki's hairy forearm. Then she leaned toward him, squeezing her breasts together between her upper arms. If an ant had been in her cleavage, it would have suffocated.

"Aw, come on," I told Matt, who half-laughed.

Flotaki made an irritated gesture to silence me, but his eyes never left Louisa. His voice deepened as he asked his ex, "Why come, sugar?"

"They could get hurt, silly." Her hand traced her neckline and he latched onto that movement, watching without blinking.

Flotaki ran his tongue under his lips, licking his teeth.

So my client appreciated spherical shapes. Did I have to witness his admiration? This was deuced uncomfortable. I glared at my colleague, who teetered on the edge between revealing his amusement and keeping his poker-straight face.

"This isn't funny, Matt."

"No. No, it's not." Matt's lips quirked.

I would bet fifty bucks—money I didn't have—that Flotaki hadn't heard us. I smacked the back of his hand, trying to get his attention.

"Hey!" he snapped at me, unfamiliar with parochial discipline.

"Can we agree the kids aren't to be in the shop without Ed?" I questioned Matt.

"Does that work for you?" Matt slanted his head towards Louisa.

Interesting to note that Matt's knees pointed away from his client, a sure sign that he did not approve of her. I had to capitalize on that. Matt's body language suggested he was onto her tricks and didn't much care for them; however, Flotaki was definitely digging her, vibrating like a tuning fork.

"Well, I don't know…" She pouted again, a well-rehearsed innocence which could have been credible if she hadn't pressed the sides of her globular boobage. Now they were oblong heaps of flesh. It would have been a real liberating, Erin Brokovich kind of moment if I thought she wasn't on the same level as my alley-cat client.

If mind games were a track and field event, Louisa finished the hurdles while Flotaki sat in the sandbox, mining for turds. I discovered my second lesson in lawyering: you don't get to pick your clients.

That kinda sucks.

"How much do you want?" I asked, tired of watching Louisa's heaving bosoms and listening to Flotaki's strangled panting. He was past getting on my nerves. Although it cut against the grain to try to wrap things up quickly when working on an hourly rate, I couldn't take any more. My retinas were already burning from seeing all this sexual heat blaze between the Abrams.

Matt cut in, playing the kid card. "It's not a question of money. It's about what's in Traylor and Curtis' best interests."

"How much?" I ignored Matt's self-righteous response. He couldn't possibly believe what he'd just said and if he did, then I felt sorry for him. Looking Louisa straight in the eye, I sent the message that this little gig of hers was up. She glared back at me, but she understood because women rarely misunderstand each other. Then she cast Flotaki a sidelong glance. That's when I knew. This wasn't just a game. She really had the hots for her ex. She wanted him to want her. And I guess even trailer trash girls in leopard spandex deserve to be wanted. God bless Louisa Abrams.

"No sense discussing support issues until we clear up custody," Matt pointed out.

"Fine. Let's talk custody. Keep it status quo, but he doesn't let the kids go to the shop. Why should his visitation be supervised, though? You drop your motion."

Louisa's lips pursed.

"What do you want?" Flotaki asked Louisa, getting to the heart of the matter.

"You gotta drop the custody fight. I need $200 more for child support." She straightened in her chair and a hardness came into her face.

"A month?" Flotaki bellowed. "Are you crazy?"

"That's not affordable."

Louisa resumed pouting then a tiny smile crawled onto her red-stained lips as her lashes fluttered at him. "Ed, you and I both know you're a good provider. All I'm asking is for you to pay a bit more of the expenses for the kids. Just a teensy bit more."

Flattery worked on him.

To drive her point home, she rubbed her red bra strap between her fingers. "Satin."

Apparently, that was code. Flotaki readjusted his seating position, and leered at Louisa.

A shiver arrowed down my spine.

"Cold?" Matt asked with fake solicitude.

I knew that he knew that we had both just pictured these two getting naked and neither one of us wanted to be in the conference room, drowning in the pheromones.

Ignoring Matt's raised brow, I nearly snapped. "How much are we talking here? Really. Bottom line. I'd like to kill this beast then go to lunch."

Parroting his client, Matt answered, "Two hundred a month."

"You're not helping here," I muttered. "How about seventy-five bucks on top of the $450?"

"I ain't got that kind of money!" My client's protests rang false. He had that kind of money from some source, probably illegal, but I didn't ask because I didn't want to know.

"You got an extra seventy-five?" I asked him, glaring at him to give me the answer I expected.

Flotaki sputtered then glared at me.

"Seventy-five? That don't cover school lunches!" Louisa argued.

"Guess everybody gets to eat sandwiches everyday." Turning to my client, I leveled with him. "Look, it's not a bad number for either one of you. Think about it."

"Sounds fair," Matt announced, "We agree the kids don't go in the shop and both motions will be dropped. We agree to modify child support to Five Hundred Twenty-Five, starting in another…let's say two months. That will give you time to adjust. Good?"

"Let us have some privacy and once Mr. Abrams and I talk, I'll give you an answer," I offered. I couldn't take my client from the conference room, because it'd ruin negotiations if I paraded him through the office with the tent in his pants. If we had any hope of settling on something favorable, I had to leave some doubt in Louisa's mind.

"Could you leave us, Mr. Bearus?"

Matt didn't smile as he ushered the vixen from the room. From reading his body language, I knew he didn't like his client, but he wasn't going to let me screw her over.

"Glad we're not playing poker," I mumbled.

"No shit, Sherlock."

I whirled on my client. "Couldn't you at least PRETEND to play hard to get?"

"Couldn't you at least PRETEND not to sell me out? Why the fuck did you agree to raising my support obligation?"

"I'm sorry. What's the going rate to pay off a blackmailer?"

He frowned. "Blackmailer? Louisa?"

"Yes. Remember you said she was going to tell your new wife, Caroline, that you two are having an affair? Don't you want to keep your lowdown on down low?" My sarcasm streak was having a field day with Flotaki.

"Damn," he whispered.

"Forgot about all that, didn't you?"

He gave a low laugh and stretched his cotton twills down his thighs. "Yeah, she got me so hot and bothered..."

"Never mind," I cut him off. If there's anything I'd rather not listen to, it's Ed Abrams giving me an explanation for his current state. "You know she's playing with you, don't you?"

"Hell yeah, but damn, she's a great screw."

"You think she painted on her clothes?" I mused aloud.

"Oh, like Farrah done? Damn, that was sexy, too."

"So, do you think you two will go celebrate after we're done here?"

Flotaki gave me a conspiratorial wink. "You won't tell my wife, will you? Caroline's the jealous type."

"Then what are you doing with your ex?"

"Some like it hot," he shrugged with a sly smile.

"You'll get burned playing with fire, you know."

Flotaki batted my warning away, showing what he thought of my advice. "So?"

"So what?"

"So, are you gonna tell Caroline about..." he quirked his eyebrows in the direction of the door. "About Louisa?"

I frowned, shaking my head. "Christ, no."

Flotaki grinned.

In that brief, brief second, I almost liked Ed Abrams.

He tapped his foot, eyed the conference door as though willing it to open. "I wish she'd hurry. I'm gonna fuck her five ways 'til Tuesday."

The slender threads of affection snapped.

"She will." I leafed through a few pages in his folder, glancing at the current court order regarding custody.

He laughed and I grimaced at the compliment I'd unwittingly given him.

"Why'd you two get divorced?"

"I dunno. She's a little on the stupid side, I guess, and after a while it got on my nerves."

My fingers stilled on the court papers. I felt a chill roll across the back of my neck, raising my fine hairs. Out of nowhere I blurted, "You better hope Caroline never suspects anything."

Matt and Louisa re-entered the conference room again. She bent over the table, jiggling her jugs a little— not quite respectable in public, but enough to promise a wonderful motorboat ride for later when they were in private. She said, "Pay five hundred fifty dollars and I'll go to lunch with you." Her smile was an invitation.

"Done!" Flotaki slapped the table with great enthusiasm, grinning from ear-to-ear. He rose and took Louisa's arm, leading her out of the conference room and towards the inevitable afternoon romp at a cheap hotel. "Draw it up, Cici," he said from the doorway, his horny eyes never leaving his ex-wife's bosom.

"Cooper," I corrected, for all the good it did me.

A thick current of lust underlaid his voice, "Let's go pick up a bucket of fried chicken! I'll slather mashed potatoes and gravy on you and lick you clean."

"Ed!" she giggled, trying to sound shocked. Then she whispered in his ear, leaning against him. Whatever she said, it made him smile bigger than Texas. I knew where the gravy was going—I just hope she didn't burn herself.

"TMI." Matt grimaced after Flotaki and Louisa left.

"What?"

"Too much information. Hey, don't worry about drafting that agreement, I'll do it."

"Great—include the provision that she's not to reveal their affair to his current wife."

"How the hell am I going to do that?" he asked.

Giggling, I stuffed the folder into my father's worn briefcase, taking a moment to trace his initials. "I don't know, but it's gotta be in there. Send it to me when you get a chance."

"Sure were a lot of hormones floating around, eh?" Matt gathered his papers, cramming them into a haphazard pile.

"And boobs."

Matt chuckled. "Use whatever works, right?"

"Yeah, the eighth mystery of the world. Go figure." I snapped the briefcase shut.

He shrugged, "Some women think all that hair's a sign of extra testosterone. Frankly, I don't see it."

I shuddered. "Yeah, well, I've pimped my chimp enough for one morning. I'd better get back to the office."

"You want to go to lunch?"

I smiled, but waved him off. "Not today. I'll have to take a rain check."

"Sure?"

"Some other time," I lied, having no intention of doing so. Something niggled that I still couldn't trust him. I might understand him, but that wasn't enough. Besides, he was married. So it ended there.

I slid behind the wheel of my Festiva, another beloved hand-me-down from my father, turning the key over a few times before it sparked to life. As it groaned awake, I tapped the steering wheel, wondering what I was going to have to do to get rid of the disturbing image of Tanny, bent over her desk. My retinas still burned from seeing her spread over her desk like that. This morning I called into the office and told Melinda I was heading straight for the mediation conference at Matt's office. Easy to avoid Tanny if we weren't in the office together. Sooner or later, though, I'd have to face her. Even though I scolded myself not to feel embarrassed—after all, I wasn't the one screwing around on my spouse, I did.

"Man, if I could afford the therapy, the things I could say on that couch."

I put the Ford in gear, took a deep breath and made for the office. Maybe Sam would be there. Maybe Tanny wouldn't mention it. Maybe. Maybe.

With hope borne, my Festiva puttered into my assigned parking stall. I entered the office with a cheery smile on my lips.

"Is that *Bronski* motion drafted?" My boss barked at me as soon as my cream slingback, open-toed pump crossed the threshold. The smile left my face as I knew this was how Lucifer wanted to play whatever would come next.

"Done." With artificial sweetness to my voice, I brought my other foot into the office and shut the door behind me. Pinning my vision to a point above Tanny's right shoulder, I nodded 'good morning.'

Our assistant, Melinda, started clicking away at her keyboard, head down, no doubt hoping to ignore our approaching cat fight.

Civility, in Tanny Whilts's book, is overrated. She commanded, "Come to my office."

No way was I going to her office. Not today, maybe not ever. Instead, I invited her to come into mine.

Melinda's head jerked up and she stared, slack-jawed, at me.

On the spot, I came up with a lie. I waltzed down the hall to my office, tossing over my shoulder, "I want to show you some vacation photos. You'll love them."

"Lovely!" Being a consummate manipulator, Tanny recovered quickly then followed. After shutting my office door, she hissed, "Are you going to tell?"

Her words, nearly and eerily identical to Ed Abrams' made me recoil. Well, no wonder they got along so well—they're cut from the same bolt of cloth.

"Tell what?" I asked with a world of nonchalance, setting down my dad's briefcase and settling behind my desk.

Tanny's smirk was back in evidence; but something about her smugness repulsed me. It'd be a good lesson for her to learn to squirm a little. So, for her own good—and my own, I freely admit, I pressed my advantage.

"As a related issue, though, the décor in my office is dismal. Some new paint, new furniture would go a long way to ensuring a certain memory from yesterday doesn't return."

Tanny fumed in silence. Her fists balled onto her hips and her knuckles whitened in anger. Curling her lips in a sneer, she gave more than a passing resemblance to that cartoon character, the Grinch.

"Extortion?" She asked in an icy tone.

"That's an ugly term," I spoke in low, measured tones, shaking my head as if her accusation saddened me. "As is my office. U-G-L-Y."

There were a few beats in silence as she glared at me.

I took up the reins again, prodding her so this damned uncomfortable interview could draw to a close. I had shit to do. Most of it the work she assigned me and I didn't want to skip lunch again today. So, if my words were terse, I couldn't help it. "Something in blue."

What was that sound? Oh, my. She was grinding her teeth. I hid a smile. Any second there'd be powder spilling from her mouth.

"Any particular shade?"

I scratched my chin, pretending to be deep in thought. "Hmmm, something Caribbean-inspired. How about Robin's Egg Blue?"

From somewhere deep inside me, a half-forgotten bird snuck out of its cage, stretched its wings and preened its feathers. Its belly filled with an enthusiastic song as its thready warbling commenced. Its singing stirred my blood, exorcising the damn, relentless fog and for a brief span of time, I was alive, fully present in the moment. Maybe my hidden talent was for extortion. I seemed to be really good at it. Rapping my knuckles on my desktop, I assured her, "Fix it up in here and you can be sure I won't tell a living soul what I saw."

Tanny shrugged with ill grace. "Fine. The re-decoration is all a business deduction, anyway."

She made a disdainful wave, her hand stilling on the doorknob as she made to leave. Then in a voice far too casual, she said, "Oh, princess—just so you know, half the cost of the makeover's coming out of your paycheck."

"What? That's not going to cut it."

Tanny gave a triumphant smirk, relishing her return of the upper hand.

"Half? Sorry, Tanny, but since *both* my eyes saw you doubled over your desk, taking it up the ass, I'm gonna have to decline. Don't forget," I reminded her, "I saw your boobies, too."

She stood at the door, seething.

Now we were getting somewhere. Or, as my sister used to say, "We're cooking with Crisco."

Then I delivered the final blow, speaking in a firm, non-negotiable voice. "Full cost for the reno is on the firm."

Tanny might be pissed, but she also couldn't be intimidated. "Don't screw with me, little girl. You have no idea what I'll do."

"Likewise, I'm sure." I'd never said that line before in my life. Don't know why it popped into my head to say it, but it seemed ideal.

Her eyes slanted to slits as she assessed her new associate. Coming to a decision, she lifted a shoulder then shrugged. Tanny tugged the door and spoke loudly enough for Melinda to listen. "Great photographs. Thanks for showing me those, Cooper."

Collapsing in my broken-back chair, I congratulated myself for the office makeover, but I couldn't help but wonder what price it came at.

Chapter 7

Sweet Bastard Angel

Sam entered my office, his fat face purple and his fleshy lips pressed together. Something had pissed him off, that was no mystery, but I hadn't expected him to fight Tanny's battles. Nor did I imagine he would take umbrage for me blackmailing his cheating wife, so what bug had crawled up his ass?

"What's the matter, Sam?"

He waved some papers in his right hand and demanded, "What *is* this?"

He referred to my *Bronski* memorandum and motion. I recognized it by its thickness.

Throwing the documents onto my desktop, he thundered, "What the hell are you trying to pull here, Coop?"

A few pages flitted off the desk and pirouetted to the floor. Chewing my bottom lip, I replayed his question, still confused. Could he be so angry about my insistence to have new office furniture and paint? What the hell?

Sam's hands raked through the few blond strands of hair he had as he gave me a belligerent stare. When he plopped into my client's chair, it creaked under the weight. In the prime of his life, Sam Hatdiff's physique left a lot to be desired. In the suit pants he wore, his ass completely disappeared. His belt hung low over his belly in the way chunky men try to kid themselves that their waist line hasn't expanded since their college years. If he'd just eat one-third smaller portions, or take a mid-morning and mid-afternoon walk around the block, he might stave off that heart attack that was headed his way.

Snapped out of these wanderings, I tried to listen to his crisp words.

"You omitted a critical point in the *Bronski* memorandum. Really, it's the only point we'll be litigating. Don't you see that?"

Alarmed, I searched my brain, cursing my stupidity for having missed something so obvious and crucial.

He leaned forward, his forearms propped on the corner of my desk and his eyebrows raised with the expectancy of a professor awaiting his pupil's answer.

I did light upon one idea, but it was so ludicrous, I dismissed it. Still searching for the answer, my confidence crumbled as I stymied. Lifting my palm in a gesture of helplessness, I muttered, "Are we supposed to litigate whether or not Mrs. Bronski's a slut—that the kid may not be the father's?"

A slow, malicious grin curled Sam's lips. He poked his finger at me. "You're getting there."

But that's as far as the steam in my train of thought would take me. How do you litigate… and *why* would you litigate whether our client is a slut? I'm pretty sure that contradicts the whole 'zealous advocate' deal we lawyers are supposed to be. I scratched my head, "Sorry, Sam. I'm just not seeing your point. Help me out here."

"Mr. and Mrs. Bronski married in September, 2005, right?"

I nodded, showing I was with him so far.

"Junior arrives in March, 2006, right?" He spoke to me as if I were learning-impaired. I hated it, but I still didn't see where he was going with this.

"So? She was pregnant when they got married. Happens a lot."

"From the notes of my interview with Mrs. Bronski," he flicked his legal pad with a squatty finger. "She tells me she had an affair with another man in June, 2005—roughly nine months before Junior's birth."

Still not following the legal implications, the words slowly drained from me, "I'm sure Mr. Bronski would gladly stipulate his soon-to-be-ex-wife is a tramp."

Sam lost patience with me and exploded out of his chair.

"If Junior ain't Mr. Bronski's biological son, he doesn't get custody or visitation, you idiot!"

I argued back, "But Junior might be his son. Mrs. Bronski was sleeping with both men at the same time."

This was the wrong thing to say.

Sam slapped his knee and swore. "Dammit, Cooper! Did you sleep through Family Law class? You need to ask for a *Roth* hearing in the damn motion and memorandum."

"A... a... a *Roth* hearing? What is that?"

"Look it up," my mentor said, biting off the words and hitching up his pants. "Re-write the motion and memorandum. Got it?"

"And ask for a *Roth* request?"

"A *Roth* hearing, you idiot!" He slammed my office door.

"Why would I do that?" I asked my gray office wall, which stood silent.

I pounded on my keyboard, searching for the *Roth* case law. After reading the landmark case and several of its progeny, I learned the purpose of a Roth hearing was to discover whether a child, otherwise considered legitimate for being born within the time of a marriage, could be bastardized. From the man's perspective (usually), a request for paternity tests is driven by the hope to dodge child support. No kid, no cash. From the woman's perspective, a request for paternity testing is a swipe against the supposed father and is a mean way to severe the bonds between father and child. No kid, no kidding.

Our client, the inestimable Mrs. Bronski, intended to divest Mr. Bronski of the joys, privileges and responsibilities of parenthood. This would be devastating to Mr. Bronski, who was deeply involved with his eight-year old son. They did many activities together and by all accounts, he was a doting father. He just didn't wish to be married to his wife anymore.

I can't say I blamed him.

Mrs. Bronski had cheated during their engagement and never stopped. Her infidelities were legion and I suspect Mr. Bronski had always wondered if he were

Junior's true father, but had obviously chosen to be his dad. Which made him a hero, in my eyes.

It also made Mrs. Bronski unchaste, which is one thing, but to deny her son a father was quite another. What a bitch. Bastardizing your son affected his inheritance rights, his ability to form trusting, loving relationships in the future, his identity—a whole host of things. The kind of person who would do that wasn't better than the host of maggots which fed off a carcass. Not sure whether I'd label Mrs. Bronski as maggots or carcass, I gave up the cerebral exercise. Did it matter? No. Not really.

I reached for the *Bronski* papers, wadded them up, cursing inwardly as I thought this was another thing law school hadn't prepared me for: the dirty, dirty fighting of a divorcing couple. Raising my arm, I tossed the ball, letting it leave my fingertips. I watched the paper land in my trash can. "Yea."

Doesn't take a fortune teller's crystal ball to see there'd be no winners in this sick, twisted game. The real loser by *my* own keystroke would be an innocent, clear-eyed, eight-year old boy. That poor, bastard angel.

Starring at my computer screen, I wonder how Junior would react upon learning that his world was now turned upside-down. His dad may not be his dad and his mom was a slut who'd rather settle a score against her ex than ensure her child's happiness.

This was rough.

Closing my eyes, I sent up a prayer. Lord, if I ever get a chance to meet our client in a dark alley late at night, please let me have an iron pipe handy. Somebody should beat the living tar out of the bitch. I hoped it could be me.

I said 'Amen.'

Groaning, I started re-typing the memorandum, hating myself with every sentence.

Instead of an iron pipe, I wished it'd be a mace, something from medieval times. Something not only lethal, but incredibly painful, too. Mrs. Bronski deserved it.

What a bitch.

***

The food pantry sure was persnickety. The policy not to accept donations from open containers made sense, but it had been a surprise. Glad to have whittled down the food stuffs that took up all the trunk and half the backseat, there was too much to cart back into the apartment. It would be asinine to throw that much away—it was perfectly fine. Rather than wasting the food, I'd find someone to give it to—poof! A little old lady wearing a knitted cozy popped into my brain.

After work, I found Mrs. Cuttlebum's house on the edge of town, a small white house with a tiny yard, which could probably be mowed with three or four swipes of the lawnmower. Having taken care of the yard as one of my childhood chores, I tended to notice those kinds of details. A narrow walkway of river stones led from the gate to the porch, flanked with crimson begonias. By the porch, another garden spread out, filled with rose bushes. The fragrance from the white, yellow, and pink roses trailed through the air, and enticed visitors to enter the house.

The floorboards of the porch were painted light green. There were worn patches to the color, making it clear everyone was to use the front entrance to the home. Shutters were painted a buttery-yellow, but they too showed signs of wear, chipping in spots. Wicker furniture with faded cushions flanked the front door. Oddly, the slightly disheveled condition of the house exuded serenity. This wasn't a show case home, where everything was neat and tidy and modernized. It was a home.

I knocked on the black screen door, bare-handed. I thought I should give her a chance to refuse my offerings, not put her on the spot. Hell, my law firm had just tried to sue her. She might want nothing to do with me. I don't know.

Mrs. Cuttlebum opened the door, her eyes squinting behind those heavy lenses in her outdated frames. Her smile was hesitant and her forehead crinkled; she didn't recognize me. Knowing that might be a good thing, I spoke up loudly, recalling her deafness. "Mrs. Cuttlebum?"

"Yes?"

"Hi, I'm Cooper Bach. We met last week in the courthouse."

She shook her head.

I didn't know what to make of that gesture, so I tried again, "I'm new in town and trying to settle into my apartment. Clearing out my cupboards, I found extra foodstuff. Could you use any of the pantry items?"

"Well, of course. I can always use foodstuff. You say you're new in town?"

"Yeah."

"Well, welcome!"

I smiled my thanks and held up my index finger, indicating she should wait while I fetched the stuff. She returned the smile, so I jogged to my Festiva and brought the first box back, setting it down on her porch.

"You're sure you want to give this away?" Mrs. Cuttlebum asked, inspecting the contents of the box like a kid on Christmas morning. "Oooh, I love pancakes!" She picked up a box of batter with her gnarled fingers, but her smile looked surprisingly youthful.

I grinned and shook my head.

"You sure you don't need this?"

"Trust me. I don't."

"What can I pay you for all this?" She replaced the mix and grabbed a bottle of Worcestershire sauce.

"Nothing."

Fiercely, she placed her hands on her hips and insisted, "Let me pay you something."

"No, it's okay. Really."

"What's up, Grandma?" A teenager dressed in jeans and t-shirt came out the front door, chewing an apple. As soon as he saw me, his eyes lit up and he leaned against the porch railing, crossing his legs at the ankle. His eyes roved over my figure in a thorough appraisal. He made no effort to hide his approval. Smiling with his eyes and his mouth, he stuck out his hand and said, "Hi. I'm Brandon Cuttlebum."

"I'm Cooper Bach."

He shook my hand, grinning so widely it was impossible to be offended by his blatant admiration. With the effort apparent, he lowered his voice and intoned, "Nice to meet you, Cooper."

Mrs. Cuttlebum frowned again then waved in the young man's direction, "This is my grandson, Brandon. He's staying with me until he goes to college next term."

Brandon took another bite from his apple, mulling it about in his mouth in a languid fashion, eyeing me the whole time.

"Could you help bring in the rest of the boxes?" I asked.

"There's more?" Mrs.Cuttlebum asked.

"Sure." He tossed his apple core into the rose bushes and fetched the rest of the boxes, placing them on the porch as Mrs. Cuttlebum and I chatted.

Watching her grandson, Mrs. Cuttlebum told me, "Brandon's going to Kansas State. Going to be an architect."

I nodded and murmured, "Impressive."

"That's the plan for now," he agreed, bringing the last box out of the car. He put it down then crossed his arms over his chest. "Which school do you go to?"

As gently as possible, I said, "I went to KU...Law School."

His eyes bugged out and he snapped into formation like a little toy soldier. His face reddened and he blurted, "You're a lawyer?"

"Hmmm."

The words, "That's pretty impressive," left his throat, as if they were being choked from him, but I recognized his attempt at being gracious and his stock went up in my eyes a few notches.

"Thanks."

Brandon turned his attention to the box, covering his discomfort. "So, what do we got here?"

"I just moved here and can't store all this stuff in my new apartment, so I thought maybe you guys could use this stuff. Can you? Use this stuff?"

He shrugged. "Sure."

Mrs. Cuttlebum tapped her grandson on the arm. "Brandon, grab a box and take it inside to the kitchen, please, then bring me my shears."

"Sure thing, Grandma."

Within a few minutes, he had done what she asked, the banging screen door the only sound as conversation between me and Mrs. Cuttlebum dwindled.

"Here you go," he said, handing her a pair of garden shears. "You want me to take the rest in now?"

"Yes, please."

Brandon took the rest of the boxes, tossing over his shoulder, "Nice to meet you, Cooper. Come around any time."

"Thanks."

Mrs. Cuttlebum clipped some roses off and hollered to Brandon to bring her some wet paper towels, which he did, grinning as he brought them outside to her.

"Man's work is never done," he said, handing them over.

"I know. I know. I use you shamelessly." She chuckled, wrapping the stems in the towels, her hands shaking so much I worried she'd snag a thorn by accident. Mrs. Cuttlebum offered them to me, saying, "I hope you enjoys roses. Allow me to say 'thank you' for thinking of us, Cooper."

I took the scarlet bouquet and inhaled. "They smell great and yes, I love roses. Thank you very much."

We moved to the porch, sitting in the wicker furniture and Brandon brought out glasses of lemonade for the three of us as we enjoyed a nice, long chat. The flowers' scent drifted in the breeze, meandering like our conversation, hitting on a variety of subjects. Brandon looked forward to attending university. His eyes lit up when he talked of architecture then became wistful as he spoke of traveling to Rome and other parts of the world to see the monuments there. From there we all chimed in on places we'd like to visit and what we imagined we'd see there. It was all in good fun; none of us had traveled abroad, except for Mrs. Cuttlebum, but since her foreign trip was limited to nursing duties in Vietnam, she had no wish to return to that place.

Twilight descended before we said our goodbyes. Tooling home in the Festiva, I realized, yet again, I'd spent worse afternoons. Being with the Cuttlebums was pretty relaxing, just sitting on a front porch, talking about this and that. No pressure. No need to perform. Just kinda…what was it? Making friends. That's what it'd been.

I groaned.

After all my resolutions, it happened and I hadn't even been aware of it at the time. Life was dragging me back into its fold, sneaky-like. Despite my intention to remain aloof, I had formed a new friendship with Mrs.

Cuttlebum and her grandson, Brandon. I was making connections. Now ain't that the stupidest thing ever?

The fragrance from the roses filled the Festiva and it annoyed me how much I enjoyed it. Realizing that might be stupider still, I parked the car at my apartment complex. I didn't want those ties that would bind me to others. I wanted to be left alone. On an island surrounded by fog. It was safer that way.

I could feel my sister prod me, shaking her head in disapproval.

"Yeah, yeah, I know."

Staring at the bouquet, I scooped the roses up then flung them into the dumpster in the parking lot.

"I'm not ready for this, Gloria. I'm not." I shrugged, noting a knot had formed between my shoulders. I took three steps before swinging back and snatching the bouquet back.

"Fine," I grumbled. "But I still don't know where I'm gonna find a vase to put these in."

***

I bolted upright in bed, my body was covered in sweat, my heartbeat racing, and the sobs I heard were my own. My watch read 4:28. Shaking, I got up and went to the restroom, trying to figure out what had just happened here. I'd had a nightmare.

Squinting to bring back the memories, the edges of recall were still in place as the rest of the picture filled out. There was blood. Everywhere. In my mind, I zoomed in on the floor where crimson droplets puddled, dripping from the gurney. I was back in the E.R. with Gloria. The scent of antiseptic once again in my nostrils along with the faint whiff of Chardonnay which lingered on her pale lips.

I kissed her. Pressing my lips against her cold mouth and tasting her last sip of wine, her last drop of blood. The ice in that kiss chilled me from the inside. Standing before my bathroom mirror, I gazed sightlessly upon my reflection, seeing only my sister's lips whiten as blood drained from her body.

I thought life would never be the same. I was right, but I didn't know how much. Looking back to that moment, it was like standing on the western cliffs of Ireland looking over the Atlantic. Sure, there was an ocean stretched before me, but I didn't realize its breadth, couldn't know how deep it would be and failed to grasp its length. My utter ignorance of what lay before me staggered. At the time Gloria passed, I never knew that event would trigger the horrific chain of events.

I splashed cold water on my face out of habit more than anything else. I glanced at my bed. It didn't exactly beckon me to return. There was no comforting welcome amid the pillows and sheets. I looked again. Sweat marked the sheets and I sniffed a faint odor.

"How long has it been since I changed the sheets?"

I cleared everything off the bed, pushing junk to the floor, which was already so cluttered, no carpet could be seen. Sloppy, wobbly towers of crap formed, like some Picasso drawing. With Herculean effort, after a lot of tugging and cussing, I peeled the sheets off the mattress. Trying to locate another set would be an exercise in futility, so I'd have to do laundry and put them back on later.

As the washer filled, I dumped in detergent, stuffed the sheets and whatever clothes I could find into the tub. It was five o'clock on a Saturday morning; that crowded kitchen called me. I answered, making myself a cup of tea before throwing myself into the task of organizing. For the rest of the day I brought order from the chaos and refused to dwell on that nightmare.

Chapter 8

Dinner by Myself

I didn't agree with the decision to bastardize a kid, but it wasn't my call. Margaret Bronski chose this course of action, despite Sam's attempt to dissuade her; to give him credit, he tried to warn her off. Realizing he'd waste his breath by appealing to the woman's sense of decency or scolding her that this would irreparably damage Junior, he cautioned a *Roth* hearing would be expensive as hell. When she still persisted, he demanded another $5,000 retainer.

She paid by credit card.

Like an annoying mosquito, an irritant niggled me. Even if Maggot (my nickname for Margaret Bronski) insisted on this, we didn't have to go along with it. Glad that Sam squeezed her for some extra juice, Maggot's retainer seemed far too cheap and too costly, all at once. Knowing the little bitch would probably shirk paying by declaring bankruptcy on her credit card bills didn't help matters. It was like being force-fed a shit sandwich. Although Tanny probably wanted me to come in and work on the case, it was Saturday and I didn't want to give up my free time to re-work the motion and supporting memorandum. Screw Tanny and Maggot. Already I'd worked 72 hours this week.

Another thing they didn't teach us in law school. Salaried positions equated to slave wages.

So instead of lawyering, I used my Saturday to haul stuff to the trash dumpster or cart it off to Goodwill. By the end of the day, the kitchen cupboards were full, but everything was off the counters and the floor. The stove top was even clear, so that I could use it. Around mid-afternoon, I tackled the bathroom and emptied the tub and gave it a good scrubbing. Cranking up the tunes, I rocked out as I folded the towels and stacked them in the narrow linen closet adjacent to my room. I place forty-four towels into a trash sack and took it to the Festiva, intending to take it to Goodwill later since it was nearly closing time.

Climbing back up the flight of stairs to the apartment, I swiped a sweaty brow. My energy felt zapped and changed my playlist to classical selections. The soothing strains of the music helped me relax as I luxuriated in a warm bath. I must have dozed for a while because the water had grown tepid. A sense of well-being enfolded me as I re-dressed. To celebrate my accomplishments, I decided to treat myself to dinner. I did a quick calculation. I could afford a bowl of soup and a glass of water at a restaurant.

Sheahan's wasn't swanky, but it was clean and offered a variety of soups and stews. Twenty-four miles into the city would find better restaurants with more ambience and specialties, but there was no need for that. Besides, I really couldn't afford the extra gas. Sheahan's would do.

The hostess, dressed in a white and green apron, escorted me to my booth and brought me a glass of ice water then told me my waiter would be there momentarily.

After the waiter introduced himself, he asked if someone would be joining me.

I gestured for him to lower his voice.

He leaned toward me and whispered, "Will you be dining alone this evening?"

Now mortified by the extra attention or sarcasm, I blushed, "Yes."

"How 'bout a beer?" He asked, friendly-like.

"Sure. Bring me a Fat Tire," I said, flustered and forgetting that was out of my price range.

As I gazed at the mahogany-paneled room, I wondered if I hadn't made a mistake in under-estimating the difficulty of eating alone. It's not for rookies. If anything's geared to bringing all latent insecurities to the surface, it's dining solitary-style.

But this was Saturday night and for the past week, my evening meals had come from a microwave: baked potato or frozen dinner. Impossible to use my kitchen, I'd nuked everything, but I was sick of restricted diet, which was probably a good sign that my appetite was returning.

Within a few minutes, the waiter returned with my beer and I thanked him. Taking a long draw, I closed my eyes, savoring the cold pale ale. This small pleasure should not be taken for granted. I took another long sip, licking my lips. I sat back against the upholstered bench seat and pictured my cleaner apartment. Some of it was tamed today. I'd whipped the jungle beasts which roamed the kitchen, linen closet, and bathroom. Sure, the rest of my apartment looked like a zoo, but at least I had established some safety zones. Being able to bathe and sleep in clean sheets would make me feel like a human being again.

I toasted the Fickle Finger of Fate. Like a monkey flinging feces, she had cast a lot of lousy, miserable shit my way recently, but I was recovering. I was fighting back. I was making my way out of jungle.

Jauntily, I raised my beer bottle in a mocking salute to Fate. "Hah."

But Fate's a bitch who bites back.

No sooner had the exclamation left my lips than a family entered the restaurant. Their chatter and laughter raise the noise level throughout the restaurant. Held by a proud father, a newborn poked through layers of pink, soft blankets, cocooned in her carrier. Beside him stood the new mother, beaming at her husband, despite her swollen ankles. Her cheeks, however, glowed like a lustrous pearl. An older gentleman—the grandfather, no doubt, spoke to the hostess while the grandmother offered the toddler a juicy cup.

I squinted for a better look at the boy, a recently ordained big brother. It was hard to examine his face since the boogar was on the move and kinda blurred. He jumped up and down on the lobby step. Chuckling to myself, remembering how Gloria and I stomped around, playacting like we were performing in the circus, walking on the high wire or leaping over the swamps filled with alligators. Or maybe he was pretending to be a grasshopper.

"Michael," I groaned, scooting down in my bench. The last time I'd seen the kid I'd made a complete ass of myself in the grocery store, calling his uncle a jerk.

I scanned the lobby. No sign of his uncle, which made me heave a sigh of relief. Recalling our debacle in the parking lot, I'd just as soon forget we ever met. If I saw him never, it would be too soon.

Ted strode through the door, smiling as he took off his coat.

My hand went to my cheek, checking to see if some of the excrement Fate was flinging landed there. Ducking behind the menu, I wonder if my luck could get any worse.

"Cooper Bach? That is your name, isn't it?"

I promised to never sneer at Fate again. Her ability to get immediate revenge was scary. Pasting on a fake smile, I slowly lowered the menu, damning that unfortunate hiding technique as I said, "Oh. Hi. Ted, isn't it?"

He held out his hand. "Yes. Thanks for remembering. Ted Danveldt."

Frantically, I cast about my hollow brain, searching for conversation. "Swedish?"

"Smorgsabord."

I smiled at his weak joke.

He shrugged, but his smile reached his eyes and it occurred to me this guy was a nice person. My gaze drifted down, drawn to that smile and I remembered that sweet kiss in the rain. It's weird, but it felt like there was a break in my mood, like sunshine piercing through a cloudy, rainy day. The mental fog that I carried burned away, rolling back those safe feelings of detachment and disconnection to allow a glimpse of life on the outside.

His mouth quirked with humor.

Embarrassed to be caught staring, my cheeks heated up.

Ted plopped down on the other side of my booth, looking pleased with himself. "You here by yourself?"

"Yeah. Just thought I'd grab a quick bite."

He craned his neck, glancing as his family sat down at their table then he turned back to me and invited me to join them.

"No, I really couldn't."

"Sure you can—just the family and you already know Michael."

I stroked my throat, hoping to squelch the rising tide of heat which pooled there and would soon travel upward. "I wouldn't want to intrude."

"You won't. Besides, I'm odd man out and having you will even up the numbers." He stood, plucked the Fat Tire from my hand and pulled me out of my seat. He helped sit me at the table then dashed away.

Panic set in. What kind of trick was this? Did he even know these people? No, he jogged back to my booth to retrieve my purse. I relaxed, smiling a little at my over-wrought imagination.

Smiling, he handed me my purse and teased, "Here, you go, Coop. Do you always forget your purse?"

"Not always," I admitted, barely halting before I revealed, 'Just with you.' That's the kind of hyperbole that could get a girl in trouble. Or give a guy an idea you were attracted to him. As if.

As if, my ass.

Sitting in the chair next to mine, he said, "Hey, everybody! This is a friend of mine, Cooper Bach. Mom, Dad—Janet and Max Danveldt to you." He indicated his parents with a casual wave then rested his other hand along the back of my chair. "My brother-in-law Ron Savitch, my sister, Karen."

Then he paused in the introductions to give me a deliberate, sidelong glance. An unmistakable gleam entered his eyes when he introduced his sister. I read that sardonic look correctly. It was a gentle gibe to remind me Karen wasn't his wife and he wasn't a cheating man-whore.

But he showed the wisdom of not actually expressing that last thought aloud. Pointing to the toddler, he finished with, "Of course, you remember Michael."

"And what's the baby's name?" I asked Karen.

Ted smacked his forehead.

"You have the attention span of a gnat, brother," Karen reached into the carrier, unfastened the belts and lifted her daughter. "This is Isabelle, who is one week old today."

"Nice to meet you all. Ted didn't ask, but would it be all right if I joined your family for dinner?"

"Oh, of course!" His mother said, smiling. Then she stretched her arms out, to indicate Karen should let her hold the baby. "We're celebrating Izzy's first outing!"

"The more the merrier," Ron said.

"It's nice to meet you," I murmured, awkward being thrust into the group.

Ted's father, Max, half-rose to shake my hand. "Pleased to make your acquaintance."

Then the waiter came for the drink order. Conversation halted as everyone chimed in with their requests.

I cupped the back of my nape. Knots started tightening there from the tension. Glancing back at my booth, I saw it now as a haven and wished I were still alone. I had nothing in common with these people. Didn't know them or the first thing about them. What on earth would I say? How could I make the next hour or so fly by as I sat here, slurping a bowl of soup?

"You can't desert me." A deep, amused voice sounded right by my ear.

I glanced at him then blinked. "What makes you say that?"

Ted shrugged. "Your shoulders are creeping toward your ears, you're so tense. Lighten up, Cooper. Roll with it."

"Roll with it."

"Yes." His eyes were brown, the color of caramel. The same color throughout the iris, undiluted by any specks or starbursts. Something steadied me about those orbs of his. Their purity, solidity made me feel grounded and secure.

Like having an anchor in troubled waters.

The light of humor left those caramel eyes, replaced with something that could have been puzzlement or concern. Maybe both.

His thumb skimmed the back of my hand, as his head came closer to my ear. "Hey. You okay?"

Withdrawing my hand, I gave a jerk of a nod. "Sure. Why wouldn't I be?"

Concentrating on the menu selections, I could feel the side of my face tingle from the intensity of his stare, but he remained silent. He sat back, removing his hand from the back of my chair. As soon as he did so, the rush of cooler air sailed over me. Funny how cozy that had been.

"What will you have for dinner?" Ted asked.

"Oh, there's a delicious stew I wanted to try."

He gave a half-smile. "Stew? Really? Why don't you try the Kansas City strip? It's really good here."

"Sirloin's pretty good, too," offered Max.

"None for you, dear," Janet reminded her husband in a sideways glance.

Max grumbled something under his breath, his ungraciousness feigned with an underlying good-heartedness.

"Dad's got high cholesterol," explained Karen, smoothing Baby Isabelle's back.

It felt so surreal, sitting here, an interloper on this family's celebratory dinner. Salads were served and devoured while I toyed with a package of crackers. By the time the appetizers came, the fog was back, covering me in layers of numbing, obscuring clouds. I listened with a mechanic smile as though in a daze. In reality, I felt plastic and hermetically sealed off from the Danveldt family. Just going through the motions.

"You all right?" Ted whispered in my ear, his voice jerking me back to awareness of my surroundings.

I returned to the 'here and now' with a jerk, startled. In the next heartbeat, a lump formed in my throat and the back of my eyes stung.

Shaking my head, I hope he understood I couldn't explain anything. Like the moon's pull over the tides, his gaze drew me.

"God, you look so vulnerable." His fingertip trailed on my cheek as he murmured, "Whatever it is, Coop, it's going to be fine."

"Is it?"

"Do you want me to take you home?"

Lowering my gaze to my lap, I shook my head.

Beneath the table, he gave my hand a good squeeze. With our fingers entwined, his bigger hand covering mine, we sat together. The thought struck me that if nothing else happened for the rest of the evening, this was enough. It was grand just holding hands. The old-fashioned word 'grand' made me smile. That wasn't at all like myself. Then again, how many evenings had I whiled away on a front porch talking with an old woman and her grandson? I'd found pleasure and contentment in those slower moments.

Maybe I was becoming a little old-fashioned.

Lifting my face, I gazed at Ron and Karen, parents of two children. Together they were a young, happy family. I watched Janet and Max talk with their kids and grandson. They looked contented. This was…this was life.

"Would you like a roll, dear?" Janet passed the basket.

"Thank you, yes." I untangled my fingers from Ted's, missing the connection. Rather than dwell on that uncomfortable fact, I smeared butter on a dinner roll.

Janet asked, "And how do you know Ted?"

About to say, "I don't," Ted interrupted me.

"Cooper's been to my bar."

I grimaced. Nobody appreciates being painted as a bar hound.

"Really? And what did you think of the place?" asked his sister, Karen.

"Yes, Cooper, what's your opinion of my place?" Ted placed both elbows on the table, eager, as though he were hanging on my every word.

Something in his cocky attitude tempted me to take him down a peg or two.

"It could use some improvement." I made a tiny, spidery smile, spinning my web to make an inviting trap for the fly that was Ted Danveldt.

"What?" His jaw dropped.

Karen snorted, rocking Isabelle. "Good one."

"In what way could it be improved?"

His dad cautioned, "Don't answer him. Let's take turns making suggestions."

Ron burst out, snapping his fingers. "The floors need to be replaced!"

"New booths!" sang Karen.

Max raised his glass and barked, "He needs new stools, by God."

"And paint it some other color—you know, something from this decade?" His mother said with a wry note, even as she beckoned for Karen to let her hold the baby again.

"*Et tu*, Brute?" Ted muttered beneath his breath.

Wrinkling my nose, I chided them. "You guys are thinking too small. It needs something big. Something like…napalm."

The whole family lost it then.

"Enough!" Ted's voice rang out imperiously, although nobody seemed to pay any attention to him. His shoulders shook with silent laughter as the waiter delivered a platter of onion rings.

"We didn't order onion rings. Did we?" Max asked his wife for confirmation.

Janet shook her head.

The waited nodded toward the kitchen. "It's on the house. You know, to celebrate the baby."

Everyone turned, looked at the kitchen and sent a holler, a 'thumbs up' or a wave.

"So, Cooper, where do you work?" Ron asked, cutting up an onion ring for Michael.

"I'm an attorney. I work for Tanny Whilts and Sam Hatdiff. They mostly do divorce work."

"Yeah," said Max with a serious tone. "She's a real work of art."

His wife gasped then scolded. "Max, mind your mouth. The children."

"Well? She is! And I'll bet Cooper's figured that out by now, haven't you, girl?"

Janet dropped her head between her hands and groaned, "Cooper's never going to want to come near this family again."

But Ron's eyes gleamed. "So, Coop, is Tanny really so bad?"

Peeling off the label on my beer bottle, I murmured, "There's not really a good answer to that, is there? If I say she's terrible, you'll think she's a lousy person. If I say she's not terrible, you'll think she's a lousy lawyer. It's a lose/lose scenario."

"Well played, Maestro." Ted clapped, his applause slow and measured.

His eyes shone with approval and whatever there was in that look of his, it sent tingling sensations down my spine.

Michael's squeal cut through the air, breaking our gaze. The toddler found a penny and carried it to his grandfather with the awe of having discovered a prized trove. Grasped between his chubby thumb and finger, he raised his hand to display his find.

Max stooped to inspect his grandson's prize. "Ah, my boy! You have found the key to love!"

"It *is*?" The boy beamed.

Karen and Ted exchanged indulgent looks, re-signed to their father's professorial ways. Ron, the son-in-law, muttered with more than a hint of exasperation, "Uh-oh, here he goes again."

Gathering Michael to sit on his lap, Max recited:

> I whispered, 'I am too young.' And then, 'I am old enough;' Wherefore I threw a penny to find out if I might find love. 'Go and love, go and love, young man, if the lady be young and fair.' Ah, penny, brown penny, brown penny, I am looped in the loops of her hair. O love is a crooked thing. There is nobody wise enough to find out all that is in it, for he would be thinking of love till the stars had run away and the shadows eaten the moon. Ah penny, brown penny, brown penny, one cannot begin it too soon."

Max patted his dewy-eyed wife's hand then kissed the top of Michael's head.

The tenderness in those actions touched me and I had a stark realization that before me sat a man, richly blessed, and who knew it. What a rarity. This was a discovery which rivaled Michael's.

"Walt Whitman!" Karen's outburst fractured the tender moment, jarring me.

Her husband wondered, "John Keats?"

Janet bit her bottom lip, unable to come up with the poet's name then asked, "It's not Robert Frost, is it?"

"No." Max shook his head and rolled his eyes, giving Michael a conspiratorial hug.

Like looking through a telescopic lens, the scene moved away from me. From a distance, I could observe this family, not yet touched by tragedy. From their banter to their hasty consumption of a touching moment, to the barrage of questions without waiting for answers, it was plain. They were blissfully ignorant, blithely arrogant in their safe cocoon of complacency; and I resented them. They had no idea. No fucking idea how extravagant they were and I wanted to scream at them.

Max ruffled his grandson's hair and said, "What a sorry lot this is, Michael. None of them recognize the great work of Irish poet—"

"William Butler Yeats." Ted and I said in unison.

All eyes turned on us. Speculation rife with his mother and sister, although his dad's mouth quirked at the corners. My cheeks were burning up and I didn't risk looking at Ted, afraid to see a mocking expression on his face.

Thank the Lord, the waiter brought our entrees then and I delved into my Irish stew. In no time, I scraped the bottom with my spoon. The rest of the evening passed without the fog rolling back in. I laughed, watching Karen and Ron, a typical married couple, bicker as they sampled one another's dinner. Michael hurried through his meal so that he could clamber beneath the table and searched for more pennies, which his grandfather thoughtfully and surreptitiously laid out for him to detect. Isabelle, the baby, made the rounds, sleeping while being adored.

It was my turn to hold her and as she snuggled against me, I breathed in her fresh, sweet baby scent. Mesmerized, I watched her tiny chest move up and down. The regular rhythm of her breathing soothed me.

She followed an unheard beat, instinctually placing herself in earth's diurnal flow. Without being taught, Isabelle had found her way in this world. Breathe in, breathe out. Hold on, let go. Somewhere between the rush and draw maybe, just maybe, you get free onion rings.

Chapter 9

LeRoy Washington,
Ladies Man

"LeRoy Washington's here to see you," Melinda announced, giving me his consultation check for a hundred dollars and putting his client intake sheet on my desk.

"Thanks," I murmured, minimizing the computer screen and straightening my desk to ensure no documents showed.

"Do you need anything?" she asked, all politeness.

"Me? No, thanks. Maybe something to drink?" It was the first time I'd ever requested someone, other than a family member, to get me something to drink. Was I experiencing white guilt because Melinda's African-American? Or was this awkward moment because, at the ripe age of twenty-five, I had acquired an older, subservient employee? How should I set the tone for an employee/employer relationship with Melinda that isn't demeaning? Would it be—

"Cooper?" She leaned over my desk, shattering my chaotic speculations. Her lips twitched with ill-concealed humor. "It's just coffee, Coop. How do you take it?"

I grinned. "Guess I over-analyzed that, eh?"

She shook her head, a slight smile still curving her ruby mouth. "Sugar and cream or black?"

"Lots of sugar. No cream."

As Melinda turned away, I called out, "Thanks."

She waved away my gratitude, but I suspect she was pleased.

I smoothed down my skirt, forced a smile, and went to greet my next client: a couple waited in the lobby. Twitching his foot, a young, wiry, African-American looked as if he were ready to launch from his chair at any second. His over-sized pants billowed around his skinny ankles. Accompanying Mr. Washington was another woman. Shoulders-hunched, she sat next to him gripping a denim purse with bony, work-worn hands. Grooves etched beside her mouth, silent testimony that during her scant decades she had lived a hard life. She wore a sundress made of thin, cheap material, which was wrinkled, witlessly building another layer to her weary appearance. Her hair was unkept and stringy, the toenails protruding from her flip-flops were unpolished. She rose to shake my hand and as the nap of cotton stretched across her belly, it was evident she was pretty pregnant.

I shook hands with them both. "Hello, I'm Cooper Bach."

"I'm Leroy Washington." He waved in the direction of his companion's direction without looking at her. "This here's Emily Reichow."

She elbowed him, and his eyes narrowed.

He nearly growled, "My fiancée."

"Please come into my office."

Emily stepped in front of LeRoy and followed me to my office, waddling with what little dignity her bloated body could muster.

"Would you like something to drink?"

"I'll take a diet cola, if you got it," Mr. Washington said.

"Just water, please," said the female.

"I'll get them," Melinda volunteered.

When she returned with the drinks, Emily and I thanked her. LeRoy took the can and popped the top.

"In there, please," I indicated my office, while I tracked into the law library and retrieved an extra chair.

As they settled in, I wrote "LeRoy Washington," the date, and my initials in the upper right hand corner of my legal pad. Once that was done, I asked, "How can I help you?"

"Are you any good?"

A slight pause before I replied in the affirmative.

Unabashed, LeRoy explained, "I hafta ax 'cause I've had lawyers before."

Another pause.

"Go on."

"They fucked me over. Ev'ry one of them."

His companion *tsked*, a sound he ignored.

"Really?" I set my pen down, keeping my motions deliberate and slow.

"Yeah." He wiped his mouth with his hand then rubbed his pant leg.

"How's so?"

"They've fucked me over, every one of them has."

111

"How have you been… err… screwed over?"

"Well, the first one was Luke something… he told me to pay LaVetta $382 a month!"

"Why?"

"Child support for Deondre. But Deondre wasn't even living with LaVetta—he was livin' over at LaVetta's mama's."

"LaVetta's the mother of Deondre?"

He nodded.

"Well, I don't know if $382 is a reasonable amount of child support or not…"

"It ain't! I can't even live on that! And now Emily here—" He jabbed his thumb at her. "Is 'pectin' in three mo' weeks. I don't know how we're gonna feed this 'un."

That's a problem.

"How much do you make a month?"

He withdrew his paystub from his shirt pocket and slapped it on my desktop.

"It's different every month. Some weeks I work fifteen hours, other times forty-five."

"Have you work here the entire year?"

"Yeah."

Using the paystub's details, I crunch the numbers. LeRoy's year-to-date was $16,784.52, yielding $2,797.42 per month. Not great, but not bad for small town Kansas—maybe a decade ago. His child support for Deondre was only 13% of gross, which was much lower—suspiciously lower—than guideline amount.

"Do you have any other debts, LeRoy?"

"Nope."

"Nothing? Not a house payment or a car payment?"

He shook his head.

"No credit card debt?"

"Nah. I bankrupted all that. We live in a trailer in the back of my grandma's yard. No rent and the trailer's paid for."

"So what's the problem with the support obligation?"

"Deondre's just $382. See where that comes out of my check?" He pointed at the deduction amounts on his paystub.

"That's standard operating procedure—garnishing."

"That's not what I'm complaining about."

"So what are you complaining about?"

"LeRoy's another $200."

Now I was totally lost. I argued, "But you're LeRoy."

"Not me, fool. Why would I pay $200 a month to support myself? Pay attention. The $200 goes to LeRoy, Junior. He's… what? Four? Five?" He turned to consult with Emily, who shook her head, as if she were too tired to guess his son's age. "Did you bring those papers?"

She murmured something, digging through her denim purse. She pulled a stack of papers, stuffed into envelopes and handed them to LeRoy, who started to take them from their envelopes, unfolding them. I held my hand out, waiting for the papers, but LeRoy wanted to read through them and put them in order first. He smashed them down, trying to keep them from furling back into their three-folds.

"The Court Trustee's office is handling my case."

"Which one? The one with Deondre or the one with LeRoy, Junior?"

"All of 'em." He shuffled through his pile. "I got six cases, but one's gonna drop off in December when J.J. turns eighteen."

"J.J.?"

He spun around. "Where's the stuff on the twins?"

"I don't know," Emily said.

LeRoy licked his thumb and flipped through the stack of papers.

"Can I look at those, please?" My arm still extended, I fought the urge to snatch the papers from him. Leroy kept shuffling, ignoring my outstretched hand.

My palm itched to give him a good smack.

Lowering my arm, I tried not to be rude. It was difficult practicing patience with this guy given his contemptuous, off-handed treatment of women. Wishing he'd performed this chore before our consultation was moot. It wouldn't have dawned on LeRoy that he wasted billable time. Finally, he shoved the papers across my desk. Studying them, I had to re-sort them into a system which made some sense to me. Half of the stuff was correspondence I wasn't interested in, so I said, "Here, keep those. I don't need the letters."

Matching case numbers, the tally ended up being six cases. That translates to support orders for six different mothers, covering seven different kids. Good Lord. Determining child support for the combined cases was a nightmare in logistics. I drew up a chart with headings for the kid, the mother, the case number, the support obligation. Between the papers and his paystub, I finished the chart without any gaps.

It was a grim picture.

Best case scenario, once taxes and support were paid, LeRoy had $560 for his use. With that money, he had to buy groceries, medicine, electricity, gas—everything. I bit the inside of my cheek. The guy wasn't too bright, but he was right about this: he was fucked.

Forty-five minutes after he first sat down in my office, I showed him my bleak calculations. He reminded me that some months he doesn't even get that much, if he doesn't work a full week.

"So, you want to reduce your child support obligations across the board?" I asked shrewdly. "With all six women?"

He nodded.

"Are any of them willing to agree to take less?"

LeRoy made a dismissive wave of his hand, slicing through empty space. "Aw man, there ain't no woman gonna do that."

"Then you have a problem."

Emily's pale face lost all trace of pigment.

Indignant, he demanded, "What? Can't you help me neither?"

"No, I can't. What's more—I'd have to charge you more in attorney fees than what I'd possibly even save for you, so it's not worth pursuing."

"You tell me there ain't nothing you can do?"

"Nothing."

"How am I supposed to live off this—five hundred, whatever?" He pounded my desk with his fist, rapping my legal pad.

"I understand you're frustrated…"

"You don't understand shit!" He snatched his papers from my hand and crammed them into Emily's saggy denim purse.

"Mr. Washington, just calm down, please, and let me explain."

"Explain what? All you attorneys are worthless. Just worthless pieces of shit. You ain't gonna help nobody but yourselves."

Emily sat mute, her knuckles tightening on her purse.

"The court can't lower child support simply because you have other kids later. Do you understand that?"

His brow lowered.

"I can't ask to lower your child support because you're having another kid."

"Why not?"

"Because that would mean the older kids got less, which isn't fair to them. The only way to reduce your support is for the mothers to earn more money—"

He scoffed at that suggestion, so I continued, "Or wait for the kids to turn eighteen."

"Wait 'til they're eighteen?"

"Yes."

"So I can't do nothing?"

"Aw, man!" he slammed his fist on my desk. "I need help. What can be done?"

"Mr. Washington, the child support worksheets show your income *lower* than what I figured for you. If I were to go in and try to get all six cases reduced, it'd probably have the opposite effect and increase your support. I can't help you."

He shook his head.

I watched Emily, whose body seemed limp. Could she possibly make it on her own? LeRoy wouldn't be able to help her, even if he wanted to and I had some serious doubts on that score.

"You can help yourself."

"How?"

"Get another job. Or a better paying job. Or both."

His glare was my answer.

"The last alternative then would be to seek to relinquish your parental rights. Give up a kid or two or three—whatever—and allow another person to adopt them."

"No!"

Resisting the impulse to counsel him about condoms and vasectomies, I returned his check for the consultation. I didn't feel right taking his money.

Besides, it'd probably bounce.

"I'm sorry I can't help you, Mr. Washington. Goodbye."

Snatching the check out of my hand, he glared at his girlfriend/fiancée. "See? Whaddiditellyew? All lawyers wanna fuck me over."

"Fare thee well! And if forever, Still forever, fare thee well," I mumbled, glad for once to return to the *Bronski* memorandum. It was something of a marvel, I thought as I began to type, to meet someone just as scandalous as George Lord Byron.

Chapter 10

Banshee from Hell

"May I ask what the hell you're doing?" The words, spoken calmly, might have fooled someone else, but they penetrated my brain as my wrists rested on my laptop.

An angry Tanny, fists clenched, stood at my door, waves of her fury rushing into my office like a tsunami. As when Sam took me to task about the original *Bronski* memorandum, I wasn't sure what I'd done wrong; the second scene of this play was growing stale. Fast. The only difference between Acts I and II seemed to be Tanny was angrier. They acted as if I'd trod across some invisible boundary, which was tantamount to trespassing on the King's territory.

What the hell, people? Lighten the fuck up.

She loomed in the doorway, her lips curling in an unattractive snarl. Most surprising were the daggers of hatred shooting from her eyes. Nothing I could fathom to justify that kind of rage.

Then it hit me.

Sam must've found out about her affair. She probably thought I'd snitched on her. Yeah, that'd explain this kind of extreme reaction.

Stabbing a path to her office, Tanny invited me to march toward it.

Steadying my nerves, I preceded her to her lair, like some recalcitrant school girl caught smoking in the girls' bathroom.

The firecracker sound of the door slamming behind me startled me out of my wits. "What are you so pissed about?"

"Tell me, Cooper Bach, do I look like Mother Teresa?"

"She's dead," I argued. "Is that some kind of trick question?"

"You watch it! I won't put up with snide remarks!" Tanny threw the stapler at me.

"What the hell?" I ducked, watching it sail past me and leave a gouge in the wall.

"You! You can't give your time away for free!"

The last part was hard to decipher, best audible for bats and dogs in that octave. Loud and high, her voice pierced my eardrum. Nice.

Realizing she wasn't angry because her affair had been uncovered, I was still at a loss why she was throwing stuff. Walking behind the chair, needing something to shield me from any more missiles, I shouted back. "What are you talking about?"

"We lose money on consultations." She explained, clipping her words. She spoke with heavy sarcasm, as though speaking to an idiot, which was similar to how Sam had treated me on the *Bronski* memorandum. My fingers curled around the top of the wingback chair. I made a mental promise that someday whenever I became a partner in a law firm, I would never speak to my associate like that. It was demoralizing. What a frickin' psycho-bitch.

I wanted to punch her in the throat, but at least I understood why she was mad. "You didn't like me giving Mr. Washington his consultation fee back?"

Tanny picked up a pen and tapped her water glass. "Ding, ding, ding! Thank you for playing, 'Let's Make Some Money!'"

Frowning, I pointed out the obvious defense. "I'm not taking his case."

She hurled the pencil at me, but without the heft of the stapler, it didn't fly past the chair, which I still used as a shield, so I wasn't in immediate danger. Relieved, I smiled. Probably not the best tactical move in my arsenal.

With both hands, Tanny shoved a stack of folders off her desk. In a single sweep, she cleared everything which had been on her desktop then stooped down to re-load. She flung her pens, pencils, and several legal pads at me. The raucous sounds reminded me of those fireworks I dreaded so much. I clamped my ears and crouched behind the chair, waiting for the barrage of office supplies to cease. When the immediate area around her emptied of potential missiles, her temper still hadn't abated, so she ripped off her stiletto and heaved it at the framed picture above me.

Shards of glass rained down, scattered on me.

I screamed.

The sound of my terror halted her tirade. She blinked, as if surprised by her own actions then propped her hip on her desk, pointed to the mess, and yelled for me to clean it up.

Sam and Melinda burst through the door, their eyes and mouths as wide as could be. "Anybody hurt?" Sam asked, red-faced and panting from the short jog.

Melinda covered her mouth to hide her shock—or maybe that was to keep her lunch down at the sickening sight, but Tanny didn't answer the pair. The office was in shambles, littered with her temper tantrum.

My legs were shaking, but I stood up and replied, as calmly as I could, "No. Nobody's hurt. But perhaps you should call the police."

Melinda's eyes widened.

Sam looked taken aback.

I refused to glance at Psycho.

I ran my fingers through my hair, loosening shards of glass. That upset me even more and my voice shook as I said, "Fuck. I'm gonna need a comb."

"We don't need the damned police," Tanny snapped.

And my fright turned to anger. I flung a finger at her and pointed. "What you just did was *criminal.* Criminally insane, probably. Clean up your own goddamn mess!" Stalking out of her office, I could almost see my father, beaming his approval down from heaven's gate.

She followed me, but seemed to be making an effort to rein in her temper. "I've not finished talking with you. Let's go to the conference room and discuss this problem regarding consultation fees."

Sam stood aside, scratching his hairless chin. My eye caught his and he looked away. No way was he going to call the police to have them arrest his wife for Property Damage, Assault and Battery. Spineless wonder, yellow-backed coward. A host of names spun around in my head, never said aloud, but I'm sure he felt the sting of my accusations.

"I need ten minutes."

"For what?" she asked.

Whirling on her, I shouted, "I'm taking ten god-damned minutes!"

Slamming the door so hard its frame shook made me feel better. Taking a couple of deep breaths helped. Firing up my computer and uploading my resumé to a few job sites improved my mood. The ten minutes passed swiftly and I took it as a good sign that nobody bothered me during that brief interim.

After combing my hair, I joined her in the conference room where a cup of tea waited for me. I assumed Melinda was responsible for that small show of kindness. Tanny drank nothing, for which I was grateful. I didn't fancy getting a face-full of coffee thrown at me or the mug. At this close range, she was bound to hit her target. I'd never considered myself a target before, strangely enough. This woman was nuts.

She asked me to close the door.

I left it open, acting as if I hadn't heard.

Shrugging as if she'd concede that minor point, she started her lecture in a soft voice which practically purred. "I blame the law schools, really those institutions are at fault. It's clear admissions standards have been allow to fall to curb-levels. In my day, course work was exacting and if you didn't have a 3.8 GPA or better, you could kiss any hope for graduating 'Goodbye.'"

Poison dripped from her tongue. Her eyes flashed a malicious gleam and she swung the leg which was cross over the other knee. Every now and again, I spotted the red sole of her heel. It was the mark of an expensive shoe. Fuming, I reassigned the value, mentally labeling it as Lucifer's mark. That pair of heels cost more than my rent.

"I'm aware you didn't graduate at the top of the class, but even a 'B' student should be able to spot legal issues. How you missed that on the *Bronski* matter amazed both Sam and me."

The nerves in my stomach knotted up until it felt like a mass of burning, roiling acid.

"Sam told me of the debacle you'd made on the *Bronski* memo."

"I think that's overstat—"

Her evil-gilded tongue lashed me again.

"Do you understand that bringing on an associate creates certain costs for us?" Smiling with demonic delight, she ticked off the arguments on each well-lacquered finger. "There's the cost of refurbishing your office. You insisted on that. Extra work places additional burdens on your secretary, Melinda. Let's not forget the cost of your salary, benefits, and payroll taxes. Vacation time, sick leave, paid holidays—" Here, she smirked. "Assuming you're still here after your probationary period."

"We never discussed probation," I clipped out the protest.

Owlishly, she blinked, trying to erect a façade of innocence, which a blind man could have detected. "Didn't we? It's for six months."

"Six months?"

Tanny pressed on. "The firm pays your bar dues, subscription fees, continuing legal education costs, and malpractice insurance, which given your less-than-dazzling start might triple our premium, thank you very much."

Those nerves were doing a samba in my belly.

"Now does your precious little brain grasp how, given our substantial investment in you, it doesn't make good business sense for you to work for free? You have to get the client's money. Please tell me Sam and I didn't tether ourselves to an imbecile!"

The last sentence exploded from her mouth.

Taking a very deep breath, I looked toward the ceiling, seeking help from the Almighty. A little divine assistance, in the form of a lightning bolt, would be just great right about now. I waited, silently calling on the Lord to send a bolt through the roof.

Come on, Lord. Show me what You got.

Tanny's flat chest heaved under the passion of her arguments. Eyes glinting with unholy mirth, she appeared giddy with triumph—orgasmically pleased with herself.

Sitting back, I watched her in amazement. This woman really was missing her marbles. A fucking, stone-cold killer.

Waiting for her to fire me, I imagined other jobs I could take where my dignity would remain intact. Something like shooting myself out of a canon, selling used cars, or dealing eight-balls to four different undercover cops. When was the prestige of being a lawyer going to kick in? Where's the respect for working my ass off in seven years of higher education? Twisting my brain to cogitate in ways unimaginable to the ordinary person—that was supposed to pay off, wasn't it? Didn't it? Shit. A waitress at Hooter's was treated better. And she wouldn't have $84,338 in student loans to repay, either.

The harsh reality was my car probably wouldn't last the distance for a longer commute. My apartment lease had ten more months left on it and I didn't see any way I could pay the funeral home without having this lousy, stinky, crummy job.

Reaching for the proverbial jar of Vaseline, I grabbed my ankles and bent over. "Point taken."

That wasn't enough for Tanny.

My subjugation wasn't complete. I suspect she harangued me for the next hour and a half as a mean-spirited payback for threatening to call the cops on her. But whatever the reason, she droned on about my incompetency, mocked my intelligence, called me lazy and lacking ambition.

Lucifer lectured, in love with the sound of her voice. By the end of that interminable tirade, I had a new schedule to last throughout my probation. Report at 6:45 a.m. to answer e-mails and return client calls. On Monday, Tuesday, Wednesday, and Friday mornings, I'd be in court, making docket calls, which typically ate up the entire morning. Thursdays and alternating Fridays were reserved for trials and hearings. During the afternoons I'd be expected to meet with clients, interview witness, prepare discovery, file motions, and write supporting memoranda.

At the end of every evening, I would give a detailed, written report to Tanny, to ensure I wasn't committing malpractice.

Lunch was a privilege no longer granted. I was required to bill out 45 hours a week, which meant I'd be working a minimum of 80 hours a week. On the bright side, my salary would remain the same.

Unable to find joy that Psycho hadn't docked my salary, I staggered out of the conference room around noon and returned to my laptop.

Tapping away at the keys, I sent Luke an email, asking him to let me know of any openings anywhere doing anything—law-related or otherwise. My situation required that I remain in this shithole until I found another job, so I set a goal of finding employment which would pay the same.

Shouldn't be too hard. In this stagnant economy. Without any prior work experience. Oh yeah. This was gonna be a cake walk.

When was God coming back from His celestial lunch? It would have been so lovely to have seen the lightning bolt hit Whilts & Hatdiff.

Chapter 11

Predator/Prey
and Other legal terms

I closed out my computer screen when Melinda marched into my office carrying a big floral bouquet. I was embarrassed she'd witnessed my ass-chewing, but touched she'd left me that cup of tea. It'd helped fortify my nerves during a demoralizing morning. I couldn't help but wonder what Tanny thought she'd actually accomplished throughout the meeting. Maybe Lucifer was trying to run me off—maybe all those demands were meant as inducements to quit. For what purpose? To prevent me from claiming unemployment benefits against the firm? Possible. She had no idea my budget wouldn't allow me less income.

Funerals are expensive.

"Look at these beauties!" Melinda exclaimed.

"Ah, you didn't have to do that."

"I didn't." Her smile took the sting out of her words as she placed the flowers on my desk. She stepped back, admired the view then checked over her shoulder to ensure a certain demon wasn't hovering in the doorway to overhear her next remarks.

"Wish I'd thought of it, though. That Tanny's mean as a rattlesnake and twice as dangerous."

Her sympathy honored me. However, I was unable to convey my gratitude, as my smile kept wobbling off my face and my throat was too tight for words to pass through it.

Melinda tutted, patted my shoulder, then delved into the bouquet to retrieve its card. She handed me the card, running her fingertips over some delicate petals and whispered, "So nice. So, who are they from?"

The scrawled writing definitely belonged to a man. The card read,

> Hitchcock Movie Marathon tonight at 8:00.
> Meet you at the theater?
>
> —Ted

I sighed and not for the first time, wished my emotions weren't so close to the surface. I flicked the card with my trimmed fingernail. "Ted. Ted Danveldt."

"Oh, I know Ted. He's a great guy. What's the problem?"

"I'm not ready to start anything. It's too soon. Too much going on."

"Coop, it's not a marriage proposal," she reminded me, sounding an awful lot like my sister, Gloria. "It's Hitchcock and from the day you're having, this is just what you need."

I stared at the bouquet, frowning.

She urged, "Call him. Go for it."

"I don't have his number," I said, glad of this narrow escape.

She wore a stern teacher's look. Her posture, crossing her arms in front of her ample chest, indicated she wouldn't tolerate my lame excuse. "He's in the phone book… under "D" for Delicious. We went to high school together. He's a really nice guy."

"Really?"

Melinda nodded, "The girls all had crushes on him—me, included. Throwing themselves at him, and he damned near caught everyone."

"So he IS a player! I pegged him right the first time I saw him! Why would I go with a guy like him?"

"Oh, quit. This is exactly what you need."

"A good lay, you mean?"

She stretched her hand across her heavy bosom, her face displaying a 'butter wouldn't melt in my mouth' expression. "I never said that! But now that you mention it…"

Glancing at the crystal clock on my desk, another graduation gift from my father, she gasped. "Uh-oh! Look at the time!"

"Shit!" I jumped up, straightened the folders on my desk. "Can you run me to court?"

"Don't forget David's sketch pad!" She snatched it up then chased me out the door.

***

The less than Honorable Judge Wilkerson presided over drug crimes. His claim to notoriety was his uncanny ability to fall asleep in jury trials. According to rumor, his rulings were the most overturned of any judge in the state. A dubious distinction, yet for some perverse reason, he seemed to take a great deal of pride in that.

Normally, you could only find such helmsmanship in the likes of Joseph Hazelwood or Tony Hayward. I imagined Wilkerson on the deck of an Alaskan Exxon ship or exploring in the Mexican Gulf for British Petroleum: he'd fit right in. Arrogance and incompetence make a deadly combination. Wilkerson took 'White Male Privilege' to its outer most edge, not giving a shit about anybody. His family came a distant second, his political party probably ran third. I had hope that his wife might be in the top ten on his list, but it was iffy. He was the kind of guy whose first wife divorced him and he never bothered to figure out why.

Waiting in the peanut gallery for David's case to be called, attorneys milled about in the courtroom. They scurried between the jail house visiting room, which was down the hall, separating those in custody from the general public and the judge's chambers. In the conference room/library, several worked out plea deals, haggling with the prosecutors in a riptide of testosterone. Neck ties were either missing or askew, agitated fingers raked through thinning hair. A deafening din of grumblings and raw cuss words carried outside as defense attorneys went about doing their jobs: cajoling the prosecutors. It's the closest thing to an open market where negotiations flew through the air in a swift volley.

Although fewer in number, it was easy to identify the prosecutors. Always seated, they drank coffee from Styrofoam cups and maintain impassive expressions as they browsed the police reports in their manilla folders.

Beneath the off-the-rack ties, beat the faint heart of a government worker-bee. The prosecutors hadn't yet risked the adversity of 'eating what they kill.' A delightful euphemism whose meaning escapes the ones who work in the public sector and are ensured a regular paycheck. In hearings, the prosecutor's job was fairly simple: occasionally prompt a witness's testimony by asking, 'Then what happened?' Pretty hard to keep your battle skills sharp when that's the extent of the workout.

'Eat what you kill,' means you gotta hustle for your cases, stay on top of the Accounts Receivables. Or starve. Every day is an exercise in survival for the defense bar. In that conference room, both sides gathered during roll call and baked under glaring fluorescent lights, arguing ways to dispose of the cases.

"Come on, Stan," nagged a public defender. "This guy's a first time offender—probation should be automatic. What's to think about here?"

The beleaguered Stan took his time answering, flipping through his sheaf of papers then spied a note. Future historians will verify western civilization now rises and falls upon Post-It notes, as evidenced from archeological digs of courthouse ruins.

Stan, the prosecutor, read the note then snapped, "No deal. Plead the bastard open."

As one, the many attorneys scowled at Stan. His words sparked a shit-storm. Pretty soon everybody was climbing onto Stan's back, beating him down, telling him such was unthinkable and to quit being a dick. They scolded him to be decent and do the right thing—

just this once, for added sting. Did I say being a prosecutor was easy? I amend that.

Stan was hounded like the proverbial cheating husband whose wife had the good fortune to possess a cast iron skillet. Being on the receiving end of a screwing without a kissing is no fun, but Stan brought his troubles on his head by expecting any self-respecting lawyer to advise his client to throw himself on the non-existent mercies of Judge Wilkinson.

First call announced the deposition of the motion: withdrawal, waiver, granted by agreement (prosecutors agreeing to a defense attorney's motion happens with the frequency of hens sprouting teeth). Holding actual hearings on motions was discouraged. Neither side uses its precious court-allotted time to argue points of law and the merits of a case. Such antiquated notions were absurd. It's common knowledge the criminal defense loses nearly all their motions. Challenging cops and their actions is practically unheard of. The public feels safer that way with the 'bad guy' losing, rather than accepting the alternative explanation that we now live in a near-police state.

Tradition forbade entering the judge's personal chambers, his *sanctum sanctorum*, without personal invitation. Wanting to know Judge Wilkerson better, I surveyed an oil painting in his lobby to get a better idea of his tastes and personality. The painting was low quality; something he probably bought at a starving artist sale. A sleek panther whose ebony coat gleamed had pounced on a floundering gazelle. Didn't take too much critical thinking to discern the guy was a real asshole. The whole predator/prey kind of thing was so Neanderthal.

After forty-five minutes of waiting, I managed to introduce myself to Judge Wilkerson. After he left the bench he ducked inside his own private bathroom. The silence was conspicuous because I didn't hear a faucet run. Suddenly, I hoped he wouldn't greet me with a handshake.

Hitching up his britches, he entered his chambers sans black robe. His assistant informed him he had a new attorney waiting to make his acquaintance. He bellowed, asking for my name. His assistant's voice came across clear as a bell. Sensing the other attorneys' eyes were on me, I wondered why the hell the twosome hadn't used an intercom system instead. He leaned back in his leather recliner and beckoned me. I entered his office. My eyes drew to the portrait directly behind him.

It was the same painting as in the lobby. Geezus. Bet he's a one-hit wonder in the bedroom, too.

"What's this nonsense?" His pudgy hand slapped a pile of papers on his desk.

"I'm Cooper Bach. New associate at Whilts & Hatdiff."

The judge threw me a look that said, 'I don't give a shit.' "You got a motion pending?"

"Yes."

"There's no prosecutor here, so don't be talking about your case. That's *ex parte* contact. Highly improper. I won't have it."

"Just wanted to introduce myself."

Clearly, there wasn't anything more to add onto that, so I left. Other attorneys streamed passed me, settling in for collegial discussions with the judge. It grated that they received a far friendlier welcome than mine.

I entered the courtroom and sat on the other side of the bar. The only person in the room was a prosecutor who sat at the counsel table, thumbing through his files.

"Hey," I said.

Grunt.

"When are they going to bring the prisoners in?"

Shrug. Grunt. He didn't raise his head, just kept glancing through the folders, trying to cram before docket call.

I sighed and waited. It didn't seem honest to bill David for the dead time I'd spent in the conference room or back lobby, but I was afraid if I didn't Psycho would subject me to another meltdown. Withdrawing David's new sketch pad, I then asked the guard if he'd deliver it to David Seltzer, my client. He smiled halfway, leaving me with the impression he didn't approve lawyers giving defendants gifts, but it was a sketch pad—not contraband.

After that duty was performed, I was bored, wishing I had brought a file to work on. Steadily, others entered the courtroom. Criminal defendants, out on bond, were easily detected by their ill-fitting, nicely pressed clothes. They were usually accompanied by their girlfriends, mothers, or wives and they sat in the back of the courtroom, distantly themselves from whatever consequences they'd have to face. The lawyers filed in and moseyed over to an empty jury box. They sat down, still murmuring or scratching out notes, finishing the details of a bargain.

I leaped to my feet upon hearing my case and approached the podium in the middle of the pit. The three minutes which passed required a disappointing and meager participation on my part.

"You're moving to reduce bond, Mrs. Bach?" Judge Wilkerson arched his brow.

"Ms," I corrected. "And yes. Mr. Seltzer has several ties to the communi—"

"What say you, Mr. Prosecutor?"

The overworked minion stood and muttered, "Fine. The people request $5,000."

"Five it is," said the judge, noting the amount on a pre-printed form. He ripped the sheet from the pad and handed it to the bailiff.

The prosecutor tossed the folder onto his slender stack and reached for another.

Taken aback by the nonchalance and speed of that 'hearing,' it was left for my client, David Seltzer, to nudge me from the podium. "That's it, boss. Not much of a dance, is it?"

All my romantic visions of waxing eloquently before the bench shriveled. There'd be no Clarence Darrow-like arguments, no poetry-like Oliver Wendel Holmes renditions, no parables similar to Abraham Lincoln's. I don't know if I could have achieved those lofty heights, but hell! I aspired to them, nevertheless.

"You got to find a surety for $500," I said, scrambling to add something of value to my client's fees.

We walked down the dim, narrow hallway to return him to the holding cell. The same doleful deputy behind us.

"I know. This ain't my first time at the rodeo, you know."

"Shhh... stuff like that doesn't help your case."

"Sure thing, boss. Hey, thanks for the sketch pad."

"You're welcome, but I guess you won't need it if you make bail."

"Nah, I'll use it. Drawing might keep me out of trouble."

"You do that," I urged with a smile. "Come see me Thursday afternoon at three o'clock, all right?"

"Thursday. Three o'clock. Sure thing, Mrs. Bach and thank you." He shook my hand and smiled.

Leaving the courthouse, I walked back to the office, smiling in the sunshine. Maybe I was happy because the weather was nice. Maybe because I was finally free of the tension in the courthouse. I suspect, though, I was happy because I had a genuinely nice person for a client, who seemed to appreciate my efforts. I grimaced. My family would freak out if they knew I considered a drug dealer a superior person over a divorceé.

That's another thing law school didn't teach me. A lot of people a lawyer must deal with are real assholes: my boss, Judge Wilkinson, Stan the Prosecutor, Flotaki, Mrs. Bronski. These folks are considered 'decent' by society, which makes me wonder: what the hell kind of society do I live in?

Chapter 12

Ingrid Bergman's a Cold Fish

Working in an empty office with no other sound than the click-clicking of my keyboard, it felt peaceful. The gentle hum of office machines was soothing white noise in the background and for the first time that day the Law Firm of Psycho & Satan was tranquil. I'd finished the last progress report for Tanny, but also got a lot of work done. I'd sent out standard discovery requests for David Seltzer's case, drawn up court orders for Junior's school and medical records in the Bronski matter. I cleared my monitor, straightened my desk, and snapped off my desk lamp. It wasn't until I took my trench coat off the hook on the back of my office door that I noticed Melinda had posted a note there.

Have fun at the movies!

—M

Understanding my receptionist-cum-secretary possessed a prepossessing but determined nature, I shook my head in mock dismay. Before I left my office, I smoothed over my hair, reapplied pink lip gloss then pinched my cheeks. Once outside, I strolled past the Festiva and continued toward the movie theater.

Ted came around the corner, whistling. His short sleeve shirt showed off his sinewy forearms and his denims hugged long, muscular thighs. With that physique and those charming caramel eyes, my gaze devoured the handsome man. My veins zinged with delight and I looked forward to our time together. This set off warning bells, which I ignored.

His face lit up with a dazzling smile when he saw me and my heartbeat quickened.

It was getting easier to ignore those warning bells.

He greeted me with enthusiasm. "Great! You're here!"

"You're sure in a good mood."

"Why wouldn't I be?" He raised two fingers to the clerk in the ticket counter, fished out his wallet then paid. "Get to watch the master story-teller Hitchcock and eat popcorn with a great-looking date. What could be better?"

A small burst of joy flared inside, drowning out the horns on those warning bells. Indulging in the rarity of listening to someone compliment me, I turned off the alarms. Melinda might be right in thinking an evening with Ted was in order.

"Here. Let's go Dutch." I tried to shove ten dollars into his hand, but he refused.

"Let's not."

He didn't smile as he escorted me through the entrance.

"Then let me buy the popcorn," I offered.

"Not a chance. This is our first date, Coop. Guy always pays on the first date, or didn't you learn that in law school?"

"Thank you for the flowers. They're pretty."

"My pleasure." He smiled and nodded toward the snack bar. "Want anything? Soda? Popcorn? JujuBeans?"

"A soda would be great. I need the caffeine."

As we waited for the drinks and popcorn, he asked how work was going.

"Been busy," I said, then added the rider, "Dodging shit."

He chuckled, thinking I'd made a joke. So he made one of his own. "I always heard lawyers slung shit, not dodged it."

"No, literally. I've been dodging stuff my boss threw at me."

At his puzzled expression, I explained. "It's how Tanny disciplines or instructs—not sure which, but she threw her stapler, pens, pencils, pads, and shoe at me then treated me to an hour and a half long tirade."

He was stunned. "Are you kidding me?"

"No. I'm not joking."

"Jesus!" A murderous scowl appear between his brows. His hand wrapped around my waist in an oddly protective gesture, which surprisingly, I didn't mind. Tanny must have really knocked me off-kilter to have abandoned my independent, career woman *persona*.

Needing to keep the conversation light, I casually diagnosed her. "I think she's psychotic."

"Undoubtedly." He tossed me an assessing look. "What set her off?"

"I consulted with a new client, declined to take his case, and returned his check."

"That's it?"

"Yep."

Ted let out a low whistle.

Settling into the theater seat, he whispered, "So, are you going to find another job?"

"I'll try, but to be honest, I don't think I'll find anything. With so much already on my plate—she wants an 80 hour workweek from me—I'm not going to have the time or energy to search."

"That sucks."

"Yeah. So, how are Michael and Isabelle?"

His lips pressed together, as though he didn't appreciate my changing the subjects, but another couple entered our aisle and stopped to chat with him.

"Hey, Ted. Good to see you."

He stood, giving them way to walk past us. "Mark, Elaine. How are things? Meet Cooper Bach—she's new in town."

Curious gazes made me squirm.

The four of us (really, the three of them) spoke briefly then Mark and Elaine moved away to find their own seats.

"Small town," he said by way of apology. "They're nosey, but all right."

We returned to our chairs and he said, "We were talking about your godawful day spent dodging staplers. Geez, that would've hurt if it'd hit you."

Shaking my head, I smiled. "Raking out broken glass from my hair really scared me."

"What?"

THE LAW FIRM OF PSYCHO & SATAN

"Her shoe. When she threw it, it hit and shattered the glass of the framed picture above me. The shards and splinters fell over me."

"Good God, Coop!"

Already I felt better. As if having another human horrified by my boss's reaction reminded me that I wasn't crazy.

"We were talking about your niece and nephew."

He gave a throaty chuckle then corrected me. "No, you asked about Michael and Izzy, but I was still wanting to talk about your traumatic day. Somebody oughta wring Tanny's neck."

"No, we're not talking about her anymore."

He winged one eyebrow—his signature move which was mocking, condescending, and funny all at once. Also sexy as hell.

Shaking my head, coming out of my stupor, he took me by surprise when his thumb brushed my hand.

"So, what do you want to know about Michael and Izzy?"

His whisper was like a magnet, drawing my gaze to his lips.

"How is she?" I stared, wondering what a real kiss from him would feel like. Invisible threads spun, looping the two of us together and tugging tighter so that the distance grew smaller. Leaning toward him, he obliged me. With a low moan, he covered my mouth in gentle brushes reminiscent of his earlier kiss in the rain. He brushed my cheek. My senses heightened to the small, abrasive feel of his calloused fingertip. Too soon he broke the kiss and pressed his forehead to mine.

"Small town," he explained.

My hazy thoughts scattered like a startled flock of birds and I jerked in my chair, sitting upright again.

His smile was crooked as he pointed out, "By ten o'clock tonight my mom's gonna know we were making out at the movies."

That made me grin. "Do you care?"

Holding my hand, he grinned. "No, but you should. I promise I'll be a perfect gentleman from now on."

"That's no fun," I grumbled, but he must have heard because he threw his head back and laughed.

"And Michael? How does he enjoy being a big brother?"

Ted's gaze softened. "It's still new. He hasn't tried to shove a bean up her nose yet. Give him time—I'm sure he will."

"Did you do that to Karen?" I asked, incredulous.

"Sure, but don't feel sorry for her. I only did it because she made me eat sand."

"Yikes."

We ate some popcorn in companionable silence then I asked, "How old were you?"

"When she made me eat sand?" The corners of his lips teased upward, recalling the memory. "I dunno, probably four or so. Karen's three years older than me. What about you?"

"What about me what?"

Ted nudged me. "Did you ever shove a bean up a brother's or sister's nose?"

"No. Just one sister—she would never have made me eat sand."

"Lucky you. What's your sister's name?"

"Gloria." Afraid my voice would crack if I said anything more, I gestured Ted to be quiet then pretended to watch the previews. My gaze fixed straight ahead, I left the moment as that fog unfurled around me and drew me away. Pulled into grief's tide, memories of times with my older sister flashed before my eyes and I re-lived a lifetime too distant. My mind numbed and my body hollowed, as if something essential to my core had been swiped away by that blasted fog.

The first movie was *Notorious* with Cary Grant and Ingrid Bergman. I don't remember when I tuned back into it, surprising to discover we were watching a movie in black and white. The screen cast a silvery glow on the audience, as if we were all waiting in the New Jerusalem instead of sitting in a theater.

Somebody told Ingrid's character—I forget the name—that her father had committed suicide and I sucked in a gasp, taking a hit to my gut. On screen, she had no reaction to this news. What a fucking, cold-hearted fish. I drummed my fingers on the arm-seat, restraining the impulse to flip her the bird.

Ted clasped my hand, stopping my staccato beating. "Do you want to leave?"

I accepted with alacrity.

He rose, too.

I waved him to remain where he was. "No, don't get up. You stay here and watch the movie."

"No, that's okay. We can go somewhere else, grab a decent bite to eat."

"Nah, I'm beat. Really. I'll catch you later." Before he said anything else, I dashed out of the theater. My chest felt heavy and tight. On the sidewalk I pulled up short to gulp air. Walk home or back to the office to get my car? Which was quicker? Without deciding, I struck out and headed east. Just gotta get someplace safe before I break down.

Something grabbed my elbow and spun me around. "Jesus Christ!"

It was Ted with an angry light in his eyes. "Where's the fire?"

Prying his fingers off, I scowled.

His brows skyrocketed as he took a backward step. With his hands on his hips, he asked, "Have I offended you?"

Trembling, I wiped my forehead, not surprised to discover it was damp. I scanned the street, looking for a way to escape. I had to find someplace safe or I was going to lose it right here.

"Coop? Cooper, are you okay?"

If anger and hurt are stored in the same jar, it would explain how quickly I could draw from that well. Lashing out, I said, "Leave me alone! Jesus!"

"What the hell?"

"You can sit there if you want and watch that cold fish, but I've had enough of this fucking shit."

His threw his hands out, flummoxed.

Glaring at the imbecile, I jabbed his chest. "Ingrid Bergman. On the plane. Cold fish."

Baffled, he stood there, holding my finger to keep from further damage to his torso. Tense, his brow furrowed over his eyes and I saw a light flicker in them. "When she'd been told her father died?"

Something shifted between us. Looking in his caramel eyes, my rage died an instant death and I was left shaking in the aftermath. Without anger to hold onto, I had nothing. Nothing to keep my composure in check, nothing to keep me afloat.

Leakage started.

The tears formed and trickled down. I maneuvered past him and trotted home, nearly breaking into a run.

"Cooper, wait!"

He caught up to me. "Oh, baby, why didn't you tell me?"

He gathered me close. Tears ran, dribbling to my chin. My body tightened as I willed my emotions to remain quiet, not giving into the temptation of howling or sobbing or wailing or anything I really wanted.

"When did your dad die, Cooper?"

There was something about the way he said it— not quite asking, just flat out saying it because he already figured it out.

I didn't want to answer. Saying it aloud made it true and I'd done such a great job of blocking it these past few weeks, I didn't want to blow it now. Not here. Not on the sidewalk in full view of everybody and the Queen. For a long, long time we remained locked in that embrace. He gently held me.

Burying into the cocoon of his body, I mumbled, "Seventy-two hours after my sister, Gloria, died."

We tilted because although my words had rocked him, he kept hold, clasping me to him. Reeling from that revelation, his voice grew hoarse, "When was that?"

A wooden voice answered. "May."

"God, you're so tense, I'm afraid you're going to crack."

I nodded, not knowing how else to respond.

"Stay with me, Coop," he said, turning me slowly around. We walked to his truck, clamped together. "Stay with me."

Soon we drove someplace—I didn't ask because I didn't care. My hands tangled in my lap, their grip tight as my hold on my emotions unraveled. The wave was coming in—a tsunami, I predicted, and I tried to brace for impact. As we drove along the street, I opened the window, taking gulps of fresh air then let the breeze cool me. In the gutter, wind played with litter and leaves, lifting them and holding them aloft. Dancing to the rhythms of an inaubible drummer, the eddies came alive, swirling like debutantes in a ballroom. The sight mesmerized me.

"They're dancing," I said, my voice filled with wonder.

"What?"

As we passed, I craned my neck to see the whirlwind scatters. They disappeared. We left them behind. Traveling through the haze, my body moved through time and space, but I don't remember that journey, save for the litter-leaf dance.

Next thing I consciously register is that somehow I sat on a couch, I suppose in Ted's living room, clutching a mug of hot tea. I stared without seeing, later aware my shoes were removed. When and how that happened, I don't know, but it seemed the most natural thing in the world for Ted to massage my feet while I sipped tea.

No physical pain present, my well of hurt had run dry. I'd escaped the tsunami, which surprised me. I'd have laid bets that I was in for another session as wrenching as the lost curler incident.

Instead of being overwhelmed, those waves of grief settled inside, lending a heaviness to my heart and limbs. Moon rocks are made of something heftier than anything on earth. I remember grasping a dark gray rock in a museum tour in my youth. Its appearance was deceptive, for it was incredibly dense. When placed in my hands, its weight caught me off-guard. My elbows straightened as my arms dropped and my knuckles scraped the floor. I'd gasped in surprise then groaned beneath the strain. Otherworldly? Sure, but that's how my body felt—shockingly dense, moon-rock-heavy.

"Gloria played volleyball in high school. She loved to spike the ball." I'd uttered the hollow-sounding words. Leaving my throat, they fell from a height, plummeted to earth and splattered.

I faced Ted, looked right at him, but didn't see him.

"She was tall. Took after Dad." One shoulder lifted on its own as I explained, unnecessarily. "I take after Mom."

Silence.

I took another sip, mechanically applying the edge of the cup to my lips and swallowed the liquid. It was tasteless, my fog too thick to allow my senses to be engaged.

"She got a full scholarship to college. It was out of state and I missed her. She left when I was fifteen and Mom and Dad had already divorced, but they hated each other. They could never talk civilly after that, so things got a little…crazy. Mom drank more—that's why Dad left, he said, but I suspect he had other reasons. His secretary was young, cute. He never admit to having an affair, but I just don't think…"

Frowning, I asked Ted, "Why else would Mom suddenly hate him?"

He shrugged and shook his head. Quietly, he reached for my empty mug and went to the kitchen to refill it.

When he returned, I continued in the same vein, "I don't think Mom realized she'd become an alcoholic. Divorce is weird. Like somebody has snuck into your home and robbed it of everything, but taking only half. You know? Half the furniture, half the income, half the people. No, that's not true. Once Dad left, it felt like he took more than half the love in the house. All the laughter. I don't remember Mom laughing after that. I think she died, heartbroken."

"Is that why you practice divorce law?"

Startled by the question, I glanced at Ted. Our eyes met. The moment stopped spinning, as if time were a ribbon, hitched on something before it could trail along into Eternity.

"What?" I asked, dazed.

"Why do you practice divorce law?"

A pause. "Somebody has to look out for the kids."

"Right."

"What is?"

"Oh, Cooper, don't look at me like that. I'm only human."

"Like what?"

"Vulnerable. Thirsty for affection. Hungry for love."

"I am."

He withdrew his arm from me to run his hand through his chestnut hair. With a sound of exasperation, he stood up and paced from the living room to the kitchen a few times. After a brief struggle, he halted, rubbed his palms together and said, "Right. Let's do this. Tell me about your sister, Gloria."

I gulped my tea then said, "Well, Mom's drinking got worse so that whenever Gloria called home, I'd beg to come live with her. I even graduated early to go live with her."

Memories swallowed me. "I dunno. Maybe I should have stayed. Maybe Mom wouldn't have died if she hadn't been left alone."

"In the end, only your mom held the key to her own happiness. It shouldn't have depended on your dad or your sister or you."

Thinking on this, I let that little pearl of wisdom sink in. He was right, of course. My mother was too fragile for this world. When life handed her a challenge, she crumpled.

While I ruminated on those matters, Ted disappeared, later returning with a plate of cheese, bologna, and crackers.

"Thank you."

Now that I'd started talking, I couldn't shut up. Nibbling as I spoke, I explained how we worked through college and law school. "Most of the time Gloria worked two jobs so we could have a little extra.

Nobody could out-work her and she always smiled. Nothing ever got her down or fazed her."

Watching him nod, I sensed he understood the indomitable spirit of my older sister.

"The girl woke up cheerful!" Spreading my hands to show my bewilderment, I demanded, "Who DOES that?"

He handed me a box of Kleenex, and I snapped out a tissue, dabbing my nose. Ted plopped down next to me and tucked me into his side.

My head fell on his shoulder and he began stroking my hair. With every brush of his hand, a few more tears released, rolling down my face and soaking his shirt. It was a quiet cry, no piercing wails, no racking sobs, but it was more devastating for its silence. This pain cut too deep to be expressed in the traditional ways. The only means of escaping the waves of despair was to roll with it, body surf-style and let it carry me away. So I mourned. I cried silently. I cried because I couldn't cry at my mother's passing and I wouldn't cry at my daddy's funeral. To cry would shatter my heart into a thousand bits. I hadn't weep for my parents until now.

Ted let me weep. His arms served as ballast, keeping me from flying into the ether. I don't know how long the storm lasted—grief diminished paltry concepts of time. Odd, that. Spent at last, I fell asleep with my head on Ted's shoulder and his arms still about me.

I awoke with a plugged nose. During the night, our positions have shifted. We were now lying on the couch, spooning. A blanket covered us. I smiled. It was sweet of him to have fetched the blanket—and the tea and crackers.

Lifting my upper body, I looked through the window. It was dawn, no longer the darkest part of the night. But it was drizzling.

As if my body held a mixture of nitroglycerin and molasses, I crept off the sofa in a slow, careful fashion. Without making a sound I gathered the used tissues then put on my coat and shoved them into the pockets. At the front door, I took another look at Ted, ruefully conceding last night had probably been the worst date of his life. His hair was tousled. Slight growth dotted his jawline. Hunched in his sleep, I worried he'd awaken with a kink in his neck. The portrait of masculine tenderness.

Smiling sadly, for what might have been, I close the door until it clicked shut. I walked through the damp morning air, grateful I'd met Ted. Sure, he was a player—probably a big time player, but he was kind. Still, I didn't need a crystal ball to know when he awoke with that stiff neck that he'd be glad I'd taken myself off. Poor guy would thank his narrow escape.

I yanked my collar to keep off soft rain and hunched my shoulders. I wished I was warm. I burrowed beneath my coat, promising myself a hot shower when I got back to the apartment. I planned on wearing a sweater to work. My footsteps struck the damp pavement, the only sound in the still-sleepy town, but as I walked home, my heartbeat thumped in sync with my steps. *Bah-bum, bah-bum, bah-bum.*

I congratulated myself for learning from Baby Isabelle how to reset my rhythms. Breathe in. Breathe out. Hold on. Let go. Somewhere between the rush and draw, there was Life.

The wind directed raindrops to softly run down my face, like my tears had done earlier. They dripped onto my lips and I tasted the Divine. Why such a quixotic thought would strike me, I don't know, but for the most absurd moment, I believed my tears had called the rain into existence.

With Mom, Dad, and Gloria gone—why wouldn't celestial choirs weep?

Chapter 13

Golden Boy, Johnny

Choosing to ignore my gritty eyes and stuffy nose, I took my first appointment with Johnny Eaton, a junior in high school. He was broad-shouldered, tall, built like a tank and blond—in other words, a real dreamboat. If anyone had ever been born to be an American football hero, it was Johnny. He was quick and moved into my office with a light tread, his green eyes scanning the layout of the room as though he were searching for his wide-end receiver. Dreamboat Johnny was starting quarterback. As a junior, that's a helluva thing.

His father came in with him. He was also tall, with a husky build and barrel chest. He had a swagger to his walk, which made me like him immediately. Mr. Eaton's handshake was firm and solid, but his eyes were red-rimmed, at odds with his tough guy image. I started to drag another chair from the library, but Johnny intercepted me and brought it to my office.

"In here?" he asked, waving the chair around like it weighed as much as a popsicle stick.

I nodded and thanked him as we settled in for a long interview. With a heavy sigh, Mr. Eaton explained what I already knew—they were here because Johnny'd been charged with raping a girl from his high school.

The star quarterback flatly denied the charges, as soon as the four letter word came up, he sliced the air with his hand.

"I didn't do it. I didn't do anything. I'd never rape a girl!"

He proceeded to explain some high schoolers were at a bonfire party in a farmer's pasture; naturally, they had a keg although Johnny didn't reveal who had brought it. He was clear, however, that he didn't bring it. I didn't care about the keg—he wasn't charged with Minor in Possession. Johnny stood around the bonfire, drinking beer all night long. Whenever he left the bonfire, it was to pee or refill his beer—not long enough to rape somebody, he'd said.

The alleged victim was Lydia Sanderson, a girl he went to school with, but didn't know well. He'd found out she was a sophomore and lived in a run-down part of town. Mr. Eaton chimed in he'd heard Lydia's dad was an alcoholic, but that was hearsay. He'd never met the man, never known him to work. Johnny repeated he didn't know Lydia, had never spoken with Lydia and certainly never touched her, let alone raped her. He had no idea why the cops arrested him, but he was concerned that Lydia had been raped and some bastard he went to school with did it.

That comment surprised me; it seemed so *honorable*. Handling divorces doesn't provide much opportunity to observe people acting honorably.

During the bonfire, there was no commotion, no signs that anybody was being attacked. Sure, there were couples making out, Johnny reported, but that was harmless, consensual stuff.

Last night after dinner, three cops came to his house, told him he was being arrested for raping Lydia Sanderson on June 3rd, handcuffed him, read his *Miranda* rights, and hauled him downtown in the back of a squad car. Johnny said at first he thought it was a joke, but when the handcuffs hit his wrist, it turned into a nightmare. As he described his arrest, his voice cracked in parts.

Without any priors, he was looking at five years in pound-in-the-butt prison, where a pretty boy like Johnny would be popular, even with his brawn. I decided to keep that detail to myself.

I asked Mr. Eaton to step out of my office and for the next hour, I grilled Johnny. Did you have sex with anyone that night? Heavy petting? See somebody's boobs? Finger bang someone? Touch somebody's groin? How drunk were you? Did you black out part of the night? Did anyone else say they saw anything? Did you see Lydia at the bonfire? Did you talk to her? Touch her? Flirt with her? Did she talk to anyone else? Flirt with anyone else?

I asked questions that would have made my father appalled and caused my mother to faint. That's another thing law school doesn't prepare you for—the loss of dignity in the pursuit of Truth.

A red-faced Johnny stammered, stuttered, and stumbled, but stuck to his main story. Yes, he'd seen Lydia at the bonfire but she wasn't somebody he'd notice. No, he didn't talk with her. No, he didn't see her talk with anyone, male or female. She stood apart, holding her arms across her chest like she was uncomfortable. No, he couldn't remember what time he saw her. No, he didn't think she'd been crying or was upset. He couldn't say whether she looked happy or sad. Her hair was down, it was dark and Johnny couldn't see her face very well, but said again she wasn't somebody you'd notice.

That's odd. Who goes to a high school bonfire to be anti-social?

Johnny answered all my questions, looking me directly in the eye. Either he was a cold-blooded sociopath or worse, he was innocent. There's nothing a criminal defense attorney hates more than an innocent client.

Johnny was shaken from my interrogation, but having been advised this was merely the beginning of a long ordeal, he braced himself. At the end of our consultation, I quoted him a huge retainer, well into the thousands. He blanched, got up, and asked his dad to re-enter. He remained standing as he explained to his father what my retainer was and offered to sell his truck.

"You're gonna have to, son, but that still won't cover the entire amount." Mr. Eaton asked if I would take payments against the retainer.

I shook my head. "Not on criminal cases, sorry."

Tanny would spit razors if I agreed to a payment plan.

"You sure about her?" Mr. Eaton asked Johnny, nodding in my direction.

Johnny looked straight at me, plunging his hands into his pockets. Without smiling, he said, "Yeah, yeah, I am."

Part of me was flattered by his confidence. A bigger part, though, realized I had undertaken the task of eating an elephant, tail-end first. If Johnny was guilty, he was taking me for a ride. If Johnny was innocent, but found guilty, this case could break my heart.

I tried not to think too far ahead.

Mr. Eaton and Johnny assured me they'd get my retainer. I told them once they had, I would get the police reports and depose Lydia and others from the bonfire. I asked Johnny for a list of who was there. We discussed the need to hire a private investigator. I told Johnny to keep his mouth shut and not say anything about the case to anybody.

"If you open your mouth, you sink your case. You got that? It doesn't matter if you tell people you're innocent. Everything you say will be used against you. Before you know it, half the high school's subpoenaed to testify about whatever you said at football practice or in chemistry lab. You got me? Trust no one. Say nothing. To anybody."

I looked at Mr. Eaton. "You and your wife are not to talk to Johnny about this case. Can I be any clearer?"

"No, ma'am. No questions. I'll tell his mom the same."

"Make sure you do. Nothing and no one is sacred in a rape investigation. Anyone can come to court and testify against Johnny." I turned back to the football star. "Keep your mouth shut. When you need to talk with anybody, you talk to me."

They left, but I figured the odds of him keeping him mouth shut were slim to none. I sighed, dropping into my chair, drained. Whatever Johnny said, I prayed it was the truth. It's always easier dealing with the truth—even if Johnny was a rapist.

***

Driven by a compulsion to move freely around my apartment, I cranked up the tunes and tackled my bedroom. Setting limits, I decided to sort through Dad's clothes tonight; it'll be harder sorting through Gloria's. I'd buried him in his best navy suit and my favorite tie, a gift from Gloria. Now I wish I hadn't done that. I would have like to have had that tie. It was red and blue silk.

Because there was no good place to start, I picked up the closest box and dumped it on the bed. Belts, ties, baseball hats, two pairs of cufflinks.

I put the cufflinks in my jewelry box, thinking I might have a son someday to give them to.

Shifting through his belongings, another wave of detachment washed over me. It was a blessing, really, to feel the numbness. Like this wasn't my dad's stuff—just items I'd found somewhere, preparing for a make-believe garage sale.

"You can do this, Coop."

I separated his ties into three piles: ugly, butt-ugly, and keepers. The first two piles were put in a box to be donated. I looked for my favorite tie, a red one with blue starbursts, but then I remembered we'd buried him in it.

"You buried him. Remember? Gloria was already dead."

The sound of my voice was accompanied by a slight buzzing. Some annoying mosquito pierced my shroud of numbness. Once it broached that protective fog, reality would rush in and I was nowhere near ready for that. I needed to remain detached, disconnected. That's how you get through sorting out your dead dad's clothes. You think of something else. You think of England.

"Now. Where's my favorite tie of Dad's?"

Sifting through the box going to Goodwill, I couldn't find that red and blue tie. Then it hit me: I'd buried him in it.

"Man, I should've kept that."

Experiencing a curious sense of déjà vu, briefly, I wondered if I hadn't already missed the tie, but it was better to keep moving and not lose momentum, so I sniffled and soldiered on.

"You can do this, Coop. It's only clothes—just sorting through clothes."

I dumped another box onto the bed. I rolled his belts up, saving his best one and putting the rest in the Goodwill box. I surveyed the 'keeper' pile of ties. It was depressingly small. There was a hideous wide brown polyester tie. Definitely not attractive, but it made the cut because Dad wore it a lot and I remember sitting on his lap and seeing it close-up. It wasn't fashion-forward, but I wanted it. The yellow polka-dotted tie Mom gave him, which he hadn't worn since the divorce, I placed in the Goodwill box.

It had been a nasty divorce.

Tactilely, I hated the feel of most his ties because they were synthetic blends. Caressing silk? That's something else entirely. That triggered a reminder to find that silk tie Gloria had given him last Christmas. It was red with blue dots.

"Now…where is it?" I searched the boxes again, looking for it. Then it hit me.

"Oh."

Anger bubbled up in my belly. Why had I buried him in that tie? For his ride into Eternity, he wouldn't have cared which tie he wore. Hell, he could have had the brown polyester tie!

Turning over the possibility of exhuming him, I only canceled that notion when I consider the cost. For that kind of money, I could easily go buy another red silk tie with blue dots on it and call it good. Right? But I wouldn't.

The radio poured out songs, I sorted Dad's clothes until midnight. With great care, I boxed up a nice wardrobe of shirts, pants, socks and underwear for Goodwill. I kissed the boxes before hauling them to the Festiva.

When I returned to my apartment, I showered then put on my dad's plaid shirt, curled up on my bed, loving the scent of freshly laundered sheets. Before my head touched the pillow, I was out.

Chapter 14

A Well Attended Funeral

Today was Mrs. Cuttlebum's funeral. As I walked into the church, the muscles in my shoulders tightened into knots. I knew sooner or later, I'd have another funeral to attend, but if I'd had my choice, later would have been better. Forty years later would be perfect.

I spotted two people I knew: Matt Bearus and Luke Winston. Sitting between them, I whispered to Luke, "How'd you know Mrs. Cuttlebum?"

"Sunday School teacher, Scout leader, school nurse—you name it. She wore a lot of hats over the years," he said.

"Oh."

There'd been more to Mrs. Cuttlebum than what met the eye. I looked around the church. The pews were roomy, but without cushions, making it easy for us to slide further right as another person took a seat next to our threesome. It got to be a little joke between me and Luke. Someone would come in, he'd whisper, 'Slide your butt down.' And I'd murmur back, 'Butt sliding,' as I edged towards the outside aisle in my pencil skirt. I decided in the future, I would always attend funerals with him; he made a scary place better.

The pianist, a middle-aged woman with the matronly paunch, worked the keyboard. Her elbows cocked as her fingers flew across the keyboard. Her sleeves wafted in response to her energetic movements—or maybe her underarm folds were wafting? Whatever, piano lady was getting busy, filling the sanctuary with music.

"Will you be my funeral buddy?" I whispered to Luke.

He put his hand over mine and pledged, "It would be my highest honor."

I smiled. The warmth of his hand felt so reassuring that when he tried to pull it away, I tugged back. He looked at me, a question in his eyes, but I smiled, "This is what funeral buddies do."

His eyes twinkled. "Good to know."

We held hands as the pianist pounded away, her face gleaming with the sheen of hard work. I scanned the program with a newfound appreciation for its brief synopsis of her life. With a shock, I realized this woman was only seventy-four years old. She seemed older than that.

A bunch of ladies showed up in red hats garnished with purple floral accessories. Naturally they sat right in front of us, their tulle and splendor obstructing our view. Luke and I exchanged horrified glances and poked our heads through a tiny space to see the eulogist.

"What can we say about a woman like Eula? She was courageous, kind, and spunky." The minister leaned forward across his podium, adjusted his glasses.

My ears pricked up at that last adjective.

Spunky? That's not how I'd describe her. Wilted, maybe. Then I thought of her amongst her roses and wilted wasn't the right adjective at all. Frowning my puzzlement, I directed my attention back to the minister.

"Eula's grandchildren told me the tale of her serving as a Chief Nurse in Vietnam. It was hot, humid work. What little air conditioning they had rarely worked. So she sometimes wet the nurses' bras and underwear at bedtime and put them in the cook's freezer when he wasn't looking. In the morning, the nurses would dress in frozen underwear, keeping themselves cool on their twelve hour shifts. She said the cook caught her doing this late one night, so she got off the hook by giving his underwear the same treatment."

"Not only did she nurse the wounded soldier back to health—her unit had a 98.5% survival rate, no doubt thanks to her contributions—but she also taught basic courses of first aid to villagers and helped inoculate orphans. At home, she taught Sunday school for thirty-eight years. Most in this congregation learned something from Eula Cuttlebum, if not through the written word of the Lord, then through her example of Christian living. She never raised her voice in anger, never heard her say an unkind word about anyone and never turned down anyone who asked for her help. She follows her husband, George, in death, as well as their youngest son, Jimmy."

I remembered how she couldn't hear worth shit, realizing her hearing had probably been damaged by artillery rounds. My head bowed, I berated myself for under-estimating Mrs. Cuttlebum. I searched for a Kleenex from my purse and dabbed at my left eye. I don't know why tears don't run at the same time. My left eye is quicker than my right—like it got a better jump out of the gate.

Luke gave my hand a squeeze.

The minister talked about the local garden club Mrs. Cuttlebum helped found, her participation in community activities, how she'd been a single parent due to her husband's early death. Brandon, her grandson, spoke briefly, his voice breaking towards the end. My heart ached for him. I knew exactly how he felt. The finality of those last goodbyes has subtle devastation. Desolation, anxiety, feelings of being bereft—these are intangible markers of grief. A human heart may not show external signs of cracking or being torn asunder, but you'll never convince your brain of that medical fact.

Sitting on the other side of me, I felt, rather than saw, Matt Bearus checking his email on his cell phone. I resisted smacking his arm or pinching him, though the urge was very strong. We rose and sang an unfamiliar hymn. Unable to read music, I hummed my way through. Gloria's and Dad's musical selections were identical. He'd helped select hers, so I figured he'd like the same songs for himself. Dad insisted on 'Ode to Joy' by Beethoven, and I didn't want to argue. It still seemed perverse to play such a cheerful, joyous song at a funeral. That was Dad. There were things about him I'll never understand.

Surroundings became blurry when the procession formed. Clutching my Kleenex, I walked through the line to hug Brandon and murmured something—I don't know what, exactly.

Before long, we left the darkness of the sanctuary and entered the glaring sunshine outside. Loitering on the sidewalk, I saw Ted Danveldt, who stood beside his sister. It'd been nearly two weeks since our debacle of a date. Ted waved and I returned a much smaller wave, pretending to be conversing with Luke. What we discussed, I haven't the foggiest idea since Ted's gaze bore holes into me.

"This morning's been tough. I need to get out of here," I told Luke before leaving.

"Catch you around."

"Yeah. Later."

Clickety, click, clack. My high heels struck the paved parking lot, uneven and rushed as I hurried to my Fiesta. I'd just sat down and was about to shut the car door when I discovered Ted had followed me.

"How you doing, Coop?"

"Cooper," I corrected, having no idea why I was being so bitchy to a guy who'd spent the last two weeks ignoring me.

"I thought we were friends?" His brow lifted in that annoyingly familiar gesture.

I didn't have a response to that, not knowing if we were friends or not.

He squatted in the tiny triangular space, his gaze coming level with mine.

"Well, I'd like to think we're friends."

I stared at him hard.

He reached for my hand, toying with my fingers. "Coop, if this is because I haven't called…"

I snatched my hand from his grasp, masking the reaction by belatedly tucking some strands behind my ear. My voice sounded high and tight as I pooh-poohed that idea "Don't be silly. I barely know you. I just prefer that you not address me as 'Coop,' okay?"

"Oh, you know me, all right." He stood, his clipped, terse voice warning I'd angered him, but oddly enough, it didn't factor.

Reaching in front of his knees, I grabbed the door handle then sent him a pointed look to move out of the way.

"You know, this ice maiden act isn't getting us anywhere."

A seismic shift occurred in that infinitesimal moment, signaled by my gasp. I felt my eyes snap open to saucer-size, then narrow to slits in half a heartbeat. "Step back! Right now!"

"Coop, I didn't mean—"

"Stop calling me Coop!"

Amidst the wreckage of grinding gears my proud but puny Festiva left the church parking lot. Through my rearview mirror, I saw Ted tug his hair in frustration.

"Name's Cooper. Cooper Bach," I muttered to anybody who cared.

Nobody did.

Chapter 15

Nothing Like You

After work, I went jogging, ignoring the forty-some boxes that cluttered my apartment, still needing to be dealt with. Aware that I was edgy, it didn't require much to psychoanalyze the reasons for it. I should never have gone to the old lady's funeral. Should never have dropped off those boxes of food or sat on her porch, drinking tea with Mrs. Cuttlebum and Brandon, talking about roses. Dammit. Was I some masochist? Hadn't I pretty much figured out the best way to get on in this world was solitary? Who gave a shit about me or my problems? Fucking nobody. Button it up, Coop. Grow up. Everybody feels isolated, some mask it better than others. Quit it. Be self-sufficient.

"Cooper!" someone yelled my name.

Ted Danveldt's truck prowled close to the curb. He waved me down, but I kept jogging. After his little 'ice maiden' comment, I had no incentive to prove otherwise, being a strong believer in Pygmalion's theory.

He ignored me ignoring him and coasted, dodging parked cars as he slowly drove down the street. His stubbornness only upped my resistance. The sun could implode before I gave in on this. Suddenly, ignoring him gave me a single-minded purpose in life. His truck purred, following curbside for four city blocks. Realizing that one of us would have to be reasonable and that this duty fell squarely on my shoulders because he was so frickin' impossible, I whirled on him. In angry frustration, I stalked to his truck, slapping my hands on the passenger's window ledge.

"Just what is your problem?"

"I'm sorry for what I said earlier today." His voice was low, sincere.

The icy walls around my heart cracked.

"Okay," I drawled, watching him closely. "Thanks."

"And I'm sorry for not getting in touch with you sooner."

I gave a short nod.

"I called the office once, but didn't leave a message."

"Right."

"Seriously, I did."

I snorted, venting my disbelief.

"And I have another problem."

Oblivious to my skepticism, his eyes danced with mirth as he parked his truck and came out to talk with me. Leaning against his hood, he said, "We could stay here all night and talk about my problems, if you want to."

"Sorry, but you need professional help. You know—with somebody who charges by the hour. Hopefully, someone very expensive."

"Well, you charge by the hour, don't you? You're a counselor. Aren't you sworn to help people with their legal problems?"

I eyed him suspiciously. "You don't have a legal problem."

"I do." His earnest tone struck me as phony, but he continued, "Look, if it's not in your field of expertise, maybe you can give me a referral?"

"I don't know."

"Let me begin and if it's outside your bailiwick, you let me know?"

With a pointed look at my watch, I said, "You got five minutes and then I'm finishing my workout."

"Yeah, okay. Sounds fair enough. You see, there's this girl I like. Beautiful, blonde type—nothing like you," he assured me with a dismissive wave.

I grit my teeth.

Ted continued, "She's kinda been a bitch to me, but I can't stop thinking about her. It's like—" He runs his hand through his hair, causing it to spike. "But then there's this soft side to her. She's not a bitch at all, just someone who's hurting."

Toeing the ground, I was at a loss for words.

"Again, nothing like you." He whispered, his voice throbbing with suppressed humor.

I slanted him a sideways look. "Flatterer you ain't."

Promptly, he replied, "She doesn't trust charmers. Thinks they're players."

"Unbelievable."

"Yeah. With her, it's real."

My head jerked up as my gaze searched his.

Warm, caramel-colored eyes assured me, "So, we have this emotional, intimate evening and poof! I wake up. She's gone. Ditched me." His voice was somber, his face serious.

The earnestness from moments before didn't seem so overdone now. "I don't have her number, don't want to pester her at work because she works for a real psycho, if you know what I mean. I hoped she'd come visit me at my bar. She'd been there once. Now it's over two weeks since I last heard from her and I'm wondering, how am I gonna get a second chance?"

Lightly, but inexorably, he tugged my wrist, bringing me against his chest. It wouldn't be long before I said something to wreck this moment, so I held my tongue. With my hand splayed across his chest, I felt his heartbeat, letting the sound of it, the heat, and scent of him soothe me. After I while, I sighed and cuddled into him.

"Forgiven?" he asked, his breath warming my cheek.

Turning my head a fraction of an inch would cause our lips to collide. Was that what he wanted? What I wanted? I didn't know. Without making the decision, my mouth tasted his. This kiss was tentative, like a sampling of a strange, new dish. By wondrous agreement, our lips parted at the same time and the kiss deepened. In broad daylight, I softened in Ted's embrace, kissing him back.

He tore himself away and in a gruff voice, told me to get into his truck. My hands shook and I would have sworn my knees buckled. With hand gestures, I directed him to my apartment, finding it impossible to speak. I don't know that I could vouch for my mental state. It wasn't quite what could be clinically termed 'delirium,' but it was by no means sane. Thoughts whirled in my head, chasing after one another without forming a conclusion. Parts of me (the area beneath my waistline) clamored for sex—screamed for it. Other parts of me (that area above the waistline) was strangely dormant. Now was not a great time for my brain to go on 'radio silence.'

The internal struggle abruptly ended when he pulled into the parking lot of my apartment complex. I fumbled for the door handle, jumping out of his truck.

"Thanks for the lift."

"Oh, no, you don't." Moving faster than you'd expect for a tall man, his lean legs swung out of the cab. "You're not getting off the hook that easily."

A rise of indignation stained my cheeks bright pink. Did he think I owed him sex? For a ride home? Really?

"Listen, buster, I don't know who you think you are, but I am not ready—nowhere near ready for whatever you have in mind."

"Buster?" He chuckled. "Shh, Coop, two weeks ago you spent the night crying in my arms. You've been through hell. Believe me, I know you're not ready for anything."

Viewing him through narrowed slits, I saw the edges of his mouth quirk. He found this amusing. Ordinarily, that would have embarrassed or angered me, but his expression reassured me. My shoulders lowered, my defensiveness crumbling.

"Don't worry, you can trust me."

"This isn't a good time."

"Yes, it is," he argued. "You need someone to take care of you; let it be me."

"Take care of me?"

"Yes." He approached as if I were some skittish woodland creature with his hands out, making calming gestures.

Closing my eyes, I made a feeble protest. "But I'm a mess."

"Sure," he agreed.

I hid my half-smile. "Thanks. I'll spot you on the emotional front, but I meant my apartment—it's a mess."

He shoved me towards my building. "I don't care. Go change. I'm taking you out to eat."

"Yeah?"

"Yeah." He flicked the tip of my nose, an affectionate gesture, but the gleam in his eye was far from avuncular.

Anxiety spiked as I unlocked my apartment door. I put out my hand to restrain him from crossing the threshold. "Before you go in, I'll warn you I'm not a hoarder. With them dying so close together, I never had a chance to…"

"Shhhh." He pressed a finger against my lips. "It's all right. You screamed at me in the middle of the grocery store, remember? I'm still here. Nothing you got is going to scare me away."

Despite my apprehensions, I opened the door. We entered my cramped residence, instantly surrounded with towers of boxes, floor to ceiling. Chaos everywhere.

Surreptitiously, I watched his face, gauging his reaction. He shrugged, as if to say, 'You weren't kidding,' but took the rest in stride.

"Ah! Land ho!" he said, spotting the clean kitchen counters. He hopped up and plopped his very fine derriere on the laminated countertop, grinning from ear to ear. "You get dressed while I wait here."

"You sure?"

"Put a move on. I'm getting hungry."

I called to him over my shoulder, "Are you always this bossy?"

"Bossy?"

I could hear the smile in his voice as I peeled off the sweaty shirt. I gave myself a quick sponge bath, splashing the way birds do.

"I'm not bossy. I just know what I want," he hollered from the kitchen.

"Yeah, right." I swiped on some deodorant, wishing I could place my hand on body splash, but I didn't want to take the time to hunt for it. Quickly, I combed my hair then applied tinted moisturizer, pink lipstick, and mascara. I smacked my lips together and checking my reflection, thought I'd do for McDonald's or Arby's.

I dashed into my bedroom, grabbed the first top I saw and stepped into fresh underwear and jeans. Jamming my feet into a pair of orange flip flops, I returned to the cardboard jungle, worried Ted might have ditched me.

"Ready?" He jumped down from the counter. "That didn't take long. You're a unicorn."

"What does that mean?"

"Low maintenance woman—you know, a creature everyone talks about but nobody's actually ever seen." He held the door open and waved me through it.

"Hardy-har-har. You're hilarious."

"Ah! My sense of humor is just one of my many good qualities," he assured me, steering with his hand at my back.

He opened the door for me, which struck me as a lot of fuss for dinner at McDonald's, but I wasn't complaining. A girl could get used to this 'being taken care of' crap even if it did run counter to my notions of being an independent, modern career woman.

Once the truck was in motion he asked, "So… are you going to give me your phone number?"

"Are you going to give me yours?"

He cast a quick glance and said huskily, "You've already got my number."

Giving me his lazy, half-lidded look, I caught my breath. A wealth of invitation warmed those caramel eyes of his as we stared at one another. Reluctantly, it seemed, he pulled his gaze away and concentrated on driving.

My breathing had mysteriously developed a small hitch and I doubted whether there'd been an invitation after all. Had that been wishful thinking on my part? What did I want to happen here? So I kissed him on the street in public view—uncharacteristic behavior. Did it signify I wasn't in my right mind or that strong chemistry existed between us? Probably the former. If it were the latter, I'd have to marvel at the ill timing. With so much on my plate, now wasn't a great time to embark on a new romance.

Ted tossed his cell phone into my lap, startling me from these cogitations.

"Here. Put your number in."

The way he'd asked for my phone number was so smooth, so practiced, that it made me think, as David Seltzer had said, 'it wasn't his first time at the rodeo.'

Cognizant that my name was joining a long list of other girls', I typed in my contact information.

He was forced to brake suddenly, swearing at the careless driver who nearly caused an accident. Glancing over to me, he muttered a hasty apology.

"Have you ever been in a wreck?"

"Yeah," he said.

I pressed for an answer. "How many?"

"How many wrecks have I been in or how many have I caused?" Ted asked.

"Wow."

He chuckled. "I'm just yanking your chain. I've had one accident—backed out of my driveway and hit the trash can on the curb. No big deal, but Mom threw a hissy over it."

"Really? That seems rather extreme…"

Shrugging, he said, "Well, I was eight at the time, so…"

Stupefied, I stared at him. "Are you kidding me?"

Reaching over to grasp my hand, he gave it a squeeze before saying, "Yes, I'm kidding. You needed something to lighten up."

That caught my attention. The bartender had the uncanny ability to take me off-guard, which was no small feat. Shaking my head in bafflement, I frowned a bit. I really was off my regular game.

His hands returned to the ten o'clock and two o'clock positions on the steering wheel. "So, given your sudden interest in car accidents, I'm curious—is that how Gloria died?"

Again, his deductive reasoning surprised me. Pain tightened my throat, but I whispered, "Yes."

"Aw, babe. I'm so sorry." Again, he took my hand, but this time he left it there. Holding hands, as old-fashioned as it sounded, was soothing. I enjoyed the warmth and security of being linked together. Ignoring my previous decision not to connect with others, I settled back in the seat and studied the passing neighborhood. The streets were lined with mature trees, the houses neatly maintained bungalows with dots of color in the front yards. He pulled into a sloping driveway. The house needed painting. A shutter stirred on a broken hinge, making a half-hearted attempt to swing in place.

"I thought we were going to McDonald's!"

"Disappointed?" Before I could answer it was a close contest between dining at Mickie Dees or here, he hurried to explain. "Look, I know the outside looks like hell, but I'm working my way through the inside first. I bought it in February and it's been a total gut job."

Pushing my reservations aside, I found my manners. Considering the mess my apartment was in, who was I to judge another person for the condition of his home? I gave him a tentative smile, hoping to assure him and that he'd forgive my earlier dismay. I didn't want Ted to think I was a snob, although entering his house felt like greeting Cerberus at the entrance to Hades.

"So you're a handy man, eh?"

His lips twitched, as if he'd heard the battle warring inside my head. Leading me up to the door, still holding my hand, he used his other to make an expansive wave. "Welcome back to El Rancho Costo Plenty."

As weird as it seemed, I had no memory of this house and would have sworn on a stack of bibles I'd never been here. That fog of grief obscured my powers of observation to an alarming degree. I had walked home the following morning at day break; yet none of the surroundings struck a chord of remembrance. My disconnect to the world scared the hell out of me. For the first time, dawning realization struck that even if life wasn't a spectator sport, I wasn't participating even as an onlooker.

The transition between the neglected exterior and the interior couldn't have been starker. The immaculate living room looked like a scene photographed for *Better Homes and Gardens* or *Architectural Digest*. The furniture, with clean lines in the contemporary style, had been arranged to best advantage. A leather, chestnut-color sofa faced the picture window and a Craftsman-style coffee table sat upon a woolen rug of muted shades. A Tiffany lamp stood over a recliner, the perfect spot for an avid reader. Unlike any bachelor pad I'd ever seen, Ted had actually taken the time to acquire coordinating throw pillows and art work. A set of three candlesticks of staggered heights had candles with burnt wicks, which cast shadows against the cream walls.

"Ted, this is really nice."

A light in his eyes danced as he accepted the compliment. "There's lots more work to do, but it's shaping up. I wanted everything to be high-quality and comfortable, but it's a slow process. Maddeningly slow."

Staring at the couch, a memory teased the corner of my mind. I had sat there as I bawled, I recalled. Glad to have found something familiar, his house didn't feel so foreign.

"Did you re-finish the hardwood floors by yourself?"

"Yeah, that was fun. Before going to the bar, I coated the floor with polyurethane then backed out of the house. While I was at work, it would dry. When I returned home, I'd sand the floors and start the process the next day. There's five coats on it."

"Well, I like the shine."

He pointed to a corner. "Something had burned over there, so I feathered in new boards. Can you tell the difference?"

Examining it, I took my time answering, not sure how he wished me to respond. Finally, I spoke the truth. "I can't see any difference between the old flooring and the part you replaced."

"Good." He gave me a one-armed hug, pleased with my compliment.

"Do you like Italian? I got a sweet red wine— Roscato, or would you prefer beer?"

"I'll try the red," I offered.

He disappeared through a frosted glass-paneled door, going, I assumed, to the kitchen. I loitered in the living room, strolling the perimeter.

"I just put the pasta on." He handed me a glass with a tiny serving of red wine. "Taste this and let me know what you think."

"Cheers," I said, taking a sip.

He watched me with that single cocked brow.

"It's good."

"Good." He poured and filled my glass. He returned to the kitchen and came back to me with his own glass of wine. "Come on, I'll give you the tour."

Turning in a small circle, he announced, "This will be the dining room. I've ordered dining room furniture, but it's not in yet."

"Where do you eat?"

He grinned, pointing to the sofa. "I use the coffee table for now."

I pulled down the corners of my mouth, acknowledging the practicality of that arrangement. I ate meals from my sofa, too. Without the luxury of a coffee table. Smiling to myself, I followed him through the frosted glass door into a huge kitchen.

"Geezus!"

Chuckling at my response, he folded his arms across his chest and grinned. The six-burner gas stove, whose name even I knew was synonymous with la-de-dah living, the oversized stainless steel refrigerator, and the Carrara marble countertops screamed, 'Gourmet kitchen!'

The wooden floor from the living room flowed into the kitchen, but Ted had stained lighter diamond shapes into the wide planks to create interest. It was stunning. The kitchen had a large pantry at one end and a mudroom at the other, near the back door. Pointing to it, I said, "That's convenient, I'll bet."

"Yeah. Karen's idea. She's given me some great advice."

I quirked a brow and he answered my unspoken question with a chuckle. "Some of it I *did* ask for and part of *that*, I actually took."

Shaking my head at the antics of siblings, I followed him through the kitchen with its gleaming pot rack and crystal stemware hanging from a cabinet made specifically for wine glasses. Going straight from college into law school, I hadn't the time to develop hobbies. Cooking was something I knew nothing about, but apparently, Ted did. He'd built this kitchen with something of an aficionado's love for detail.

Tallying up the facts I'd learned about him, I made a quick inventory: kind, gentlemanly, compassionate, well-educated, businessman, renovator/contractor, great kisser. Commendable qualities, but another factor weighed heavily against those: he was a player. No sense entering into a long term relationship with a player—might as well try to drive a bus to Hawaii. It wasn't going anywhere.

Frowning, I wondered what I was going to do with this guy. Keep him in the friend zone? Make him a fuck buddy? Sideline the whole thing? Sex complicated stuff and if there's one thing I needed less, it was another complication, but to ignore our sizzling chemistry seemed unlikely. Wiping my palms on my jeans, it didn't surprise me that the mere idea of having sex with Ted Danveldt would make me sweaty. Once again, I questioned my sanity.

A large room ran the width of the house, but it was bare and stripped to its essence. A chest-high stack of drywall sat on the north end, a film of dust covered the rest of the floor. Three exposed light bulbs dangled from electrical wires, swaying as the house "breathed." Ted's footsteps creaked across the unvarnished narrow planks as he passed.

"This is going to be the family room. Does that surprise you?"

I shrugged, this new revelation not jiving with the inventory I'd earlier done for him. "I just assumed you'd want to remain a bachelor for a while. Unless…"

"Unless?"

"Are you planning to flip this house?"

His lips pursed. "No, I'm not working my ass off just so I can turn the house over to somebody else."

"Oh."

"What's the matter, Coop?"

"Nothing. I just figured you enjoyed playing the field."

"In other words, you don't think I'm the marrying kind, is that it?"

Scrunching my forehead, I pretended to give it some thought.

He laughed without mirth. "Forget it."

"No, no." I said, speaking in mystical tones, pretending to hold a crystal ball as my other hand span it. "I can see the future. Your future. It's very bright, indeed. Filled with…"

"Cooper."

His quiet admonition made me leave off the joking. "Seriously, I could see you with a little girl, maybe an ornery son, too. Giving piggy-back rides and bubble baths and reading bedtime stories."

"Sounds good, doesn't it?"

"Yeah." Turning away so he couldn't see the pain these images brought me, I flicked one of the light bulbs. "Family's important."

He stuffed his hands in his pockets and flicked the switch off, signaling the end to this particularly awkward moment. The mood turned quiet and subdued as he showed me the rest of his house at a meandering rate. The bathroom was spa-like with a sculptured, stand-alone bath tub. The tile work turned out great, being a white basket weave with a black square inset. He admitted it had taken patience.

"I'd say it was worth the effort, don't you?"

"Oh, yeah. It's gorgeous."

Four wide, squatty candles graced the windowsill. An arrangement of bottles were within arm's reach of the tub, sitting on an old wooden fruit crate. "This really does look like something out of a design magazine, Ted. Did you design this yourself? Tell me honestly."

"I did."

My eyes narrowed in suspicion.

"What?" He picked up on my skepticism.

"Then why is your house is so beautiful and the bar so...not?"

He threw his head back to laugh. After his bout of hilarity calmed, he wiped his eyes, glanced in my direction then ripped into gales of laughter again.

Feigning patience, I waited for him to regain his equilibrium. Obviously, different people had designed the two places—that answer was clear from his reaction. My gaze scudded the house. Definitely it had a woman's touch. Someone who cared enough for him to ensure he lived in luxurious settings. His sister, Karen? Or another girlfriend? My lips pressed together. The house was too recently decorated in the fully finished rooms for that relationship to be finished, so I left the bathroom with the goal of returning to the kitchen. I was hungry. I'd eat a dinner then leave. No big thing.

"Coop? Baby, are you all right?"

The endearment was nearly my undoing. In a ragged whisper, I asked, "Why are you playing with me?"

He stilled. "What do you mean?"

"Look, right now, it's taking everything I've got to stay afloat. You get it?"

"Where's all this coming from?"

We stood in the hallway, staring at each other.

"I asked to take care of you, Coop. I meant that. Tonight, I'm feeding you a nice dinner, and plying you with wine in the hopes you'll be able to relax. That's all. That's all that's going on here. I promise."

My shoulders lowered.

He smiled and gave me a half-hug. "I'm not playing you, okay?"

"Okay." Shifting anxiety into low-gear, I decide not to read too much into the curbside kiss. Sure, there was chemistry here, but that didn't mean we had to act on it. Ted appeared to take everything in stride and so I would, too. With a shaky laugh, I said, "Well, let's continue the tour—unless dinner's ready?"

"This way."

We peeped inside a spare bedroom, painted a tranquil baby blue with crisp white bed linens. No pictures decorated the walls, no knick knacks rested on the furniture. It was a spare bed waiting for the chance to be used. Another bedroom was painted a soft apricot color, a drop cloth served as carpet and I smelled fresh paint. The bare room boasted some beautiful crown molding and thick baseboards, stained dark.

"Peach?"

"What's wrong with peach?"

I shrugged. "Not what most bachelors would pick out."

"Don't forget Karen's influence."

"You were right."

He leaned against the door jamb, giving me a lazy look. "You'll find that I usually am, but what, specifically, do you mean?"

"At the grocery store when you warned Michael his mother had wussified you."

His lips twitched, spreading into a wide smile as his caramel eyes danced; Ted Danveldt was quite an attractive man, especially when he smiled. He was one of those people who smiled with his whole face, a particularly bright light entering his eyes. He might prove to be a unicorn, too. A kind, decent guy. God knows I'd dealt with some real assholes in my time.

"So, what's for dinner?"

"There's one room you haven't seen yet. I'm kinda surprised by your lack of curiosity, counselor." A wicked gleam sprang into his brown eyes.

The prickling sensation was there again, sending an aura of awareness across the surface of my sensitized skin. Nervously, I licked my suddenly-dry lips. Ted might be a nice guy, but there was no mistaking that ornery look.

"Don't you want to see my bedroom, Cooper?"

Knowing if I saw him in his bedroom, that I'd be imagining him there every night for the next week, I shook my head. "No. No, that's all right. Tour's over."

He chuckled. "Don't be scared. No torture apparatuses, I swear."

"Scared? I'm not scared. Why would I be scared?"

"Here." He brought me to the threshold of the sumptuous master bedroom outfitted in khaki, cream, and small touches of black. Silk cream drapes flanked the bay window, which would be an idyllic spot to read a good book with all the inviting pillows of different shapes and sizes. A small nook had just enough room for an overstuffed chair, an ottoman, and a side table with a lamp. The upholstery was tan with a houndstooth pattern.

"Wow."

"You like?"

"Yeah. It's lovely—the whole house."

"Do you really like it or just trying to be polite?"

"Oh, no. I'm never that polite. It's all very well done, Ted."

"Thank you for the compliment." He signaled me to follow him through to the kitchen and asked over his shoulder, "Are you ready for dinner now? We still need to make the sauce."

"Yes, I'm starving." I tossed the salad as he made the sauce. It was nice working in a kitchen large enough for two people to maneuver. He'd spared no expense in outfitting the appliances, cookware, glasses, and plates. My brow pleated, as it occurred to me Ted picked everything I would have selected, had I the money to afford this stuff. His home was a work-in-progress, but excellence shown in the rooms he'd already finished. I wondered how beautiful the house would feel once it was completed, but then such curiosity wasn't healthy. In all likelihood, Ted and I wouldn't be seeing each other by that future date.

Strange as it may be, that thought liberated me, allowing me to unwind. Believing Ted and I inhabited this particular bubble of time and space made me stop over-analyzing things. Bubbles were fun, but not long-lasting. I'd enjoy this time, roll with it—whatever. This was just dinner.

We ate on the sofa, over the coffee table, as informally as teenagers would do. Ted drank one glass of wine to my two.

I'd teased him when I saw his bottle opener. "And here you nearly had me fooled thinking you were some classy guy."

Color burnished his cheeks, as he guffawed. "Lola, you mean? Don't ridicule her—she's my best girl."

The bottle opener was made of pewter shaped like a woman's hourglass figure. As the corkscrew turned, her legs lifted high and wide. Sure, it was risqué, maybe even raunchy given how her sleeve drooped low over one breast to reveal the areola, but the sight was comforting, as well. Ted Danveldt might be near perfect were it not for Lola. Perfection, even in a lawyer, is intimidating and I had enough crap to deal with, thanks all the same.

The edgy feeling which hounded me since Mrs. Cuttlebum's funeral evaporated while we ate and conversed. We talked about the rest of his plans for the house, his business, our favorite books and movies. I discovered Ted loved heavy metal bands and hip hop, which I couldn't stand. He shuddered when I told him I liked classical music. We both agreed the Top Forty was a total sell-out and R.E.M. was a reason for rapture. When he wasn't playing handyman, he was out on the links, playing golf. I'd only played the miniature kind. Throughout this lengthy discussion, he struck me as an ambitious person, a hard worker, but laid back, too. Interesting. He didn't fit any mold of any other man I'd met. I wasn't sure if that were a good thing or not, but it intrigued me.

Near midnight, he returned me to my place, walking me to the door. In his low voice he prodded, "This is where you say, 'It's been a great evening, Ted. Let's do it again soon.'"

Playing indignant, I said, "Have you got a script for me? It'd be so much easier to read it."

"Ah, there she is—that little pissy pain-in-the-ass I first met."

"Pissy?"

He kissed my forehead. "Yes, but that's okay. I can handle pissy when I know the reason why."

Lowering my head, I muttered into his shirt, "I can be sarcastic, but I'm normally not pissy. I don't know…"

"Shh. Don't over-think things, Coop. And quit making the moves on me."

Mortified, he removed both my hands from the waistband of his jeans. I had no memory of doing that. Geez, was I ready to jump his bones on the landing outside my apartment door? Was grief some kind of aphrodisiac? My brain couldn't manufacture anything witty, so I nipped my bottom lip. "Why not?"

"Why not what?"

"Why not have sex? I don't want to be alone. You could come in, stay for a little while, make me feel better."

He groaned and closed his eyes.

"Are you praying?" I asked.

"Yes," he muttered. "God give me strength."

"Ouch." Rejection stung.

"Look at me."

When I was reluctant to do so, he tilted my chin and lifted my face. Staring into my eyes, he reminded me, "Cooper, I would love to come in with you, strip the clothes from your body, and find pleasure together. Nothing better, in fact." His strained smile assured me of his sincerity. "But sex complicates things and you are not at a place in your life where you need to borrow more problems. I'm not a saint. I won't lie and tell you I've never had one-night stands—I have, but that's not what I want from you. I need more from you, but now we're going to take it slow."

"You make abstinence sound noble."

"You're accusing me? You're the one who warned me not to play with you." He looked at his watch. "About three hours ago."

He was right. Tucking a strand of hair behind my ear, I sighed. I'd try everything to forget my emotional pain. Everything except a great screw. Instinctively, I knew Ted could give me that. Why wouldn't he cooperate, dammit?

"Look, would it help to know you tempt the hell out of me? You're smart, beautiful, and tough. You've taken blows which would level others, and you're still standing. I admire that quality in you. I like the steel in you."

Shaking my head, I refuted all he'd said. "It's not like that. I'm not strong. Not at all."

"Yes, you are."

I nodded, still not trusting that I wouldn't tackle him like a hyena in heat.

"I'll call you and we'll go to dinner again. Are you free Tuesday?"

"Yeah."

"Great. I'll see you Tuesday." Pressing a hard kiss on my mouth, he muttered something about nobility, spun on his heel, and left.

I stared after him, bewildered.

Chapter 16

A Rose, an Egg, and a Kid

David Seltzer was waiting for me when I entered to the office the next day. I'd forgotten we had an appointment. I apologized for the brain fart. He assured me he didn't mind.

"In fact, I took the opportunity to draw." He raised his sketch pad.

Smiling, I led him into my office, anxious to see whether he had any talent, but also worried Tanny would harangue us.

"Ugh!" he said, as soon as he saw my office, which made me laugh.

"I know, I know. A painter's coming next week."

"Are you replacing the furniture, too?" He ran his hand along its top. "This is terrible! It looks like a room at the state mental facility!"

"Are you gay?"

"What?" His asked, eyes round.

"You have quite an eye for the aesthetic. Most straight guys don't."

"I'm straight." Then he chuckled. "Not sober, but straight."

I stomped my foot, twisting my shoe into the gray berber carpet. "Aw, David! How can you be using so soon?"

"Relax. A little pot ain't gonna hurt."

I slapped my hand down on my ugly metal desk. "A little pot is still illegal in Kansas! And can be detected in the U.A.'s! And you'll get your bond revoked if you test positive."

He rolled his eyes and sighed. "Okay, Mrs. Bach. I promise not to use any more marijuana while this case is pending."

"Or anything else?"

He crossed his heart and promised. "Or anything else."

I leaned back, "Okay, hot stuff. Show me what you got."

A wide grin broke out when he opened his sketch book. He'd drawn flowers, roses, in particular, with raw eggs peeping out behind the petals. Only pencil drawings, but the detail was exquisite, the lines and proportions masterful. Turning each page was a revelation of aching, soulful beauty.

"These are beautiful," I whispered as if I were in church. The lyrics from 'Ode to Joy' sprang to mind, *Hearts unfold like flowers before Thee.* I wiped a tear away, hoping he hadn't noticed.

"You think?" he asked, tilting his head. He acted casual, as if my response weren't a big deal, but that merely proved how much it did matter to him.

"No, not what I *think,* what I *feel*—does that make sense? Your drawings are precious and evocative. Beautiful."

"Glad you like them. Take the whole damn book."

"What?"

He nodded. "Go on, if you enjoy them. I can always draw more."

"Really?" A happy flame danced in my chest.

"Really."

"David, have you ever studied professionally?"

"What? You mean art?"

"No, auto mechanics, you idiot! Of course, art! These are really, really good."

He shrugged. "School's not for me. I was the stoner in high school."

"But you don't need to be!"

"That's all I am."

"That's all you've been," I corrected him. "You have a lot more to offer the world than fewer brain cells, champ."

"You really think so?"

I grinned then pointed to a picture of a rose, off-centered. An egg rested in the foreground. "This is my favorite."

"What does that say to you?"

"I don't think I should tell you. What if I see something you hadn't? Will you be mad at me?"

"Do you see anything?"

"Yes. I see beauty and life, hope and immortality."

"Okay, now you're just bullshitting me."

"No," I said. "The egg represents a birth, a soul. The rose signifies beauty and its thorn, pain. You've encapsulated life."

An uncomfortable silence floated mid-air between us until he cleared his throat and said, "I'll go down for four. Talk to the prosecutor. But I'm not giving anybody up."

"Are you sure? Four years is a long time."

He gave a wry smile and stood up. "Ah, I don't know. With good time I'll be out in three. That's the same time it takes to get through grad school, right?"

"Not the same place, though," I said dryly.

"I'll be all right. I've got my drawings. There'll be a library—stuff. Maybe every now and again, you could send books with pictures for me to copy? I doubt my family will do much to help."

I couldn't explain the lump in my throat. "So, this is a self-imposed artist's exile, eh?"

"Oh, yeah. It's all self-imposed. You know, I've been thinking. I didn't have to make Roland's job so easy for him."

He saw my confusion and prompted my memory. "Roland, the undercover cop. The guy I went to grade school with?"

"Right. Okay. I'll talk to the D.A. See what I can do. It shouldn't be too much trouble." I escorted him from my office. In the lobby, I asked, "When do you want to start the sentence?"

"Let's say thirty days from now. The sooner it's over, the better, but make them understand that I won't turn anybody over—I'll never make it inside if I squeal."

I shook David's hand. "Okay. I'll let you know by the end of the week. We can waive the pre-sentence investigation, but the prosecutor's probably going to want an NCIC check, at least."

David nodded, his eyes glowed. "Goodbye, Mrs. Bach."

"Okay, David. Talk with you later."

I hollered after him, as he crossed the front door's threshold. "And David? Thanks for the sketches."

He waved off my thanks. "No problem."

And then he was gone, his boyish grin lingering in my memory.

***

Sam Hatdiff, the husband and junior partner, accompanied me to court on the *Bronski* motion. We came to see if our request for the *Ross* hearing would be granted. In essence, the judge had to decide if it was in Junior's best interests to have a paternity test done. No brainer, right? We were going to have our asses handed to us. After trying to talk Mrs. Bronski out of this horrible idea, we conceded defeat. We drew the perfect judge—not. She was female, not prone to smiling and not known for showing mercy to idiots. Sam and I exchanged worried looks.

"Wonder what I'll look like once Waterman strips ten pounds off my ass," Sam muttered.

"Is it gonna be so bad?"

He leveled me a look which said he pitied my naiveté.

"Mark my words, Cooper. Judge Waterman is the short stick in this draw."

Within ten minutes of meeting Judge Waterman, I understood what my boss tried to tell me. With her gravelly voice, spiky platinum hair, and high IQ, she was Mrs. Bronski's complete opposite. No high-flown dramatics, no screaming protests, no screeched warnings. Judge Waterman wouldn't show a lot of sympathy to Mrs. Bronski's whoring. Our client wouldn't find a sympathetic ear here.

Sam had taken me into Waterman' chambers before the hearing, introducing me.

"Fresh out of law school, eh?" She asked, shaking my hand firmly. "From where did you matriculate?"

"K.U."

"Me, too," she nodded. "Fine law school. Almost as good as the basketball team, eh?"

I grinned.

"I'm sorry to hear of the double deaths in your family. That must be terribly hard on you."

The jolt of hearing the phrase, 'double deaths' shook me to the core. I'd never thought of it that way before. For something so obvious to have escaped my notice, well, that spoke measures of its own, didn't it?

"People talk." I said, rather than asked.

She looked apologetic as she explained, "Yes, but it's not gossip. This is a small town and the lawyers all know everybody, but I am for sorry your losses."

Reading her steady gaze, we shared a moment of kindred understanding. People who lose a loved one have a certain tightness around the mouth. Maybe it comes from grimly accepting time marches on—despite wishing it wouldn't. The sadness leaks into the tender skin by the eyes, creating tiny wrinkles. No matter how much time passes, those physical reminders of grief don't fade. Judge Waterman had those tight, drawn marks of bereavement. She knew.

Gruffly, I managed to mumble 'thank you,' as I seated myself.

Without much delicacy, Sam launched into the reasons for the *Bronski* motion.

Shutters flew over the judge's face, making me promise to never play poker with her.

She asked, "How old is this child?"

"Nine," Sam said.

"Actually, eight," I said.

Sam glared at my correction, which was easy to ignore. He'd made me write that damned memorandum twice. I knew all the salient facts by heart. If he didn't appreciate that, he could go suck an egg.

Although Judge Waterman' eyebrows met her hairline, she said nothing. I'd have bet ten dollars Judge Waterman used to beat up cheerleaders at her high school, too. In my gut, I knew we'd already lost the *Ross* request. No way was this judge going to chance bastardizing an eight-year old. The psychological damage to the child at this age could be irrevocable. Not, I remembered, that that had seemed to bother our client, damn the Maggot.

The judge turned the conversation, asking if Sam was going on vacation. We learned more of his travel arrangements than we could possibly want to know, but it seemed as long as the judge kept Sam talking of inconsequential things, it was a comfortable conversation.

After leaving chambers, I murmured to Sam, "I totally get what you were trying to tell me about losing this hearing."

He smiled without humor or pleasure.

Shifting my weight from one foot to another, I broached him with a tentative solution. "Could we negotiate something with opposing counsel?"

"We can't. Our damned client wants her pound of flesh and day in court. I've tried talking her out of this until I'm hoarse, but she won't authorize anything."

"She'd not going to like losing, either."

"How's her retainer?" He asked, changing the subject so rapidly it made me blink.

"Half burned up, I guess. After today's hearing, it should be gone."

"Good. I'll withdraw right afterwards." Sam held the courtroom door open for me and warned, "All we can do in the meantime is hope it won't go too badly."

We took our places at counsel table. Mrs. Bronski sat sandwiched between us. Maggot (my pet name for her proved to be permanent) wore cloying perfume, which nearly made me gag. Her thick make-up was expertly applied and she'd worn an expensive, elegant dress. Carrying it off with a sleek sexuality that shouldn't be trusted, our client sat back in her chair and twitched her ankle, marking time. The hem of her skirt rode up, skimming her thighs in a calculated play. Her dark hair and trim figure, courtesy of color stylist and liposuction specialists, were magazine-perfect. She fidgeted with a charm bracelet, causing the trinkets to jingle a warning to the cuckholded husband.

When Mr. Bronski strode into the courtroom with his lawyer, I gasped. He was H-O-T! Broad shoulders, narrow-hips with muscular, his blond, masculine beauty rivaled the Norse god, Thor. He was that rare man whose sensuality appealed to women of all ages. He was the kind of man every man wished to be. His mantel of beauty was worn with ease, as if he truly were some demi-god.

My gaze swiveled to my client. My incredibly vindictive, silicone-enhanced, stupid client whose eyes glittered with hatred. She was a highly attractive woman, but her beauty had already begun to fade. Even at her zenith, she had married above herself, looks-wise. In fact, on paper, this was a couple seriously off-balance. She wasn't his equal in looks, in fortune, in education, or temperament. Just what the hell had Mr. Bronski seen in Maggot? And why hadn't Maggot thanked her lucky stars every day of her marriage? Why was *she* throwing *this* guy to the curb? Why had *she* cheated on *him*?

Then it clicked. No wonder she sat, twisting her bracelet like a stiletto into his heart. This man was Maggot's pinnacle. She'd never have such a hottie husband again, so she did what petty people do: she punished him. Conveniently forgetting her unfaithful conduct caused the demise of their marriage, she wanted to punish him for divorcing her. Viewed through those lenses, it was easy to understand her bitterness. It didn't make me like her; in fact, I thought less of her.

From my spot at counselor's table, I noted how the lines of tension appeared grooved into Mr. Bronski's face. It didn't detract from his handsomeness. He was a good father to Junior. A good role model.

And here I was, trying to bastardize this man's son. My stomach protested and I placed my palm on my midriff. Too late to ask if we could swap clients, but dang it—I wanted to.

Instead, I shuffled folders on the table top, trying to think of a way to avert what was bound to be a catastrophic hearing. I got nothing.

The bailiff announced the formidable Judge Waterman' arrival over my gurgling belly. With distant courtesy, Judge Waterman asked the attorneys to introduce themselves and their clients. Hearing these announcements, she called the matter to order, avoiding eye contact with everyone save the bailiff. To him, she delivered a cool smile.

After this brief fanfare, the blood sport began. Because we were the movant, Sam began with his opening statement, wielding his gladiator sword with precise words, non-offending demeanor, and careful recitation of the evidence. Working methodically, breathing life into my crafty arguments with stealthy movements. He called forth Mrs. Bronski as a witness after opposing counsel waived his opening statement.

Sam returned to the table for the purpose of collecting his notes for the direct examination of his client, but he gave me a look, to which I answered, "Something's not right—it's too easy."

"Yeah," he said, turning away but not before he advised me to watch the judge.

So instead of taking notes, I set down my pen and observed Judge Waterman. My gaze flickered to opposing counsel's table every now and again. Mr. Bronski frowned a lot, in varying degrees of severity to his wife's testimony, but his attorney carried himself with enviable savoir faire.

Opposing counsel, Mr. Damore's demeanor unnerved me. Not sure if he had successfully found a new way to fuck with my head or if he had a Hiroshima-esque bomb about to unload, I didn't know what to make of it. This whole hearing had a sense of inevitability unfolding.

"Mrs. Bronski," Sam started the direct examination. "Please tell us when you married Mr. Bronski."

"September 8, 2005." Her voice was breathless.

What's up with that? Then it hit me. Maggot was trying to sound like some breathy teenager. I shook my head. This judge wasn't going to be impressed by that act.

"Did you have a long engagement?"

"Well, it seemed like an eternity at the time."

"During your engagement were you chaste?"

"No, we were not. Bill and I were extremely attracted to each other." She peeped at opposing table from beneath her lashes.

Mr. Bronski missed his wife's sultry glance, scribbling notes again. Just as well.

"Your son, Bill Junior, was born when?"

"March 19, 2006."

"Was your son premature?"

"Objection."

"Sustained."

"Exception."

Judge Waterman' lifted her brows, but merely asked Sam, "Is Mrs. Bronski an expert in obstetrics, counselor?"

"No, ma'am."

"Then any testimony you solicit regarding matters of medicine can't come in through lay testimony," Judge Waterman explained in a carefully modulated tone which boded ill for our entire case.

Sam stood, looking stumped for a minute before turning to Mrs. Bronski and asking, "How long were you pregnant?"

"The regular time. Nine months."

I grimaced. Her answer was too general to be helpful and we didn't have an OB/GYN doctor on the witness list. I saw now that was an error on our part in pinpointing the dates of conception.

"Bill and I had premarital sex. Lots of times."

Mr. Damore rose. "Objection!"

The judge removed her glasses and said, "You are to answer the questions as they are asked of you, Mrs. Bronski. Nothing more, do you understand? That last statement will be stricken as non-responsive. Carry on with your direct examination, Mr. Hatdiff."

"Before you became pregnant, when was your last menstrual cycle?"

"Objection, your Honor!"

"Sustained." Glaring at Sam, Judge Waterman scolded him. "Counselor, it's already been ruled that this person is not educated in obstetrical matters and there can be no basis for soliciting such testimony."

"It's her own experience of which I seek to discover—"

"So that this court may make assumptions not based on expert testimony regarding the procreative process? I think not, Mr. Hatdiff. In your pretrial order, you have not listed an expert upon which you rely to establish the date of conception, or am I mistaken?"

"No, your Honor. That's correct."

"Then you seek to circumvent the pretrial order?"

"Objection," Mr. Damore added for good measure.

But the judge already had the matter well in hand and didn't need him to chime in at the moment, so she waved him off.

"Do you, Mr. Hatdiff, have an expert witness to proffer testimony who can pinpoint the date of conception with a reasonable degree of medical certainty?"

"We do not," Sam mumbled.

"Then further testimony regarding that date cannot be admitted at this hearing, sir."

Inwardly, I quailed. There went our entire case. We were seriously fucked.

"I don't care." Mrs. Bronski's silicon-inflated chest lifted with indignation. "Bill and I had sex before we married. And I also had sex with—"

"OBJECTION!"

"Mrs. Bronski, I've already admonished you once about responding to questions not put forth to you. I want no more outbursts. Do you understand?"

Panic widened Maggot's eyes as she stared at Sam, not sure what was happening, but sensing things weren't going well.

"Did you have sexual relations with another man besides Bill Bronski?"

"Objection," Mr. Damore said. "Irrelevant."

"Sustained." Judge Waterman glanced at Sam. "Counselor, you have already confessed you cannot establish the critical time of conception. There is no other time at issue in today's hearing which holds any relevancy on this issue, so I will strike any such testimony solicited for that purpose."

"Certainly, ma'am." Sam then faced his client and began again, "In the nine months prior to Junior's birth—"

"Objection, your Honor."

"Yes, I am aware. The objection is sustained."

Dammit, we were toast.

"Do you doubt Mr. Bronski's parentage of your son?"

No objection.

I breathed a sigh of relief.

"Yes. Yes, I do."

"What do you base this belief upon?" Sam asked.

"Objection, your Honor."

"I'll allow it so long as it doesn't intrude upon the perimeters already mentioned."

Our client had a 'deer in the headlights' look about her.

Sam picked up the thread of the direct examination and took control of the slippery greased pig by asking, "What color is Junior's hair?"

Which was a mistake. Never, never, never ask a question you don't know the answer to — Law School Basics 101.

"Blonde," Maggot said.

Because the answer could devastate your whole damned case.

"Objection."

Judge Waterman dismissed that objection without ruling upon it.

"Bill Bronski, your husband, has what color hair?"

"Brown."

"Does Mr. Bronski have any unusual mannerisms?"

"Objection."

"Based upon what?" Judge Waterman scowled at Mr. Damore.

"Speculation. The term 'unusual' is subject to vast interpretation and cannot be replicated."

Judge Waterman shrugged. "I'll allow it."

Mr. Damore said, "Exception."

"Noted," bit off the judge.

"Bill lifts one of his shoulders when he shrugs," Maggot testified.

"Does your son have this attribute?"

"No, he does not."

"Any other difference in coloring or mannerism between your husband and your son?"

"Objection. Already asked and answered."

"Sustained."

"Based on your personal observations of the differences between your husband and son, why are you now requesting paternity tests?"

"Because I don't think Bill is Junior's real father."

"Objection."

"To what?"

Taken aback by the judge's sharp tone, Mr. Damore sat in his chair and mumbled, "Withdrawn."

Mrs. Bronski leaned forward and said, "Bill isn't the real father and he doesn't deserve to have to pay support for a child that doesn't belong to him." The flash of triumph lit Maggot's eyes with a hard brilliance.

Judge Waterman, in her first 'telltale' response of the hearing, darted an angry glance at the witness.

I flinched, knowing Maggot might as well have a label stamped in ink on her narrow forehead as 'opportunist.' No way could we wrap this turd in clean linen and present it to the court—don't know why we even tried.

Retainer. Ah, yes. I'd forgotten we'd been paid to be hired guns. Wishing I didn't have this irrational desire to shower, I tried to listen to Maggot's testimony.

"Do you believe it's in Junior's best interests to have this paternity test taken?" Sam asked.

"Objection!" Mr. Damore hollered, not because he had a basis for the objection, but because it was so damaging to hear what the whore had to say.

"Overruled."

Casting her eyes downward in a demure fashion, Maggot said, "Oh yes. Bill shouldn't pay for a child that's not his and he shouldn't be burdened with those other responsibilities. I fear he may come to resent Junior for it—"

"Move to strike! Calls for speculation!"

"Indeed, it does." Judge Waterman banged her gavel. "Mrs. Bronski, please confine your answers to the question put forth to you. Answer only that."

Sam wrapped up the direct examination after that and we took a short recess, prepared for a grueling cross-examination.

It didn't come.

When we returned to the courtroom, Mr. Damore was invited to present his evidence. Instead, he argued for an immediate dismissal. "The movant has failed to proffer testimony regarding any actual evidence that Mr. Bronski is not the biological father of Bill Bronski, Junior. Nor has movant, other than saying his son doesn't shrug like him, provided sufficient basis for that opinion. Mr. Hatdiff failed to prove by a preponderance of the evidence—let alone a clear and convincing standard—that a paternity test would be in the child's best interest."

Once more we took a break and stepped outside the courtroom as the judge gathered the file and her thoughts.

"What the hell, Sam?" Mrs. Bronski hissed. "Is he saying we should have had a doctor testify?"

"Apparently. To establish the dates you were likely fertile and then you could have testified that you and this other guy from the bar had sex during that window, as well as Bill."

"How the hell am I supposed to remember when I fucked the bartender from nine years ago?"

"Well, exactly. You see, how impossible it is to prove?"

"You told me we'd have a hearing!"

"I told you it wasn't a good idea to have a hearing," he corrected her.

"How is it a hearing if I'm the only one allowed to speak and half of everything I wanted to say didn't get heard?"

I put my finger in my ear, quelling the pain her piercing shrieks caused.

"Look, you don't want to be cross-examined by this guy." I thumbed toward the closed door to indicate Mr. Damore on the other side. "He'll crucify you."

"So what?" Maggot lifted her chin, her face frozen in lines of hatred. "I want Bill to know I fucked around on him from the get go and never let up."

How noble.

The bailiff opened the door, popped his head around and asked us to return. An uneasy quiet greeted us. The atmosphere in the courtroom shifted. My gaze took in Mr. Bronski. His hands covered his forehead, shielding his eyes. In a flash of insight, I realized he'd been crying. I'd never felt so low. That retainer Maggot gave us seemed like blood money now and I wished to hell I'd never met her. Wished I hadn't come to court with Sam. Wished…well, that I'd never met either one of them.

As soon as the judge was seated, Maggot remained standing and addressed the court. "Your Honor, I want to tell you how unsatisfied I am with the progression of today's hearing—"

Sam stepped on Maggot's foot, but she glared at him and continued, "Obviously, my counsel no longer represents me, their incompetence being revealed—"

Again, Sam stepped on her foot and cleared his throat to cover her sound of pain.

"Your Honor, I would ask, as my last act as counsel for the movant, that we have another break—"

"You promised me a hearing! And I didn't get one!"

"Be quiet," he snarled in an undertone.

Maggot recoiled and snapped, "Don't tell me to shut up!"

"I didn't tell you to shut up," Sam corrected, "I asked you to be quiet."

"Enough!" Judge Waterman banged her gavel to restore order. Directing her remarks to our former client, she asked, "Am I to understand during this last break you have fired Mr. Hatdiff and Ms. Bach as your attorneys?"

"I have!" she lied.

"Would you wish to precede with this matter or do you request an adjournment?"

"Your Honor, I have to object—" Mr. Damore, a man of few words, repeated again.

"Understood." Judge Waterman flung her palm at him. "Your answer, Mrs. Bronski?"

The woman squirmed for a moment and then took a step forward. "I wish to continue and shall represent myself for the remainder of this hearing."

"Oh God," Sam groaned. "Your Honor—"

"You're fired! Sit your ass back there!"

The judge responded, "Mrs. Bronski, if you insist on representing yourself, you must do so in accordance with the rules of professional conduct, which includes civility to the tribunal and counsel. Do you understand?"

"Yes, your honor." A blithe promise easily made.

Opposing counsel said, "Your honor, as to my motion for dismissal…"

"I'd like to shoot you!" Mrs. Bronski spat out at Mr. Damore.

The bailiff's hand went to his holster.

"Like the rabid dog you are."

The bailiff rushed from the courtroom.

"I beg your pardon?" Judge Waterman asked, icily. "Are you threatening Mr. Damore's life?"

Even Maggot knew that was beyond the pale, so she gave a condescending wave and demanded the hearing continue because, "I'm not done talking."

From the side of his mouth, Sam muttered, "For God's sake, shut it, woman."

At this moment, the bailiff returned with a small army. They dispersed along the edges of the courtroom, circling Maggot as an icy fist of iron clenched my gut. I almost felt sorry for Maggot.

Judge Waterman gave a nod, and the sentinels approached Mrs. Bronski. The bailiff whipped out his handcuffs and cautiously approached the litigant.

"What? What's the meaning of this?" She twisted, now realizing that maybe smarting off to Mr. Damore hadn't been her wisest move. She was trapped by her own bombastic stupidity.

"Your presence to this hearing is disruptive. Making death threats against opposing counsel is criminal, as well, Mrs. Bronski. For the safety of the participants in this proceeding, which you initiated, by the way, I command these officers to place you under arrest for Obstructing Justice. You will be arraigned later this afternoon by some other judge, and I will sign any affidavits necessary to effect your arrest."

As the judge ruled, Mrs. Bronski was handcuffed behind her back and led from the courtroom, an angry, writhing woman, spewing epithets which disparaged the lineage of every man's mother. Mr. Bronski shook his head sorrowfully, but heeded his attorney's nonverbal caution and restrained himself from saying anything that would only worsen the explosive situation.

In the silence of her removal, my stomach cramped. I felt sick. Judge Waterman, however, showed no sign of discomposure. She was, as always, cool and unflustered as she announced, "In light of the fact that the movant has left this proceeding, I order you, Mr. Hatdiff, to continue representing her until this matter has been journalized." Sam nodded his understanding, and she continued, "I'm prepared to hearing further arguments on your verbal motion to dismiss, Mr. Damore."

"Your Honor, the requirements for a *Ross* request have not been met, even viewing Mrs. Bronski's evidence in the best possible light; therefore, I respectfully ask that her motion be denied and for attorney fees in the amount of $5,500.00."

"Are there any other requests on Mr. Bronski's behalf?" She asked, scratching the tip of her nose but maintaining a closed expression.

I could nearly hear the vertebrates in Sam's back-bone stiffen. Mr. Bronski conferred with his attorney and vehemently nodded, slashes of crimson color crossing his cheeks, chasing his paleness away. Mr. Bronski scribbled something on paper then jammed the pad into his lawyer's hand, his movements jerky. His attorney leaned closer, whispered another question in his ear and Mr. Bronski sliced his hand in the air, indicating his disagreement with whatever proposal he'd just been given. Straightening, his attorney arched his eyebrows, saw that his client was not going to change his directions then returned to the podium.

Taking a brief moment to collect his thoughts, Mr. Damore said, "Your Honor, considering Junior's best interests, we believe the father should have residential custody, not the mother. Given the movant's antagonism, this court should make that finding and rule for a change in custody. We would ask the court order the parties into mediation to set the mother's visiting schedule."

"Any other requests?" Judge Waterman invited.

Opposing counsel had a blank expression on his face, then lit up. "If this Honorable Court changes custody, we would ask to terminate child support from the father to the mother and for the Court to establish child support be paid according to the Guidelines by the mother."

Sam jumped from his chair. "Now, wait a minute here, your Honor. This is moving along far too fast. There's no need to change custody or the child support obligation. There's no finding that present arrangements are not in the child's best interests."

"Has there been any finding that the present arrangements *are* in the child's best interests?" The judge looked above the rims of her spectacles. "No? I believe the current arrangement was put into effect upon Mrs. Bronski's filing an *ex parte* order, which I believe Mr. Bronski contested. Are there any other arguments you wish to make, Mr. Hatdiff, on your client's behalf?"

The nightmare that unfolded over the course of the next twenty minutes was like dropping into a pit of quicksand, sinking with inevitable finality. Sure, Sam sputtered out some arguments, raised his voice, banged on the table, but nothing dissuaded Judge Waterman. All the showboating in the world couldn't stop her. She employed several tricky tactics to impose her will on us, like listening, re-directing, and patiently waiting as Sam blustered on, throwing up feeble arguments. When the *Sturm und Drang* subsided, only then did she proceed with rendering her rulings, politely bulldozing our protestations. Plowing calmly ahead, Judge Waterman emasculated Sam with a nonchalance that would have been humorous if it weren't directed at us.

By the end of the afternoon break, Mrs. Bronski was cooling her heels in jail, the *Ross* motion was denied, custody was changed from wife to husband, child support terminated for husband, child support established for wife, neither side was awarded attorney fees against the other, and both parties were ordered not to discuss paternity with the child. Mrs. Bronski received the standard, 'blue plate special' visitation schedule: Wednesday evenings and alternating weekends.

Like whipped dogs, Sam and I slunk out of the courtroom with our figurative tails tucked between our legs. Let's face it—we didn't like our client, didn't believe in the cause, but nobody enjoys getting their ass kicked. With a heaviness that comes from suffering a humiliating defeat, Sam said, "I'll go visit the jail and give her the rulings, recommend a criminal attorney for her."

"Do you want me to come with you?" I gulped, crossing my fingers and hoping he'd say no.

He shook his head and I heaved a sigh of relief.

"That was a spanking," I jerked my thumb towards the courthouse. "I almost feel sorry for her, losing her kid."

"She lost a bargaining chip." Sam picked up his briefcase and gestured me to precede him. "Anyway, she'll be out by the end of the day and will, no doubt, rush to tell Junior Mr. Bronski isn't his real father."

I gasped. "But the judge specifically ordered her not to do that!"

Sam gave a mirthless laugh. "She's not going to play by the rules. This is war. Winning at all costs. She'll do it—mark my words."

"But…but that's her son!" A stupid argument, but I made it, nonetheless.

Throwing me an exasperated look, Sam said, "What the fuck made you think she gives a rat's ass about her son? She'd done everything but rent out a sign that shows she doesn't."

It took a moment to digest this unnatural phenomenon. "Should we warn opposing counsel?"

"Why?" His bushy eyebrows veered into his forehead. "We're out of the case."

"But that isn't right…"

"Cooper, Mrs. Bronski is no longer our problem, and Junior never was." His steel blue eyes pinned me as he asked, "Got it?"

I studied the folds of his pink flesh as they tumbled from his chin to chest, the coldness in Sam's eyes.

So this is what a person without a soul looks like. And…God help me, he's my boss. My frickin' boss.

I wanted to throw up.

"Got it."

Chapter 17

Forgotten Purse

Fifteen boxes later, I cleared out Dad's shaving kit, jackets, overcoats, hats, gloves, boots and shoes. I kept his sky blue cardigan because its threads had absorbed the scent of his tobacco; I couldn't part with that. The smell of him was so comforting that I buried my head in the sweater, wrapping it around me like a cocoon. Some basic hand tools were salvaged and stored under the kitchen sink, but I didn't know what to do with his jigsaw, circular saw, and planer. I couldn't see myself using those tools. Dad's tools weren't family heirlooms—they were Sears Craftsman brands, but it'd probably be wise to sell them and pay down my credit card bill.

I thought of listing the tools online, but the idea of handing my dad's tools over to a stranger didn't sit well. Plus, a single girl couldn't be too careful about posting stuff for sale online. I put them aside, deferring that decision for another day. I shifted through more boxes of clothes, finishing Dad's and starting on my sister's. Thankfully, that feeling of detachment descended on me and my hands moved automatically, sorting through her belongings.

Yesterday, in the courthouse, somebody called out, 'Gloria.' I spun around, heart pounding, scanning for my sister. After a nasty bolt of reality hit, I realized she wasn't going to answer. That one incident was like a guerilla attack. I retreated to the ladies room, shutting myself into a stall until I regained composure.

The hell of it was random moments like this happened all the time. Two nights ago, 'Ode to Joy' drifted over the airways on the public broadcasting channel. This triggered an hour crying jaunt with me curled into the now-familiar fetal position under my covers.

I miss the foggy days.

I hated these surprise attacks of grief. Unlike nursing a physical wound, mourning the loss of a loved one has no upward trend. There's no linear progress, day to day. Every hour could hold nasty surprises. Emotions can scatter like marbles on ice. Some days there were no meltdowns; some days it was all I could do to keep breathing. Simple tasks overwhelmed me. Twice Melinda brought me my purse, finding it in the compact refrigerator at work. Once I discovered my nail polish in a cereal box. During the good days, I'd lull myself into complacency, half-wishing, half-believing life was returning to normal. I caught a glimpse of peaceful acceptance and reached for it with both hands, only to find it was a mirage. That realization left me with a sour taste and bile churning my stomach. In the next heartbeat, those invisible expectations shattered, struck down by hurricane-force winds. What else was there to do at such times except curse at the universe and rage at a god who had forgotten me?

***

"Cooper?" Melinda's knock on my office door was tentative, her face pinched.

"Yes?" I gave a little smile to show she was welcome, even though her nervousness worried me.

What has Tanny done now?

Melinda's nimble fingers smoothed the soft material of her skirt, her eyes lowered to the hemline. I waited, curiosity aroused.

"Um... it's about David. David Seltzer." She roughly cleared her throat, and before she uttered her next words, I knew. In the way the hairs on the back of my neck raised, in the way my gut clenched. It can never be wholly explained or described, but I knew. Instinctively, I held out my hand to stay her next words, to stop the bad news from arriving. If she spoke the words, it would be true, but as long as Melinda didn't say anything, then it didn't happen.

She must not say it.

"He's dead."

I wanted to scream at her careless stupidity. How I wished for Superman's strength so I could stop the world on its axis and go backwards in time. Unsay those damning words! Like a blazing bolt of lightning, my common sense returned, draining me of foolish desires, however well-meaning. My head dropped. In a hollow voice I asked, "How?"

Melinda's explanation came in halting words. He'd been found dead in the nude on his apartment floor.

We'd have to wait for an autopsy, but from all accounts, it looked like an overdose.

After he'd promised me he'd stay clean.

The words struck a blow to my heart, a shaft of disappointment stole my breath away. Struggling for normalcy, I took up my pen and directed a steady gaze towards my assistant. I concentrated on taking a deep breath and letting it out slowly. "Thank you for telling me. I know it couldn't have been easy for you."

The tension in her face broke for the first time since she'd approached my door. "Yeah, it wasn't. I wasn't expecting you to take it so well. You know, after…" her words trailed off as her fingers fidgeted with her skirt once again. With a grimace, she shut the door.

Returning to my keyboard, I finished the interrogatories on the next case Tanny had dumped in my lap then spent the rest of the day preparing for the deposition of Lydia Sanderson. Thank God for my ability to focus.

There were parts of that afternoon, however, that I never remembered.

***

Next to my sister's smiling picture, resting on my bedroom bureau, was David's sketch pad, displaying a page of his rose and egg drawing. Picking it up, I slowly flipped through the penciled art work.

Imagine what he could have done with oils.

It was ironic that these two strangers held place of pride in my apartment, sharing the dubious distinction of having their young lives cut short. I thumbed through the entire body of work, now painfully slim before noticing an inscription on the back cover.

To Mrs. Bach- Thanks for believing in me.

PS: My supplier is Gerald Drue.

Jackpot! I kicked up my heels, hollering in excitement. News like that was meant to be shared, so I crawled over the boxes, snatched up the phone and called Ted at the bar.

"Hello. Tipping Cows. How can I help you?" the waitress asked.

"Can I speak with Ted? Tell him it's Cooper."

A brief pause followed Ted's cheerful greeting. "Hey, Coop! How you doing?"

"Crummy. Really shitty day in court. Got our ass kicked in a custody case."

"You don't sound too upset about it."

"I'm not. I had a client die."

There was a brief pause on the other end of the line. "Why don't you start at the beginning? I feel like I'm missing something here."

I chuckled. "I'll do better than that. I'm coming right down."

"Great. See you soon."

Fifteen minutes found me bar side, tossing David's sketch pad to Ted. He leaned forward and planted a quick kiss on my mouth. "Hey."

His caramel brown eyes glowed warm and inviting. Which of his stellar attributes should I consider on first: the smooth lines of his face, his broad shoulders or muscled biceps? Eventually, I gave up and let my gaze roam his entire body. Damn, the man was built!

He picked up the artist's book and lightly slapped my wrist with it. "Cut it out."

"Those are David's, my client," I pointed to the drawings. Ted thumbed through them, squinting his eyes in an appreciative manner.

"They're good. The boy's got talent."

Heaving a deep sigh, "He did."

Ted's face scrunched up. "This is the client you were telling me about? The one who died?"

"Yeah."

Ted placed the pad next to me then poured me a beer. "Fat Tire," he said, handing it to me.

"Thanks." I raised the glass in a silent toast as he tilted his head to the side, waiting for some explanation.

"Look here," I said, pointing to the inscription on the back. "What do you make of that?"

Ted craned his neck to read David's writing. Slowly, a smile dawned over his face. "I'd say this David was a funny guy."

"Huh?"

"Gerald Drue," he snorted.

"Yeah, I know," I lowered my voice. "He didn't want to give anybody up, but what if his dealer didn't know that? What if he panicked and decided to off David while he was out on bond? What if he—"

Ted interrupted me, "Coop, how well did you know this guy?"

"What?"

"He was a client, right?"

"Y… yeah," I stammered.

"For what?"

"Criminal case—drug possession charges."

"And he died?"

"Yeah, they just found him last night."

"Found him where? How?"

"Naked. In his apartment. They suspect overdose, but I think—"

Ted held up his hand. "Slow down, Coop." He filled another order, slapping the beers on the waitress' tray with what could only be irritation.

What's he pissed off about?

"Come on, Coop. Gerald Drue." He said the words as if they should carry a special meaning.

"What's your point?" It was my turn to be irritated.

"Gerald Drue is an anagram."

"For?" Too late I realized how belligerent I sounded.

Ted grabbed a pen from behind the counter, and wrote "Gerald Drue" on a napkin, then rewrote, "Drug Dealer."

"Oh." Ridiculous how such a tiny word can convey such a huge feeling of loss. "So you don't think David was telling me something in secret code?"

Ted shook his head, "No, honey, I think he was pulling your chain."

I frowned. David didn't strike me as a smartass. Besides, this joke was cruel. David wasn't cruel.

Is it possible such a sensitive artist could be cruel?

It didn't make sense. My bubble of euphoria sprang a leak; I came back to earth at an alarming rate. Ted laid one hand over mine.

"I'm sorry, Coop. I didn't mean to hurt you."

"You didn't."

He looked at me and after a while seemed to come to a decision. "Come on."

"Where?"

"My office. Time I took a break."

He tugged me through the bar's swinging, stainless steel door through a cramped hallway and back to a small office. Once he threw the bolt across the door, though, an electric current coursed through me. It took a moment to recognize the sensation, it had been forgotten, but it was a thrill.

Ted gathered me into an embrace then dropped a kiss on my forehead. Very anti-climatic. His hands rested on my shoulders as he spun me around so that I faced the beige office wall. He massaged my nape, his strong, powerful hands gliding across my shoulders and kneading the tense muscles.

"That feels so good." My head lolled forward.

Time froze. Fragile threads connected us and carried us from one breathless moment to the next. Somewhere in that journey, I sensed a change in the tenor of his touch.

"Cooper?" he breathed into my ear.

Never before had my name felt like a caress upon my skin. Slowly he turned me, placing his hands at my waist. My arms snaked up his chest, skimming over broad muscles before grasping his shoulders. Ted's head lowered and he kissed me. Endlessly. Deeply. I kissed him back with everything I had. All my rage, my loneliness, my yearnings—I put them all in my answer. My hands gripped his shoulders, roamed through his hair then snaked to his waistband and busied with the task of un-doing his belt.

He walked me backward until I leaned against the desk, an incredible, sexy move. "You're so beautiful." Ted kissed my throat then landed on the pulse which beat at the base.

Just what I needed, wanted to hear. Ted was here, giving me everything I needed. The sound of his zipping coming down was inordinately loud.

Panting, he drew away and grabbed my wrists. "Cooper. No."

It was difficult to focus; desire hazed my vision. Eventually the silence penetrated the layers of fog. "No?"

"I'm sorry—"

"You're sorry?" My question came out in a squeak which would have made Maggot Bronski proud.

Ted straightened, closed his eyes then moved away. As the distance increased between us, cold air rushed in to fan my heated cheeks. Every part of me seemed to have chilled, as if I'd been dipped into a vat of ice water. I shook my head.

Tucking in his shirt—for he'd already re-zipped his fly and buckled his belt without my registering those facts, he said in a steady voice without any trace of tremors, "I want you—denying that would be pointless. But sex complicates things and I don't want to go there with you yet."

Wow. That statement struck with the force of a bomb. My head jerked back, as if he'd struck me.

"I'm sorry—" Trained as a female to utter apologies whenever situations got out of hand, I stopped myself.

Why the fuck should I be sorry when *he's* the one who's rejecting *me?*

Lowering my head to hide the anger I was convinced would flash in my eyes and the hurt which was certain to be written all over my face, I stood mute.

"Coop, I'm the one who should apologize, not you."

"This should never have happened." I spied my purse and picked it up, congratulating myself for that small victory of keeping track of it. "I'll see myself out."

My shoulders squared, my backbone stiffened as I left the office, strode down the hallway, picked up the pace as I entered the bar. Only after the front door shut behind me did I slow my progress. Climbing into my Ford Festiva, I cranked up the tunes. He'd hollered something—I don't know what. Hell, I couldn't even tell you what tone he'd used. I'd concentrated on getting the hell out of there. I had concentrated on an exit strategy.

That's when it occurred to me. Focus is the one thing which could save my life. It might be the only thing to save it because—sure as shit—I was heading for a nervous breakdown. A breakdown I couldn't afford. I'd lose my crappy job, the messy apartment, even this hand-me-down car. I was that close to the edge, teetering. There was only one thing to pull me back from the brink.

My ability to focus.

Focus on the horizon, on where I want to be. Then work on getting there. Fuck everything else. Fuck everybody else.

Focus on breathing, pulling in and letting go.

Focus.

Chapter 18

A Witness Crumbles

Lydia Sanderson arrived late at the prosecutor's office for her deposition. Her hair was lank and tangled while the dark circles beneath her eyes told me she hadn't slept well. The prosecutor had agreed to the victim's deposition so long as Johnny wouldn't attend. It was a crumb, but all defense attorneys would be grateful for it. It was rare for the State to allow its witness to talk with defense counsel on the record. However, there was a disturbing revelation that Lydia had recanted her story and the prosecutor, Jim Hedgmon, wanted to straighten out the facts before taking the case to court. He was conscientious, not wanting to chase down a dubious conviction. Jim was a rarity amongst our profession: a man of integrity.

Johnny wished Lydia hadn't accused him of raping her, not wishing for the butt-pounding in prison he'd get for a crime he didn't commit, but that's secondary in criminal cases. The prosecution's main objective is to protect its astronomically ridiculous conviction rate; it's not usually overly-concerned with ensuring justice. If I expressed a skepticism on that point, the older, white male lawyers shook their heads and straightened me out in rapid fashion.

After going through the preliminaries of the deposition, I asked Lydia open-ended questions, allowing the fifteen-year old girl to talk about her family and home. Instead, she spoke of school, which was fine. I wanted to put her at ease, knowing I'd get more information if she were relaxed, but she was stilted, pale, and her hands shook. This was one nervous teenager. At one point, I wondered if she were anemic, her pallor seemed so unhealthy. As she talked about high school, it became clear she enjoyed accounting. She'd done pretty well on the ACT exam, but not enough to win scholarships, so she'd have to work through college if she wanted an advanced degree. She'd already applied for after-school jobs, and had a teacher's recommendation. I followed up and her eyes brightened, showing the first sign of animation.

"I want a full-time job next summer. Even now while school's in session, I want to work."

"How many hours would be ideal for you?"

"Twenty. Even thirty." She shrugged.

"Wouldn't that interfere with your other activities?"

"Nah." She waved, dismissing a high schooler's social life as it weren't important. "I don't belong to clubs."

"What about music? Band? Do you sing? Play an instrument?"

She smiled, a tiny lifting of the lips and as mysterious as Mona Lisa's. "I can't carry a tune in a bucket. Heck, I don't even know which end of the flute to use."

"Student government? Chess club?"

Again, she shook her head. "No. Nothing."

That smile slipped off her face. Lydia looked out the window, as if wishing she could escape. There was a tightness to her mouth, a bleakness to her eyes. Shocking to see in such a young person. Glancing at Jim Hedgmon, I wondered if he noticed it, too.

Jim's pen stilled.

Something was off here. As I stared at the teenager who stared at the window, it suddenly hit me. Lydia was sad.

A rape victim, especially a young woman with a promising future, shouldn't be sad. No, she'd be angry, enraged, furious. What was going on here?

Lydia didn't act like a typical rape victim—and yeah, I know there's no such a thing as a 'typical rape victim,' but this girl wasn't walking around with fresh wounds, exposed and raw. No. She hadn't been freshly traumatized.

She seemed… dammit. I couldn't put it in words. Something nagged at me that the pieces didn't fit together. I was missing something, overlooking something. My instincts searched for an answer, but finding none, I had to keep digging, poking, prodding.

"Do you date?" I already knew the answer.

Lydia's eyes grew wide, moisture gathering in the corners.

"N..n..no," she stammered, turning splotchy with embarrassment.

"Pretty girl like you?" I arched my eyebrow, exaggerating my disbelief in an effort to draw more out of her.

And instantly hated myself.

That blush fled from her cheeks, leaving her drained of all color so that I could see the bluish veins beneath her skin. Lydia grabbed her stomach.

Was she going to vomit?

Her head whipped around, first left then right. She rose from her chair so fast, it fell over.

Jim leapt to his feet, extending his hand, which she ignored.

Like a spooked horse, she backed away, making for the door. Her eyes loomed in her face as she shook her head in jerky motions.

Is she leaving? That appeared to be her plan.

"Calm down, Lydia," I spoke, doubting I could feel any more of a giant turd if I'd been dipped in raw sewage. This kid was terrified and I had triggered that.

With a touch of authority, Jim said, "Sit down, Lydia. Please." His head bowed to the vacant chair. "Let's finish this, okay?"

"You're safe." I don't know why I said these words. It seemed ridiculous in modern day America that these words would occur to me, but it was absolutely what Lydia needed to hear.

Her shoulders returned to their normal height. Her chest bellowed out as she inhaled a long, calming breath. She closed her eyes—silent prayer? Then opened them and her owlish, fearful look was gone.

I relaxed then, too. The gears of my brain unlocked, spinning to find the trigger I'd inadvertently pulled.

I'd just asked about dating, said she was a pretty girl.

Lydia sat down, then Jim, then me.

Looking down at my notes, I scanned the topics I'd wanted to discuss, but the words swam before my eyes. Fine hairs raised on the back of my neck. I closed my eyes, willing myself to focus.

I remembered Lydia clutching her stomach, looking nauseous.

My eyelids flew up.

"Are you pregnant?"

For a fraction of a second Lydia did nothing, said nothing. Then a sobbing wail burst from her lips. She collapsed against the table top, keening like a wounded animal. Her forehead skidded along the surface as she sobbed in anguish.

What. The. Fuck?

Jim snapped, "We're off record—take a break." He glared at the court reporter then glared at me.

I nodded to the reporter and said, "It's all right. Leave us."

The man ducked out of the conference room, quietly shutting the door on the painful scene. I imagine he felt relieved to be away from all of us. I know I wanted to skedaddle.

Jim wouldn't look at me. He sat there, tight-lipped for the longest time. He'd already scooted the box of tissues toward Lydia, but she missed the kind gesture. Once her wails subsided, he quietly asked her if she was okay. He touched her shoulder.

What an idiot. Now it was my turn to glare at him. As predicted, Lydia scrambled away. Her look of despair fell away, replaced with an expression of revulsion.

No foolish than the ordinary man, Jim gave Lydia plenty of space.

"You're safe," he said, using my phrase.

Lydia folded her knees up to her chest, and rocked in the chair. She sniffed, helped herself to a tissue, and kept rocking.

"Was it Johnny?" The husky timber in my voice surprised Jim, who looked at me.

"N..n..no." Lydia hiccupped.

We waited.

"I…never had sex with Johnny. He didn't rape me."

Jim flexed his hand, trying to regain his composure. "Why did you say you had then?" His words may have been quiet, but the anger beneath the surface was clear.

"Jim," I warned, placing a hand on his arm, but he shook it off.

He barked out, "This isn't a game, Lydia! A man's life may have been ruined. I would have put him in prison for five years and done so gladly. On your say so! Now you say Johnny didn't rape you?"

He stood, shoving his chair back from the table in a violent start.

Lydia hid her face in the crook of her folded arms; her shoulders shuddered, her breathing was loud and ragged.

My mind whirled. My chest felt like a weight had been dragged across it. Recalling Sam Hatdiff's words, 'she's not our problem anymore,' I toyed with picking up my papers, stuffing them inside the sheaf, and leaving. With Johnny's innocence established, Jim would dismiss the rape charges. He wasn't an asshole. I could walk out, call him next week. Wrap it up in a journal entry.

Instead, I remained seated.

Jim pinched the bridge of his nose.

"Who impregnated you, Lydia?"

"What does THAT matter?" Jim shoved his hands in his pockets.

Ignoring him, I turned toward the teenager. "Why did you say it'd been Johnny?

She hiccupped. "Be...because he's so..."

I prodded, "Hmm?"

"So nice." Lydia twisted the tissue until it settled into frayed pieces on the table. Using her hand, she swept the bits onto the floor. "And cute. And strong. Every girl's in love with him, you know." She sighed, tucking a strand of her tangled hair behind her ear and the wistful look on her face tore at my heart. "He's one of the nicest guys I've ever met."

Not sure how these attributes qualified him for being accused of raping her, I said slowly, "He is."

"They call him the Golden Boy," she continued, her pale face stony.

"The Golden Boy."

Jim rested his splayed hands on the table. "Who got you pregnant, Lydia? When are you due?"

She shook her head.

"Who, Lydia?"

Jim and I had, without planning it, fallen into Good cop/Bad cop mode.

"I'm not having this baby," she whispered. She covered her mouth, as if the words surprised her.

"Who, Lydia?"

"He'll kill me if I tell." She flung her head back into the crook of her arms. "It'll look like a freak! Probably have two heads and three arms or something."

Jim stared, stunned.

Both hands rubbed my temples as I tried to keep my chaotic thoughts from exploding out of my head. Those hairs on my nape still wouldn't lay flat. Something was terribly wrong here.

Lydia's thready voice spiraled around us. "He's done it for years. Comes into my room. At night. After Mama goes to sleep. Sissy's down the hall. He tells me if I tell, he'll kill them both."

Jim fell into his chair, his body dead weight.

That rush of adrenalin made my own hands shake as I watched Lydia struggle.

Her voice droned on in a hollow, eerie fashion. "He likes me to wear underwear so he can take them off. Then he slides his fingers in, grabs my pussy. Moves inside me. The whole time I feel dirty and he keeps calling me, 'Daddy's pretty girl.' I hate him. I hate him."

No one spoke. I doubt if any of us drew breath.

After a lengthy delay, I felt the upstart of bile swelling in my stomach and threatening to escape my mouth. Hurriedly, I gulped my glass of water, hoping to neutralize the acids. Then I thought, why the hell am I thinking of pH balances, for God's sake? It's strange where a shocked mind will lead...

Lydia lifted her head from the cradle of her bent arms. Her eyes glittered before the teenager blinked twice. "I wanted to pretend it could have been Johnny's, not my disgusting father's."

"Sonuvabitch."

Jim read my mind.

Chapter 19

Shitbags and Autopsies

The coroner confirmed he died of a drug overdose; David's two front teeth were badly chipped. I questioned the findings as soon as I heard of them. OD'ing on pills just wasn't David's style. The D.A. decided not to investigate further because, as Prosecutor Wilson painstakingly explained to me, who cares what happens to shitbags?

Who indeed?

Except to me, David wasn't a shitbag. He was a decent person with a drug addiction. Long after I hung up the telephone receiver, I stared at nothing. I wish I'd asked the coroner's assistant if tooth fragments had been found in David's stomach. That'd make all the difference to me. After several unbillable minutes of wondering, I picked up the receiver again and dialed Jim Hedgmon's direct line.

A brief delay and Jim answered. "Hedgmon. How can I help you?"

"Jim? It's me, Cooper. Cooper Bach."

"Hey, Coop." I could almost see his fingers pinching the bridge of his nose, his weariness coming across the telephone line.

"I need a favor," I nibbled on my lower lip, suddenly nervous of his taciturn ways.

"I've already dismissed the charges on Eaton. What more do you want?"

"An autopsy."

A sudden intake of breath and a muttered curse. "Jesus. Who'd you kill?"

"Not me, you idiot. It's for David Seltzer. Former client of mine. Drug addict."

"When'd he die?"

"Thursday the 18th, last month." I held my breath and crossed my fingers.

"Why do you need an autopsy?"

"I don't think his drug overdose was an accident."

"Drug overdose?"

"That's what they're saying, but his front teeth were chipped off." I rubbed the notch above my eyebrows, wondering if permanent wrinkles would settle in before my thirtieth birthday.

"You think something was shoved down his throat?"

I nodded then realized he couldn't see my action. "Yeah, I kinda do. The guy snorted coke; he didn't ingest ice. Besides, he told me he was clean, except for a little bit of pot."

"Shit, Coop. You can't believe an addict when they tell you they're clean. If you're that gullible, wanna buy some oceanfront property in Arizona? The Brooklyn Bridge? Any of this sinking in?"

"Funny, har-har."

He let out an exasperated breath.

Heaving a sigh, I said, "Because David's one of the few clients I actually liked. He died after I got him out on bond, but now I wish I'd left him in the county jail. His supplier probably got nervous that David was going to sing like a canary—"

"Would he have?"

"Maybe, but probably not. I'll bet the murderer's trail leads to the kingpin drug dealer. Think what wonders that could do for your career."

"I have plenty job security," he cut in.

Wondering if I should beg, I considered it before Jim spoke. "I'll get the coroner to open up the stomach and search for contents. That good enough for you?"

Aware of the honor he'd paid me, I pressed my luck a teeniest bit farther. "And a tox screen?"

In the silence after that, I would have bet fifty dollars his cheeks were blow out and he was pinched the bridge of his nose.

"Fine. I'll order a tox screen. Anything else, princess?"

He was gonna kill me, but I had to ask. "Hair follicle?"

He cussed under his breath, something I'm sure he'd never say in front of his mother. I held the phone's receiver away from my ear.

When the tirade was finished, I chirped. "I owe you one, Jim. Thanks."

In a sharp rebuke, he informed me that what I owed was $700 to the county.

"Write it off on your expense account. I don't have that kind of money."

"Private practice ain't all it's cracked up to be?"

"Not at all. Hey, do you know anyone named Gerald Drue?"

There was another beat of silence. Jim cleared his throat then asked, "Was that David's contact?"

"Yep."

"How do you know that?"

"He wrote it on the back of a sketchbook."

"Where's the book now?"

"I got it."

"Okay, bring it in. I'll look at it."

"I will. Seriously, Jim, I owe you one."

"Yeah, right. If I had a dime for every time one of you dumbass defense attorneys told me that…"

"Jim?"

"Yeah?"

"You're not such a dumbass yourself." I rested the receiver in its cradle, still hearing the echo of his chuckling. Jim Hedgmon was all bark, little bite.

Shitbag or not, David deserved better than to be ignored in death. I wasn't willing to throw him away.

Chapter 20

Fall From a Mountain

"Girl, I don't know what you're doing, but keep it up. Definitely keep it up!" Melinda brought in another floral bouquet. There were fuchsia and orange Gerber daisies, some white flowers I couldn't name, and bright sunflowers in an orange vase tied with a bright pink ribbon.

"From Ted, right?" The receptionist's eyes gleamed. "These are gorgeous! How's he affording this?"

That remark made me feel guilty. No one's ever bought me flowers before, except Dad on my birthday.

How expensive were they?

"Doesn't your husband bring you flowers?"

Melinda rolled her eyes then explained, "We've been married eight years."

"And he only sends flowers when he's screwed up, right?"

"He better not screw up." Her plum-stained lips tightened momentarily, then she switched gears and asked, "What's the card say?"

Taking the card out of its tailored envelop, I gazed at his now-familiar scrawl.

We golf tomorrow.
Tee time is 7:30 a.m.
I'll bring the coffee.

—Ted

"I can't believe it. He wants to take me golfing."

"Careful, honey. I can see your tonsils from here." Melinda frowned. "What's he up to? Doesn't he know no woman wants to golf on Saturday mornings?"

"Yeah, I don't get it. I had him pegged as a player, but this is—"

"Lame," Melinda snorted.

I shrugged in agreement. "Why would he think I can golf? Or that I'd even want to?"

Tanny sauntered to my office's doorway, leaned against the doorjamb and sucked the joy from the room. She arched an eyebrow, staring at my bouquet. "Flowers? Again?"

"Yeah. He wants to go golfing."

"Rain's in the forecast," Melinda chimed in, but our boss had already cut her off.

Tanny snorted the word, "Golfing."

Shaking her head in mock pity, my boss said, "You're being placed in the friend zone."

Melinda, my homegirl, demanded, "Then why send the flowers if he ain't hot for her?"

"Trust me," Tanny flicked her wrist, scorning my floral tribute. "This is an outing between friends. Don't read anything romantic into it."

My facial muscles froze as I watched my boss saunter away. Melinda trailed after her.

Digging through correspondence and client files, I tried to keep busy, but thoughts of Ted kept popping into my head. Since that little make-out session, which ended so abruptly, he'd sent three bouquets. Talk about mixed signals. The man had me utterly confused. He didn't want sex, so what was his deal? And to make a date—or friendly outing—for golf? I didn't know what to make of that, either. My brows pulled down as I considered matters. Golfing, outdoor sport, was conducted in public. Maybe Psycho was right. Maybe Ted merely wanted to be friends with me. Platonic friends. I heaved a sigh. I didn't need platonic—I needed a good lay.

Watching the clock, I waited to call Ted until I was sure he was working at the bar. It'd be easier to leave a message on his cell phone than to speak with him. So I thanked him for the bouquet, keeping my message short. It was time for me to take a step back and let my libido cool. Chiding myself inwardly, I wondered what made me think during my double-grieving process, I'd be able to conduct a sizzling love affair. Now wasn't the time. I needed space for my emotions to catch up with me. Later, I could date somebody. Hopefully, by that time, I wouldn't need a cane to hobble around on, either.

***

Six-thirty on Saturday morning comes way too early. I snatched up my cell phone, saw that Ted had sent me three texts last night. Pulling the curtains back,

I was relieved to find that it was raining hard. 'Felines and Hounds' as Gloria would say. I smiled, remembering how squirrelly, but utterly adorable she was. God, I missed her. Dealing with Psycho and Satan would be so much easier because Gloria would have joined me in making fun of them. Even Dad's death wouldn't have been so horrible. We could have muddled through it together.

She shouldn't have died so young. Thoughts of a perpetual twenty-six year old Gloria were unnatural. My cherished sister would never age. She'd stand on a river bank as I flowed downstream on the tides of time.

The loud shrill of my phone ringing made me flinch. "Hello?"

"Hey, Coop. Doesn't look like the golfing was such a great idea after all," Ted said. "Rain check?"

The edges of my mouth twitched in a reluctant smile. "Sure."

"So, you want to do something else today?"

An image popped into my head of our naked, sweaty bodies entwined in rumpled sheets before I banished it. Platonic friends, remember?

"Nah, I need to sort through these boxes."

"Want some help?"

"No, thanks."

He persisted, "How 'bout lunch?"

"Nah. I know you've got work to do on your house, too. I really just want to tackle this mess and see if I can't tame some of it."

"Why didn't you answer any of my texts?"

"I didn't check my phone."

"Why not?"

"Hey, Ted, I loved the flowers, but you really shouldn't send any more."

"Let me help, Coop. Let me take care of you."

There was silence then he asked, "So this means no lunch today?"

"Not today. Thanks, anyway. Bye." I ended the call then turned on the mute button. I looked at my phone, feeling like I just lost something special again, before I tossed it onto the dresser.

Time to do what I do best: *focus.*

Much later in the afternoon, my gaze roamed my living room. I was pleased with my progress. There was a path throughout the room, the sofa and cocktail tables were cleared, and I'd reclaimed a few square feet in my bedroom so I could dress without contorting my body. I'd washed my comforter, located a second set of sheet, and put them on, appreciating their yellow, cheerful color.

Things were definitely looking up.

During the hours of sorting, I found the source of a mysterious odor—putrid water leftover from a vase of flowers. I dumped the flowers, cleaned the vase then tossed it into the common recycling bin with a sense of euphoria. Ridiculous how de-cluttering could feel so good. I jogged back upstairs to my apartment. My steps faltered when I spied a man leaning against my door.

A wave of joy struck me when I first saw Ted. The intensity of that rush caused my feet to drag. I really, really didn't want to be friends with him. I wanted so much more than that. I wanted the whole ticket: house, kids, marriage, sitting side-by-side in rocking chairs, growing old together. I didn't know that was what I wanted until it flashed between my eyes. This was so not good. Smoothing damp palms over my jeans, I avoided his gaze.

Knowing my aspirations diverged from his, I knew these next few moments were going to be damned awkward.

Focus.

"Hey."

"Hey, yourself." I hoped I didn't sound breathless. With any luck, maybe he'd chalk it down to my recent jog up the stairs.

He leaned down and kissed my cheek.

A friendly salutation made in the public hallway. Great. Just dandy.

Silently promising to research the price of lobotomies later and work it into my budget, I invited him inside. "Come see what I've done. I cleared out a lot of stuff."

"Wow." He whistled. "You've been working really hard."

He motioned to the volleyball trophy on the mantel. "Gloria's?"

"Yeah."

Rubbing his palms together, he said, "Okay, so I'm here to work. Tell me what to do."

"Are you kidding me?"

"I told you I'd help. I meant it."

"Wow."

He tapped my nose. "If you're a good girl and work very, very hard, I'll give you the kiss I really wanted to give you when I first saw you today."

I threw back my head and laughed. It had been months since I'd laughed so hard. I felt happy knowing he wanted to kiss me. Before I blinked, though, he stepped back a few paces and pointed to the power tools I'd set along the wall.

"What are your plans for those?"

I shrugged. "Do you need them? I'll probably never use them, but they belonged to Dad."

"Sure, I'll use them, but how about if I just store them at my place? If you need them, just let me know and I'll bring them back."

"Sounds good."

So he loaded the tools and took them to his house. I asked him to bring back some empty boxes so that I could store more stuff and he went one better. He brought a stack of empties and a pizza.

The rest of the afternoon we cranked up the tunes, packed things for Goodwill, or tossed them into the dumpster. We discussed a variety of topics from teenage crushes to the Kansas City Chiefs' chance of going to the Super Bowl, both equally ridiculous, but the lighthearted conversations kept my mind occupied while my hands busied doing the packing. And I laughed. I laughed probably more than I had during the three grueling years of law school.

By seven o'clock that evening, I was astounded, not only by the progress we'd made, but that I hadn't had a break down all day. Sure, I misted up a few times, but Ted listened and I recovered.

"Whew!" Wiping the sweat from my brow, I flopped onto the couch, grateful I didn't have to move stuff out of the way to sit down.

"You're sweating," Ted said.

Shaking my head, I corrected him, "Horses sweat. Women glow. Men perspire."

"Right. Well, gorgeous, you're definitely glowing."

I sniffed and waved my hand in front of my nose. "Daannng, kid."

He gave a short laugh. "You don't like Eau de Pew?"

Afraid I'd blurt out that my fondest wish would be to lick the sweat off him, I jumped up from the couch and asked if he'd like a glass of water. "I have clean glasses now."

"Nah. Let's go out to eat. We're both too tired to cook."

"True. I'm beat, but I'm not sure if I feel up to going out."

"Suck it up, buttercup. We can't stay in."

Puzzled, I cast him an inquiring look, forcing him to explain. "If we stay in, it'll be a small second before I throw you down on the bed. I've been fighting the impulse all damned day."

Somehow we were in each other's arms, bodies pressed so tightly together the air molecules squished. We kissed. Actually, he drizzled kisses into my mouth and I devoured the sweetness. Ted was solid, warm, gentle. Until…he wasn't.

He wrenched away, combing his fingers through his hair until it spiked. "Wait. Wait. I didn't mean for this to go so far."

"Me, either." A presentiment caused a shiver to snake down my spine. I knew whatever he had to say next, wasn't going to thrill me.

"Maybe we need some limits on whatever this is." He motioned from himself to me.

"Limits? Whatever this is?"

His hand sliced the air. "Dammit, Coop, I'm not going to label it. Don't ask me to."

"You want something platonic from me."

He frowned, disliking that idea as much I did. "You're not ready—"

"Are you sure you're the one who's not ready?" I went on the offense.

Upon hearing my crisp tones, he snapped, "This isn't about me—it's about you."

"Why do you get to decide?"

"Because you're not yourself!"

"Look, you're the one who was ready to throw me down. Well, that's fine by me. We're two consenting..."

"That was my mistake, but I was just being honest."

"You're pushing me away and pulling me close. What's your deal?"

From his stillness, I knew he didn't like my argument; so I pressed harder.

"You send me flowers *three* times. You spend the day with me going through my family's belongings. You kiss like a dream. And now you're backing away because you don't want to have sex?"

"I do want to have sex with you, dammit. I just don't think we should be lovers yet."

"So fine. Let's not be lovers."

"But still have sex?" His caramel eyes narrowed to slits.

"Friends with benefits," I urged him.

245

"You're making this hard on me, I won't lie. It's tempting as hell."

"Come on. Let's get naked." My smile tilted as I waggled my brows at him.

Shaking his head until his answering smile faded, he said, "No. The timing's not right and I don't want to push it. If things between us don't work out—and so you'll know, I've never had a relationship that 'worked out,' you're going to end up hurt. And I don't want to be the asshole who adds to the mountain of pain you're already loaded with."

Blinking, my mind raced, trying to think of some reply. There wasn't any.

From the door, he waved to me, a sad smile on his face. "I'll see you around, Coop."

There was the soft snap of the door closing, heavy footsteps traipsing down the hall until faint thuds sounded on the stairwell. My world was reduced to sounds. All my other senses had stopped.

Chapter 21

Saved by Starbucks

Surprising how much work you can get done on so little sleep. The next day was the hardest, passing in a blur. My skills stayed sharp, though, and I didn't miss much of whatever it was my clients told me. I didn't pay much attention to Tanny's daily bitches about my case progress reports. Over the next week or so, she called me into her office numerous times to read me the riot act for this, that or the other. I'd stand as still as a stone statue the entire time she harangued me. I felt like I'd been sprayed with liquid plastic, a permeable coating that allowed me to see, breathe and speak, but nothing else could get through to me. My core was safe, hermetically sealed off behind this sturdy membrane. During her rants, I didn't respond much. My wooden replies assured her I was miserable, confirming I was on the same baseline as any other young associate, so she must be correctly supervising me.

I'd returned to the Land of Fog, embracing those feelings of disconnection. Going through the motions, I logged more billable hours than the rest of the staff combined. I researched motions, wrote memorandums, drew up discovery requests, and churned out proposed property settlement agreements like they were going out of style. I wasn't just focused—I was a goddamned human laser.

After five weeks of this relentless pace, Tanny sniffed something might be out of whack. Sensitive soul that she was, she called me out, claiming my billables were so astronomical, they could only be gigged.

"No, that's all accurate, right down to the quarter hour."

"Hmmm…" she tapped a red tipped acrylic nail on her teeth. "I haven't seen these kinds of numbers since before I was married."

I smiled, hoping to disarm her.

"The first time I was married."

That surprised me. "Oh? I didn't realize Sam wasn't your first husband."

"Sam wasn't my first anything," she drawled.

Wow.

Tanny pressed her hand to her chest, a parody of melodrama poses. "Ah, the pangs of unrequited love." Switching gears, a sliver of sympathy passes in her eyes before she banished the weakness. "So lover boy didn't pull through for you, eh? Well, don't sweat it. You'll get over it in time. We all do."

Not for all the money in China did I wish to discuss my private love life with Psycho, so I stayed mute.

"A person becomes stronger after having her heart broken." She offered the wisdom in ponderous tones, but her gaze shifted to the window and I sensed she saw nothing of the view as she paid a visit to her past love.

Her shoulders slouched in an uncharacteristic sign of defeat. I frowned. Her silence had continued so long, it became worrisome. Eventually, I floated this idea out there. "Stronger or just alone?"

She laughed without humor, peeling her gaze from the dirty glass pane to skim over me. "We all die alone and we are what we are until that moment arrives."

It may have been the first time she said something without being sarcastic. It was as unsettling as it was comforting, discovering something in my psychotic boss that echoed within me.

Tanny straightened a few items on her desk. "Anyone can promise everything, but it's wiser to count only on yourself." She paused then added, "Not that you won't disappoint yourself now and again, but once you learn to forgive yourself, life is so much easier."

***

Since Ted had uttered the 'See you around,' line, I'd lost twelve pounds. To compensate for my pallor and thinness, I applied more blush and wore loose-fitting clothes, but didn't fool Melinda. She took the reins and provided extensive Starbucks therapy. Every morning she brought me a cheese Danish and Tall Double Chocolate Chip Frappuccino. At lunch, she encouraged me to eat potatoes or pasta or both. In the afternoons, if I was in the office, she'd force me to eat an energy bar. She emailed me funny photos or jokes—anything to pull me out of the doldrums.

Most importantly, she never mentioned Ted Danveldt's name.

Others noticed a change, too. Matthew Bearus called and demanded to know what the hell was going on. "Lunch, Cooper. Today. I'll pick you up at 11:45."

Before I could protest, he'd already hung up.

Matthew and Luke took me to a hamburger joint and insisted on buying lunch. I let them, figuring I was a cheap date. After settling into the booth, Matthew plowed in, demanding to know if I wanted him to talk with Tanny or Sam about easing up on my long work hours.

"Nah, not necessary. I find it easier to keep busy." I doused my fries with ketchup, wishing I hadn't come. The last thing I needed was an ass-chewing.

"But you can't keep on like this, Cooper," he insisted. "Just this week, I received discovery requests from you in two matters and you revised the last Abrams' custody order three different times. Keep up this pace and it'll kill you."

"Nobody ever died of working too hard," I protested.

"Does the name John Henry mean anything to you?"

A blank look crossed my face then comprehension dawn and I had a hard time keeping my lips from twitching.

Matthew growled, slapping an angry palm on the formica table top. "Keep sending me this shit and I'll kill you."

I laughed.

"Slowly and painfully," Matt explained. "And I'd make it look like an accident."

I stopped laughing. "Shit."

"Now you're getting it."

Luke gave this wry observation. "Great, Matt, you've just established pre-mediation. Shall I notify the police now or later?"

Matt speared a french fry. "That doesn't leave this table."

"How old are you, Cooper? Twenty-five?" Luke asked.

"Six," I said, removing the pickles from my burger.

"Too young to bury yourself in the office for 120 hours a week."

Chomping into my cheeseburger, I was hampered from making a reply while my mouth was full.

"What about a hobby? Do you run? You could run with me, if you like," Matt offered, thinking he'd given me a treat.

"I don't run marathons. You have to be a maniac to do that."

"I run sixteen miles every day, rain or shine."

Luke and I exchanged glances.

"What?" Matt asked, clueless.

I explained, "You say that like you think it's normal—it ain't."

"Says you," Matt snapped.

Luke flung out his palm. "So eloquent, counselor. Here, finish my fries, you rotten bastard."

"So you guys think I should find a hobby?"

"Yeah. Seriously, kid, I'm worried about you. Tanny's a slave driver and Sam's too weak to put an end to her nonsense."

"True enough."

Matthew flung his burger onto his plastic wrapper. "That Tanny Whilts is something else, ain't she?"

"A work in progress," Luke supplied, but I remained silent.

Tanny had by no means earned my loyalty, but still, it was impolitic to badmouth the one who signs your paycheck, meager as they were.

"What I need is a way to make more money." The words surprised me even after they'd left my mouth. "I don't get paid on an hourly rate and right now I'm working for beans. I got $16,000 I owe to the funeral home plus my student loans. Like having a mortgage without the house to go with it."

"You don't need a hobby, you need a second job."

"Or a better paying job," Luke said.

We finished lunch, still debating ways for me to make more money. As we exited the restaurant, Matthew steered me with a proprietary hand to my back. It felt intrusive. I maneuvered out of reach. That was something else that had changed. Anybody's touch repelled me now. I blame Ted entirely for that since it didn't happen until our breakup—if it could even be called a breakup. Whatever it was, I smiled grimly as I recalled his refusal to define our relationship.

Once in the car, Matthew agreed with Luke's assessment. "A second job doesn't help because you'd still be working too many hours. I'll ask around to see if there are any associate openings anywhere else in town."

Thanking them both, I stared out the window, oblivious to the passing scenery.

Matt dropped Luke off at his office and we headed to court. Armed with briefcases, we invaded the courthouse, prepared for combat at docket call. Equivalent to chain mail and helm, my skirt and ballet slippers were in place, secured for the upcoming battle.

Throughout several hearings that afternoon, motions to modify temporary orders, requests for specific parenting time, and the ever-present request for attorney fees, I thanked heaven for the courtroom brigade. It was a blessed distraction, which I needed. Working myself ragged wasn't the worse, though. No, the difficulty came in having to sustain this pace for the next thirty years. Surely a merciful god would kill me before longevity set in?

As the afternoon drew to a close, Judge Powers kindly invited me into his chambers by barking out, "Ms. Bach! My chambers! Now!"

How could I ignore such a polite summons? Biting the retort, 'You bellowed, sir?' I dragged into his chamber.

The judge removed his robe, placed it carefully on a padded hanger then flung it over the back of a chair. He stood, considering me with a baleful stare, then snatched his glasses off his face. He motioned me to take a seat. "How are you?"

"F… fine," I stammered, suddenly nervous.

He remained standing, with his hands clasped behind his back. The picture of any stern schoolmaster. "You've lost weight. You look exhausted. You're working all the hours the good Lord gives us. I'm worried about you."

"Worried about what?" I asked with a nonchalance I was far from feeling. "My clients are fine. My employers are happy. Everything's good."

He adjusted his glasses so that he could more effectively look down his nose at me. It was one of his favorite ways of alerting lawyers his bullshit detector was going off.

I sighed. "Is this really necessary?"

"Cooper, there are no secrets in small towns. You know that, don't you?"

Afraid where this was going, I froze in place.

"You're headed for a nervous breakdown."

Whatever blood remained in my face drained away at this drastic conclusion. "What? Like hell I am!" Recalling that I was in the judge's chambers, I groaned, wishing I could rescind those last words. Every lawyer cusses. Every judge cusses. Just not in front of the other. On the scale of impropriety, it rates right up there with farting in church. Big time *faux pas*.

"You're going to work yourself into the grave if you keep this up."

I winced at his poor word choice.

"Sorry," he muttered, finally lowering into his leather chair. "Cooper, hear me out. This is for your own good. Several of us are concerned about you."

Judge Powers waited for a response that wasn't forthcoming, so he waved his hand and continued, "You got dark circles under your eyes. Hell, you've lost enough weight you could get a gig working as a scarecrow."

Uncomfortable pinpricks bit into the back of my eyeballs. I pressed fingers against my lips and chin to stop the trembling. Please God, don't let me break down here. I will never forgive myself if I cry in front of a judge. It just isn't done. Another mortifying *faux pas*.

"Dammit, Coop." He turned tender, making it damned near impossible for me not to cry. "Tell me what the problem is and let me help you."

"Why should you?"

"I figured if you don't pay your associates, you should at least back them up, but with Tanny and Sam being who they are..." He cleared his throat, realizing his indiscretion too late. "You need someone to stand *in loco parentis*. It might as well be me."

My eye brows lifted toward my hair line.

"And," he continued wryly, "I drew the short straw at the judge's lunch today."

I chuckled.

"Good. Now tell me what's eating at you."

"Where to start?" I decided he didn't want to hear about my pathetic love life, so I laid out the financial strain I was under, telling him I was paying for two funerals.

"Your father didn't have life insurance?"

I shook my head. "Nope. I make monthly payments to the funeral home."

"What are those payments?"

I told him.

Judge Powers whistled.

"They want it paid off in a year."

He cocked an eyebrow. "What's the interest?"

Amazed at my ignorance—I was a contracts whiz in law school, I could only say, "This sounds stupid, but I don't know."

"Car payment?" he asked.

I indicated a negative response.

"That's something, at least," he muttered, not particularly grateful for small favors.

"My Ford Festiva's fourteen years old."

"Hang in there. Student loans." He said the words, rather than asked.

"Naturally." At his silent question, I supplied the answer, "$840.00 a month."

"What was the name of the funeral home, again?"

I told him.

He made a note on his iPad then shut it. "I can't promise anything, but I'll look into re-financing that mortuary debt for you. Maybe see if you perform some free legal work in exchange for a reduction."

I flexed my hands to maintain my focus; otherwise, I was going to cry.

"As for the student loans—that's the price of admission to this circus. Everybody pays it, so hunker down on those. Are you willing to take night court cases? 'Cause I know our lawyers will toss you a few. Those fees stay in your pocket, not Tanny's and Sam's."

"That'd be great. I'm not afraid to work hard."

"No one's thought that."

"Will Tanny mind about the moonlighting?"

"Not if you don't tell her."

He stood up, signaling the interview was finished. "Run along, Cooper Bach. I'm a busy man."

"Thank you, Judge Powers."

"Run along," he repeated.

I could have sworn he almost smiled.

***

By the end of the week, I'd picked up four hundred dollars in traffic court, working 'til midnight. By the end of the month, the funeral home sent me a new payment plan, lowering the monthly amount by $275.00. The interest rate decreased from 18% to 4%. The balance reduced by $4,740.00.

Happy as I was to open that particular bill, I had to ask Judge Powers if there'd been a mistake in calculating the principal. He said, no. The attorneys had 'passed the hat' and donated that amount for the funeral costs.

"Sam put in the forty bucks. Cheap sonuvabitch," he muttered beneath his breath.

I tried not to smile, but wasn't successful, so I turned the topic. "I should write 'thank you' notes. Tell me their names and I'll get on it."

"I'm a busy man, Ms. Bach. I don't have time for such foolishness. Run along."

"Yes, your Honor and thank you, Judge Powers."

He waved off my thanks, but this time I was certain he'd smiled.

Chapter 22

Say it Ain't so, Joe

I didn't want to make a spectacle of myself, but sometimes that's what a girl's got to do. Six weeks of waiting for nothing to happen nearly killed me. It was time to force the issue with Ted, even if that meant I'd lose the home field advantage. This pushed me to become wily, quick. Maneuvering into offensive mode, I put on my best tight dress, fixed my make-up to 'killer mode,' and headed towards Tipping Cows with the resoluteness of a Norman invading Hastings.

Exiting my car in the parking lot, I saw him approach. He wasn't alone. Some willowy brunette clung to his arm like some damned limpet. They were leaving the bar together.

Finally, something pierced that foggy wilderness in which I'd lived. An iron shaft driven straight to my heart would account for it. Rage and pain so intense, I couldn't even think of a cuss word to express my frustration.

Shadows obscured Ted's face, but unless he'd grown two extra arms and legs, it was plain the two forms pressed against each other. They moved toward his truck. He helped her inside and before he shut the door, she flung her arms around his neck then drew him between her knees to kiss him.

With an inward groan, I ducked behind an SUV, squatting out of sight, but heels aren't made for such moves; the heel broke. Teetering on the damned shoes, I waited for the sound of his engine revving to life then listened as it faded away. After I was certain they were gone, I stood, shucked off the heels and walked, bare-footed back to my Festiva. Impervious to the rough pavement, I trod on the scattered stones before sliding into my car seat. My hands shook so hard, it was difficult to insert the key in the ignition. Sensing something, I glanced down, surprised to find blood on the gas pedal. My stroll across the parking lot had cut my feet. In King Lear, William Shakespeare wrote, *When the mind's free the body's delicate: the tempest in my mind doth take all else feeling.*

I'd been right when I'd pegged him as a player. Bracing my shoulders, I instilled some starch into my backbone. About time I faced reality: Ted had his own life, which would be separate from mine, but I wasn't going to break down and cry. I'd sobbed enough for a lifetime already. So what now? For some reason, King Lear didn't have any advice for me, but Lady MacBeth sure did. *Things without all remedy should be without regard: what's done is done.*

Shakespeare was right. He always was—the perennial 'go-to' guy.

***

No matter how bad you think your life, it can get worse. Fate's a cruel bitch and she lobbed another giant turd in the pre-dawn hours. Nothing good comes from an early morning phone call, today was no exception. Shrill ringing jolted me awake from a disturbed sleep where I imagined Ted Danveldt with his new girlfriend, so it felt as if I'd only caught two or three minutes of sleep.

I threw my cell, swearing a long, loud string of expletives at it, but within five minutes it went off again. On the third ring, I picked up.

"Cooper?" A tearful voice began.

"Yeah?" Not knowing who it was.

"Coop, it's me. Melinda. You need to come to the office. Right now, sugar."

"What is it?"

"Just get here quick," she said.

Another bout of cussing followed as I got dressed. Foregoing make-up, I grabbed my keys and jetted to the office. A block from my destination, I saw the coroner's van, an ambulance, and six police cars with their lights flashing in angry, throbbing red. I parked then walked toward the building. I saw Melinda talking to a cop. Her hands twisting around each other then dashed at a trickle running down her cheek then back to hand-wringing.

Sam sat on the curb. He wore dress slacks and a white t-shirt. Paler than usual, he drew on a cigarette. He stared at the ground.

"Coop!" Melinda flung her arm toward me.

I took her hand then squeezed, trying to reassure her. "What's going on?"

The cop asked her, "Who's this?"

"Our associate, Cooper Bach," Melinda introduced. "Cooper, something terrible's happened. Tanny's been shot."

Time slowed. Her words floated through my head.

"Fatally?" I asked, having a hard time comprehending what the presence of so many police and the coroner's van were telling me.

Melinda nodded.

"Oh my God. Why? How?"

The officer pointed towards the building, the source for answering those questions. "It's pretty bad."

Melinda folded her arms beneath her bosom, as if she were trying to literally hold the pieces of her body together.

Turning, I stumbled to where Sam still sat on the concrete curb then plopped beside him. For a long while, I couldn't think of anything to say. Condolences hadn't even begun to form in my brain.

Sam drew on the cigarette, its end glowing red like the flashing lights on the squad cars.

"What the hell happened?"

He flicked the butt away. We watched it skid across the road, mesmerized by its progress, not surprised when its journey ended as it rolled sideways and lost momentum. With red-rimmed eyes, he coldly asked, "Did you know the cunt was fucking around on me?"

Avoiding his scrutiny, I said nothing, hoping it'd been a rhetorical question.

"Did you do it? Did you shoot her?" As the words left me, I wanted to take them back—too late. Good lawyers don't ask those questions because they don't want to know the answers. I craned my neck, checking whether anybody overheard my stupid solicitation for incriminating evidence.

"Fuck no!" He drew a package of cigarettes from his pocket, tapped it on his knee and muttered, "Wish I had, though."

"No, you don't."

He neither nodded nor shook his head. Instead, he drew on another cigarette, using the nicotine for comfort. After a few shaky sucks, he pointed toward a bleach-blonde who'd been cuffed and stuffed into the back of another squad car. Her face was splotchy and she was screaming. I'm not sure who she was talking about, but somebody's lineage was greatly disparaged.

"Who's that?" I asked, jerking my head in the direction of the vehicle.

Melinda and the cop joined us curbside. Melinda crumpled to the grass, huddling next to me with her feet tucked beneath her.

"That's Caroline Abrams," the officer said.

Melinda chipped in, "She's married to Ed Abrams."

"Flotaki?"

She nodded, knowing we were talking about the same person.

Another barrage of screaming and swearing about unfaithful husbands blasted from the female suspect.

"What the hell happened?" I asked again as my mind refused to connect the dots so glaringly obvious to everybody else.

"Can't you haul her out of here, for God's sakes?" Sam snapped at the officer.

"Will do, Mr. Hatdiff." He touched the brim of his hat.

Sam tapped his cigarette. Ashes fell upon the curb. "Fuck me." Sam clasped his head then let it drop between his knees.

Across his hunched back, Melinda and I exchanged meaningful looks. She shook her head, signaling me to stay quiet. Then she smoothed her hand over him shoulders, making small circles and murmuring nonsensical sounds.

I lit him another cigarette and handed it to him.

Another officer, one in plain clothes, approached, asking if Sam would identify the body.

Sam's shoulders shuddered in grief as he openly wept into his hands.

"I'll do it."

Melinda flashed me a grateful look, but of the two of us, I was the better choice. Sam needed her with him at the moment. Besides, I had experience in identifying corpses, for fuck's sake.

My footsteps were heavy as I trotted alongside the detective. He opened the door to the office then passed through it, waiting for me to follow. Oblivious to his lack of manners, he strode through the foyer and toward Tanny's private office. A man in a haz-mat suit wheeled a gurney through the doorway, staying when the detective flung up his palm.

A crisp, white sheet draped over a body was revealed before hidden from view by the small army of investigators. They swarmed between Tanny's office and the foyer, busy with tasks that I have no knowledge of.

"You ready?" The detective asked me.

I inhaled then nodded.

He signaled to the haz-mat guy to tug the sheet from the corpse's face.

I took a deep breath, braced my shoulders and stared. The coroner's hands were aged, showing raised veins through the thin latex gloves. They moved slowly, unveiling the crown of dark hair then a wide, intelligent forehead. My breath hitched, but the coroner didn't pause in drawing down the sheet.

Pale cheeks. The tip of an upturned nose. Blue, thin lips. A rounded chin.

No need to look any further, but something beckoned me closer, just as I was drawn Gloria's lifeless body. Compelled for no reason I can explain, I took the corner of the white sheet and tugged it down the cold, naked skin. The gunshot wound was in her side, painted on a pearlized canvas with raw, bloody edges. Frozen fingers jerked the sheet back to her chin then I ran the back of my fingers over a cool cheek.

Tanny's words echoed in my brain: Once you learn to forgive yourself, life gets much easier.

Leaning over her, I caught a whiff of that familiar musky perfume. Separate from the metallic scent of blood, just like it'd been with Gloria, the two smells were distinct. Without a living host, they'd lost their ability to mingle.

"What happened to you, Tanny?"

Proving he was more attuned to his scientific nature than to his humanity, the coroner answered the question quite literally. He pointed a gloved finger toward her office. "Shot with a semiautomatic at close range, caught in *flagrante delicto*. We recovered the weapon."

That explained how Sam found out Tanny had been having an affair. Really no way to cover this up and sweep it under the rug.

"Where's her partner? What happened to him?"

"Ambulance. He'll pull through. Shot in the upper shoulder."

The detective tapped my shoulder. "Make it official, please. Then we can get out of here."

I swallowed hard. "Yes, that's Tanny Whilts."

"Fine."

The coroner wheeled the gurney out of the lobby. The detective held the door open. Other investigators jostled me as I became rooted to that particular spot. A heaviness weighed me down so that my feet couldn't move.

I'd seen death before with my sister, Gloria. I remember how my dad looked as he laid in the coffin and could even tell you the dress Mom wore for her funeral. Those pictures flip through my mind's eye from time to time, never-changing. I could now add Tanny's pale face to that collection.

Somehow my body brought me to inside Tanny's office where experts collected information like worker bees around the hive. A photographer took snapshots of the scene, training his lens on blood spots and the sprayed gore, which clung to everything. One man and another woman examined casings, picking them up with tweezers and bagging them. Quietly, they talked to each other, putting their heads together as they worked on gathering evidence.

I stared at the circle of blood on the carpet. My gaze trailed up the walls to the splatters.

Another hawk-eyed stranger strolled into the office. He peered at the divot in the back wall and rubbed his chin. Pulling a pencil from his shirt pocket, he circled the area. That was the mark her stapler made when she'd hurled it at me, but I didn't explain it.

He moved to draw on another part of the wall, this time circling an area gummed with remains. "Joe, make sure you get this one." He squatted next to Tanny's panties and scooped them up with pencil. The detective dangled them in mid-air. "There's spooge in the crotch—bag 'em."

Stumbling back outside, I joined Sam and Melinda on the curb. Throughout dawn breaking, we remained huddled together, sharing some damned moment like a KumBaYa fest.

We didn't know what else to do. There wasn't anything left to do.

I couldn't even pray.

Chapter 23

Bringing Up the Rear

Once the clock struck 8:00 a.m., Melinda and I called clients, opposing counsel, and talked with judges to continue every one of Tanny's and Sam's cases for the next three weeks. We told them Tanny died that morning without going into further detail. Some were curious and pressed with questions, but we managed to deflect the worst of it. Early in the morning, Melinda alerted Sam's brother, Steve, but had to leave a message. He later returned the call and talked with me. Steve asked if I would collect him from the airport on the late afternoon flight. During our phone conversation I told the story, as much as I knew. It appeared Mrs. Abrams planned to kill her cheating husband, thinking he was having an affair with his attorney. She shot both lovers, only afterwards realizing the man who'd been caught red-handed with Tanny wasn't, in fact, Flotaki Abrams. It was some guy named Brooks, who I didn't know. He wasn't our client. I didn't even know if Brooks was his first name or last.

"Good God!" Steve's bass voice boomed through the line. "How's my brother taking all this?"

"Not great. Lousy way to discover your spouse is cheating on you. He has a lot to process."

"His phone's turned off, so tell him I'm coming."

"He needs his family around right now for support. Thanks for coming."

"Yep, we'll get it sorted out all in good time."

Feeling relieved that Steve had a solid head on his shoulders, I hung up the phone to find Ted Danveldt standing in my office doorway.

"Hey," he said, looking so good it made my chest tighten.

"Hey."

He scrutinized me, those shoulders lifting in concern. "I came as soon as I heard."

"Melinda."

He nodded and approached me with his arms opened. Without thinking, I moved into his embrace and burrowed against him, feeling safe at once. Ted folded me into him, smoothing my hair and bringing me such comfort I nearly came undone. "God, honey, I'm sorry."

My head moved up and down in the crook of his arms, but I didn't pull away. It was too snuggly here, cocooned in Ted's warmth.

After several minutes of savoring the heat and smell of him, I said, "Thanks, but I have to go to court." I pulled away, straightening my skirt to keep my hands busy so I wouldn't reach out for him again.

"Sure?"

Nodding with an unnatural jerk, I explained, "I have to appear for Tanny and Sam today, as some cases couldn't be reset. It's going to be crazy around here for a while."

"You look like hell."

That made me snap my head up. "Gee, thanks. You can go now and take your silver tongue with you."

"That's not what I meant and you know it." He brushed the hair behind my ear. "You're a sight for sore eyes, Cooper Bach. God, I've missed you."

"I have to go. See you around, Ted."

I left my office, snatching my brief case on the way out then paused at Melinda's desk. "I'll walk to court. You got enough to hold down here."

It was jarring to see Tanny's door closed with 'Caution' tape across it. That had to be unnerving for Melinda, sitting so close to it. God, the smell was enough to roil my stomach. I shook my head, wishing to rid myself of those thoughts. "We need to get some baking soda and scented candles—something."

"Let me drop you off," Ted volunteered.

Gritting my teeth, I demurred. "That's okay. I can walk."

"This will save you time," he smiled, grabbing my elbow and guiding me to the office door.

The drive was made in silence. His truck pulled up to the curb by the courthouse and he shifted it into 'Park' before swiveling to face me. "I want to see you. Tonight."

Instinctively, I shook my head as I opened the door. "Sorry, but I can't. There's no way I'll be finished at the office before midnight, probably. But thanks for the lift."

"Back to the ice maiden act?"

If looks could incinerate, he'd be a pile of ash. I slammed the door then walked away. Waiting in the security line, he startled me when his hand clamped on my shoulder.

"Hey!" I protested.

"Easy, Coop. Look, I'm sorry." We were jostled, and Ted waved a person ahead of us, inviting them to play through. His gaze slued toward me, and I saw the light of determination and something else indefinable there. "I'm taking you to dinner tonight. Okay?"

"I have to work."

"You have to eat, too."

Standing in front of me, he grabbed my upper arms and gave a slight shake.

"I'm taking you out for dinner," he reiterated. "I'll pick you up at seven at your apartment. Give you a chance to catch your breath. Understood?" He leaned over and whispered into my ear, softly threatening. "Seven o'clock."

Too angry to respond, I nodded.

Satisfied with that, he wished me luck at court, stepped out of line, and left the building.

***

In the history of horticulture never has a floral bouquet incited such rage, but today was a red-lettered day. Fireworks erupted when I saw Ted's offering. There he stood, a goofy, grinning idiot on my threshold clasping a bundle of pink roses.

"You might as well turn around and take those back to the florist, buddy. Go on." I made a 'shooing' motion.

My afternoon had been worse than any nightmare I could have imagined. The news of Tanny's murder had already spread through the courthouse like wildfire and everybody stopped me to ask for salacious details. Trying to maintain some dignity in this ridiculous situation tested my patience so that when Ted waved the roses, it was the metaphorical plucking and breaking of my last, frayed nerve.

"Better yet—give them to your new girlfriend."

I tried to shut the door in his face, but his foot wedged inside, preventing it from closing. "What the hell are you talking about?"

His indignant bellow sounded sincere, but…

"Are we going to fight right here? God, your neighbor's pulled his cell phone out—sonuvabitch's probably posting this on Instagram."

I poked my head out the door to scold the neighbor. "Mind your own business, Gavin!" I snapped before tugging the front of Ted's shirt and hauling him inside.

"What the hell did you mean—" He started with a full head of steam then caught himself when he glanced around the apartment. Stunned, he said, "Hey. It looks great in here. You've been busy."

His gear shifting struck me as funny until I imagined him getting BUSY with a certain brunette. "You've been pretty busy yourself, haven't you, Ted?"

"What are you talking about?"

"Well?"

He flung his hands out. "Well what?"

"Who's the brunette bimbo?"

He frowned. "What brunette bimbo?"

271

Rolling my eyes, I snapped out, "The girl I saw you with last night in the parking lot of Tipping Cows."

A blank look crossed his countenance before it was replaced with a mocking one. A mischievous light entered those caramel eyes as his voice lowered when he asked, "Jealous?"

Seething, I searched for something I could throw at him. Ideally, it'd be something heavy and capable of inflicting great damage. Gloria's volleyball trophy would do.

He sidestepped me on his way to the kitchen, deftly taking the trophy out of my hands and replacing it back on the shelf. Incredibly, he then rummaged through the cabinets before spying what he needed. He filled a vase with water then unwrapped the roses.

"You like pink?" he asked.

My mouth gaped open as I watched him, speechless.

Chuckling, he ignored my reaction and mocked, "Stalking me, Coop? I'm not sure how I feel about that—one part is me is flattered, naturally. But the other? Well, it's a bit overwhelming, don't you think?"

"Out. Get out."

"Without dinner? What kind of gentleman would I be to go back on my word to a lady?"

"Cut the crap, Ted. Thanks for the roses. Now leave."

All traces of amusement vanished from his voice as he ran a hand over his face. With a sigh, he signaled to the sofa. "Have a seat, Coop. Let's get this out of the way."

"I don't want to sit…"

"Humor me." His smile held no warmth.

Grudgingly, I sat on the edge of the sofa. He planted himself on the cocktail table, our knees touching.

"You would happen to see me last night and put the worse connotation on the incident," he muttered.

I arched my eyebrows.

"Last night I drove Nanette Richardson home as she was too drunk to do so. I didn't want to wait for the taxi because she was picking fights with folks in the bar. Also, she happens to be married to a friend of mine, John, and I didn't want to embarrass him. God knows she was so horny she probably would have jumped the taxi driver. I didn't come onto her and I sure as hell wouldn't fool around with a married woman, let alone my friend's wife."

He appeared so earnest, I wanted to believe him, but...

"You don't believe me."

I shrugged. "Listen, it's been six weeks since we last saw each other. What you do with your life is—"

"I haven't been with another woman since I met you, Cooper Bach."

That surprised me.

Grimly, he passed a hand over his brow. "God only knows what you saw. I shoved her into my truck and she kissed me."

I nodded.

"You saw that? Shit."

My brows arched again.

Upon seeing the disbelief, he snapped, "She was drunk. She kissed me! I didn't kiss her. I'm not interested in Nanette and never was. All I did was take her home to her husband!"

Anger drove him to his feet. I watched his hands run through his hair as he mumbled a string of profanities at Nanette Richardson. He paced the length of the apartment.

Pursing my lips, I wondered what would happen next. Glancing at the apartment door, I wondered if Gavin were listening to this exchange. "Look, I'm grateful for the explanation. You certainly didn't have to say that. And I like your roses, so thanks for those, but…"

"But you want me to leave you alone."

The sad note of defeat in his voice made it feel so final between us, it left me paralyzed. Alone was such an ugly word.

He stepped toward me, his gaze pinning me with an intensity that burned. A shaky forefinger skimmed my cheek in the softest caress. His warm breath skidded over my skin. He pressed a reverential kiss on my forehead then placed his head against mine. "Don't you know I'm crazy about you? I haven't looked at another woman since you stumbled into my life. I want you. You with your sweet kisses, hot temper, and sucky apologies. I want to be with you all the time. Don't kick me out."

I needed instructions how to breathe just then as I totally forgot how.

"Cooper? Talk to me. Tell me, have I left it too late?"

Stepping back to better look at him, I asked with anguish in my voice, "Why did you leave? Why did you stay away so long?"

"Honey, what was I supposed to do? I'd tried taking it slow, but it didn't work. Anytime I'm around you, it's ten seconds before I go up in flames. I've never wanted anybody so much as I want you, but you were nowhere near ready for a relationship. Even under the best of circumstances, I've never had a relationship last more than a couple of years. Some of the break-ups I didn't mind, sometimes not, but I couldn't take the chance of getting involved then hurting you if it fell apart down the road. You've had enough pain to last a lifetime."

"True."

"Your sister and dad dying—that broke your heart."

I nodded, a lump in my throat.

"How could you love anybody while your heart was still shattered? You needed time to heal, Cooper."

"What are you saying?"

He shook me by the shoulders, but not hard. "Haven't you been listening? Staying away from you these past six weeks, three days and…" He checked his watch. "Two hours has been the hardest thing I've ever done. And I don't want to be apart from you anymore."

"You want to be with me?" I felt a grin breaking forth from nowhere.

"Yes, Cooper. With all my heart." And then he kissed me.

My arms entwined around his neck and I kissed him back. He'd mastered the kiss, that's for sure, taking it to a deep, sweet place. His kisses were like molasses, pouring into my mouth with slow pleasure.

"Are you ready for this? Do you think this is a good time for us?"

I took a long time considering my reply. "Life doesn't wait until you're ready. Fate is going to throw down whatever it's got, whenever it wants. Yes, I do want to be with you. Not because I've lost Dad and Gloria and Mom. Not because I need you to fill the gaping holes their absence has created. But because..." I cupped his cheek. "Just because, I guess."

His hold tightened. "Me, too."

Another long kiss followed, a silent pledge to explore each other and see where this new journey would take us. When we broke apart, he asked, "Did it upset you? Seeing Tanny?"

"It was painful, but it wasn't the same as it was with Gloria. I suppose because we weren't close."

"Or perhaps because she threw staplers and shoes at you?"

A smile flickered on my lips before I explained, "Sure, that, too, but looking at another corpse again...well, I worried it would set me off."

"It didn't?"

"No, it didn't." I scrunched my nose, trying to describe how sad it felt, but also how distant. "Almost as if all pain had sailed away on a boat. I can still see it, bobbing on the horizon, but the tides are taking it further out to sea. With Dad and Gloria, I have some days like that. Not every day. Not even most days. But with Tanny, it was already like that."

"Sounds healthy."

I snuggled against him.

"Look, we probably ought to go now."

"Go? Don't go."

"I don't want to pressure—"

"You're not! Please. Please stay."

He cocked the one eyebrow and my heart leapt in joy. God, I'd missed that.

"Do you want to talk about Tanny anymore? Or us? Or Sam? Or anything?" He nuzzled on my neck.

"No. No, I don't want to talk anymore."

"Good." Ted scooped me into his arms and carried me to the bed. Gently he laid me on the covers then waggled his brows. "Because as of right now, you are officially boarding the Pleasure Train."

"Gawd, that's corny!" I laughed. "You're the conductor, I suppose?"

"Oh, yeah." He peeled off his shirt then took mine off, smiling while his eyes glittered with desire.

"What does that make me?" My hands went to his waistband then took off his jeans. I wiggled out of mine. When we lay skin-to-skin, he gathered me close. His hands gripped my buttocks and gave a hard squeeze.

"The caboose, baby. The caboose."

Chapter 24

Bubbles

In the days after Tanny's murder, Ted and I spent most of our spare time together either laughing, making sweet love or both. I'd become addicted to his honeyed kisses, which was equal parts comforting and terrifying. Afraid this season of enchantment would be torn from my greedy little grasp, I tried to keep those dark thoughts at bay and do what I do best: focus.

Facing canons at work, my usual laser approach was too much, too little at the same time. Everything but the kitchen sink was thrown at Melinda and me. On top of aiding the police investigation, the insurance companies pounded us with requests for information, never happy with the first response. And it wasn't just one insurance company we had to deal with—there were five. Like the heads of a Hydra: Malpractice, Life, Business Continuation, Accidental Death and Disability (for Sam), and Homeowner's. We'd cut one head, answer the interrogatories of a company, and three more sprouted in its place. Client notifications had to be sent out, their retainers calculated, billings done. Referrals to be made for those who wanted to leave the firm and conflicts of interest to avoid in sending the client folders to new counsel. Letters had to be sent to area judges, local attorneys, the state Supreme Court, the Office of Disciplinary Administrator, the local bar. Calendars updated on multiple levels.

That was just the business side of practicing law.

On the flip side, we still had clients. Feeling very much like the chump-bait in a shark feeding frenzy, Melinda and I had to deal with anxious clients. They didn't nibble—they devoured. With questions, demands, complaints, and more demands. We spent hours, one-on-one, addressing those concerns. It was draining in ways I'd never imagined.

After having lost every member in my family, I placed a premium on family ties somewhere a bit higher than Mount Everest's summit. To witness the tearing asunder of those vows, the breaking up of a family caused me to wonder if human decency existed. My disdain grew, making it more difficult to extricate these folks from problems they'd created. Less and less I cared about my clients. More and more tempted to curse them, "You're a fucking idiot!" My 'hand holding' skills weren't great before Tanny's murder—now they sucked.

"What's worrying you now?" Ted asked, placing a plate of spaghetti in front of me. I'd driven to his place so we could spend a short hour or so together before he started work.

Not even bothering to deny it, I set my utensils down. "The cleaners came today. To remove the mess of the crime scene. Thank God they ripped out the carpet, but it still smells in the whole damned office."

Ted shuddered.

"Everything is awkward, as if there's something…" I trailed off, not knowing how to describe the unsettling sensation of having to work within a stone's throw of a murder scene.

"Something?"

"Evil."

"Well, there's a reason stigmatized real estate doesn't sell. So what does Sam intend to do as the sole partner now?"

Turning the options over in my mind, I admitted I had no idea. "He could offer me a buy-in or keep me as associate with a different pay-out schedule to offset my increased workload, but here's the catch: I can't afford to buy-in and I'm not sure I want to, either."

"Why not?"

"I don't like divorce work, which is ninety percent of Tanny's practice."

He narrowed his eyes, considering that dilemma. "Would you remain as an associate if he paid you more?"

"That's just it. With Sam, there's no guarantee he'd paid me more, despite the heavier workload I'm handling."

"Cheap?"

I nodded. "Miser."

"I figured Tanny was the one who was tight-fisted." He frowned.

"Sam's no prize." I wiped my face, tired beyond belief. "Even so, I feel terrible for the skinflint. You won't believe how vicious the gossips have been!"

He refilled my wine glass as I continued, "How many hours have Melinda and I wasted on fielding their questions? They think they're entitled to hear every salacious details. Tell me, was Tanny giving the guy head?'"

Ted flung his palm out. "Skip it. I get the picture. Besides, I've heard it all at the bar."

"Oh. Right." I shoved my plate away as my appetite had vanished. "Are Matt Bearus and Luke Winston prying you for details?"

"Nothing I can't handle. Do you want me to tell them to back off? Are they bugging you?"

"Everybody's bugging me," I mumbled.

"That's it." He rose from the table, stretching out his hand to me. "Come with me."

"Where are we going?"

Tugging me from the table down the hallway, he strode toward the bathroom. He opened both spigots, dumped in lavender salts then twirled his finger, indicating I should turn around. Smiling, he untucked my blouse then unzipped my skirt. I wiggled out of it then kicked it away from my ankles. He lifted the blouse over my head and massaged my back. An involuntary series of moans escaped me and my head lolled forward. His hands started to wander, as did mine. Within a few short panted breaths, we had tumbled into the tub filled with bubbles, laughing. Wet skin slid against wet skin and I straddled him as he held my hips in place, his head resting against the tub's rim. Hot and yet so sweet. It wasn't gentle. Afterward, we laughingly mopped the floor. He was forced to rush to dress for work, but at the front door, he spun around, a wide grin on his face.

"What?" I asked, startled by his sudden stop.

He jogged to me, lifted me until my feet dangled then squeezed me. He gave me another long, deep kiss before tapping on my nose. "Stay here tonight?"

"Yeah. Sure."

"Good." Then he gave me another quick, hard kiss and left.

I stood there, watching the front door for a long while before stirring. I cleared the table and did the dishes, the mindless tasks soothing. As I reflected on our dinner conversation, it struck me that Ted hadn't offered platitudes or advice or 'man-splained' the situation to me. He'd listened to my concerns, validated them. The huge grin on his face was the most un-playerlike thing I'd ever witnessed. By showing such enthusiasm, he had definitely surrendered the upper hand in the relationship. Funny how it didn't feel as if I had him in my power; no, it felt more like he'd enthralled me equally effectively. That heart stopping kiss before leaving? Those shudders when he'd come? They delighted me, turned me inside out and upside down.

"There's something about him that I can't seem to get enough of—and I'm beginning to suspect I never will." I spoke aloud, hoping my wry thoughts would coalesce once brought into the open.

Where was this thing with Ted heading? Would we end up married, living at El Rancho Costo Plenty? I shuffled from room to room, picturing the future. A little boy with dark hair, a little girl with curls and caramel eyes. Finishing the wine, I washed my glass, rinsed it then set it out to air dry.

Crawling into bed sometime later, my head filled with visions of family life, two things struck me in the solar plexus: the first was how afraid these notions made me—not that they would come true, but that that they might not. Fate had been such a little bitch to me, I more than half-expected her to pop my bubble of happiness. The second thing which hit me later was that while I worried about losing something I didn't have, I hadn't thought of the troubles at work.

I was determined to rest, even for a few hours. When Ted returned around three o'clock, I'd want to be awake and say 'hi' before we returned to sleep. When we were together, whether we were having sex or not, he made me feel like the real me, the one who wasn't hermetically sealed off from the rest of humanity. The one who laughed. The one who'd just mopped three inches of foamy bubbles from the bathroom floor.

I'm pretty sure the grin on my face matched the one I'd sent him off with.

**

Eight days after Mrs. Bronski's botched plan for revenge, Ted and I sat together in the same church where we'd gathered for Mrs. Cuttlebum's funeral. Luke, my official funeral buddy, sat on my other side. He'd teasingly tried to hold my hand, but Ted quirked his eyebrow at him so he dropped it. I rolled my eyes at both of them.

How bizarre that Tanny would so closely follow the older woman in death. I could imagine that toilet paper cozy tilted on Mrs. Cuttlebum's head, her eyes boggling behind her thick eyeglasses. Picturing the two women meeting in heaven, Tanny on the outside, St. Peter standing at the pearly gates, and Mrs. Cuttlebum peering at the new arrival from the inside, it was hard not to laugh. Conversation would be brief.

"Are you kidding me?" The olive cozy would tip in Tanny's direction as the former Vietnam nurse asked the Apostle.

St. Peter would shake his head, running his pencil down the roster, checking for Psycho's name on the roll.

"Look again," Tanny trailed her forefinger down St. Peter's clipboard, horning in on his job.

Mrs. Cuttlebum and St. Peter exchanged meaningful looks.

The gig was up.

St. Peter reached for a bell pull which had gone unnoticed then tugged it.

Tanny, now realizing what was about to happen, stepped backward and shook her head. "No. No."

Lowering her gaze, Mrs. Cuttlebum walked away, disappearing into the clouds as the lawyer stumbled then fell, her lips formed a wide circle, making a soundless scream.

"What's that?" Ted asked.

I hadn't realized I'd spoken the line aloud. Leaning closer to Ted, I whispered the Shakespearean quote, "And when he falls, he falls like Lucifer, never to hope again."

"Shh," he said, jerking his head toward the reverend, who'd just taken his place at the pulpit.

Nearly everyone in the legal community attended Tanny's funeral; I wondered if any had the decency to squirm for the mean-spirited things they'd said that week. Everyone maintained expressions which were appropriately dignified for the occasion, wonders of wonder.

Sam slumped on the front row, his brother's arm around his shoulder, his sister-in-law sitting next to Steve. My boss's head shone with perspiration, but that's all I could see of the fellow. Except for the brief visits to his house to get his signature on papers, I hadn't seen much of Sam since that dreadful dawn. Looking at the magnificent floral arrangement atop Tanny's casket, the corners of my mouth lifted. I applauded Sam taking the high road and sending his wife off in style. Sure, it might have been better than Tanny deserved, but Sam's generosity impressed me.

My attention turned to the reverend, different from the one who'd presided over Mrs. Cuttlebum's services. His reminiscences of the deceased weren't tinged with that underlying note of affection that Mrs. Cuttlebum received. The first part of his eulogy was little more than reading aloud the obituary. Apparently, Tanny had been unknown to him, which was hardly surprising, I suppose. I tried not to be miffed at his lack of professionalism, wryly noting attorneys' reputations for perfectionism were well-earned. Taking calming breaths, I sat through a diatribe about the wages of sin. That fodder might apply to the decedent, but she wasn't here and that condemnation didn't comfort anyone within the four walls of the church.

Angry for Sam's sake, I wanted to slap some duct tape across the reverend's mouth. He was heaping coals of shame onto Tanny's head, but it was Sam who was getting burnt. As miserable, cold, and calculating that he was, Sam didn't deserve that. He'd been humiliated him enough. Half the bar association mocked him for being cuckholded. I thought about walking out, but remained, glaring at the reverend instead. He finished sermonizing, made to sit down then returned to the podium to add this throwaway remark—"Let's pray for the soul of the dearly departed."

At this point, Matt Bearus had a choking fit. I cast a sideway glance at Luke, whose frame shook with smothered laughter. Neither could be glared into silence.

"Shut up," I hissed beneath my breath.

Seeing my scowl, both Luke and Matt sobered.

As we filed out of the pews, Ted muttered, "Pompous idiots."

He got it.

Jim Hedgmon approached, touched me on the arm. "I'm sorry, Cooper. If you need anything…"

Blinking back tears of anger, I thanked him.

Jim was a class act. Days after the funeral, I ran into him outside the bank of elevators at the courthouse.

"Hello, Cooper."

"Hi."

"How's Sam?"

My shrug must have conveyed something of my feelings because he answered with a knowing look and said nothing more. We stepped into the carpeted elevator and rode up in momentary silence.

"Anything from David Seltzer's tox screen and hair follicle?"

Jim slid his finger under the collar of his shirt, as if his tie were strangling him. "Bad news on that count, kid."

"What?"

Jim rolled his eyes. "Wilson's not gonna prosecute."

"Why not?"

"Discretionary judgment on her part—you know that, Coop."

"She's gonna let someone get away with murder?"

"I don't like it either, dammit, but Seltzer wasn't my case. It's Wilson's and she's not going to investigate his homicide."

"Because he did drugs." It wasn't a question.

Jim nodded his answer anyway.

"Apparently, that makes him a shitbag."

"No," Jim objected.

I glared at him a moment then muttered, "That sucks."

"I hope you make more eloquent arguments than that, counselor."

"Shut up," I said with a smile.

"You liked him, huh?"

"Yeah." Frowning, I said. "Yeah. I really did."

He paused a beat before concluding, "You must have some pretty shitty clients."

"You're pretty eloquent yourself."

We laughed.

"What about Lydia Sanderson?" I asked. "The rape victim on the Johnny Eaton case? What are you doing there?"

His lips firmed. "I'm going after that shitbag father of hers for First Degree Rape."

"Good, good."

He rubbed the back of his neck. "That is, as soon as I can find Lydia. She's dropped out of school and won't answer my subpoena. Hell, I even sent Jeff over to talk with her."

"Reluctant to testify, eh?"

"Guess so."

"But there's another daughter in the house…"

"Yeah. So I gotta move forward on the old man before he fucks that one, too, if he isn't already."

The elevator stopped at his floor and he muttered goodbye.

"Nail him to the wall, Jim."

His face grim, he gave me a nod before he stalked off. Jim Hedgmon was about to slay a dragon. On his own. Without his prime witness. It was like sending a knight into battle with a switchblade and Tupperware lid, not a broadsword and iron shield.

Impossible, our jobs. Fucking impossible.

Frustration made me punch the elevator buttons harder than warranted. With another lurch, it proceeded its upward climb to Judge Powers' courtroom where another unhappy pair waited for me to snip their bonds of matrimony.

"Where the hell are you, Lydia?"

Chapter 25

At Last Prayers

Ted planned a low-key date for us: dinner at Sheahan's and attending the first high school football game of the season.

The contrast between our first meeting at the restaurant and this one was marked. Before I'd felt like an outsider, staring in at the rest of the world. This time I joked with the waiter and talked with Ted. Through mystical osmosis, I had taken a sense of peace from Ted. Puzzling over why that should be, I dug into the onion rings. I glanced at Ted, who was laughing at something. He'd thrown his head back and I gazed at the tendons in his neck, the pulse at the base of his throat. My gaze slued away. The revelation struck like a thunderbolt.

Being with Ted was like coming home. I felt safe, secure, happy when we were together.

Ted sprang from his chair to thump my back, trying to help me dislodge the onion ring I'd choked on.

"You okay?"

Dabbing my watery eyes, I didn't think it was the right time to blurt out 'I love you,' so I managed to gasp, "Wrong pipe."

His shoulders leveled upon hearing the explanation, but he gave me an intent stare. With Ted's vaulted powers of observation I panicked that he might uncover my secret. Contrary to popular sentiment, newly discovered love does not need to be shouted from the rooftops.

That fickle finger of Fate flung a spanner into the spokes of my wheel. I needed time to ruminate, come to grips with this startling discovery. Well, I thought wryly, time and tequila. If sobriety couldn't lead me to the answers, Mother Inebriation surely would.

The liveliness of the evening drained away, leaving me inordinately quiet and restless, bending my elbow more than usual.

"Ready?" Ted asked, holding his hand toward me.

"Sure," I said, grabbing my bag and standing.

His eyes narrowed. "What's wrong?"

"Nothing. I'm just worrying over nothing."

"Relax, will ya?" We strolled to the parking lot, hand in hand. His thumb caressed my wrist in smooth, circular motions. "Wait till we get home. I think I know a few ways to make you relax."

Hot blood coursed through my veins. Where his hand was on my back tingled.

I pushed my anxieties aside as we chatted during the drive to the high school stadium. Yeah, maybe I realized in Sheahan's that I love Ted, but here's a detail that just registered: he wasn't letting me loose. Maybe the guy loved me back?

Walking through the crowd, Ted kept me close. We wended our way through the throng to take our seats without his hands leaving my body. The constant contact made me happy. Glowing from within, I felt as if I'd been lit on fire by a secret source of fuel.

We sat on the aluminum bench. I skimmed the top of his thigh, my hand trailing over the denim.

"Behave," he admonished, but the corner of an uplifted lip made a lie of his stern tone.

Maybe yes? I couldn't be a hundred percent sure, but it was starting to encourage me.

"Mrs. Bach?"

Reluctantly, I withdrew my hand from Ted's leg and looked at my former rape client, Johnny Eaton. He was so tall, I had to crane my neck to look at him. He wore a decorated letter jacket and scruffy blue jeans.

"Hey, Johnny. How's it going? Johnny Eaton, this is Ted Danveldt. Ted, Johnny," I introduced them. Scooting over to make space, I invited Johnny to join us.

The quarterback sat down, easing his long legs into the aisle. "You're looking good, Mrs. Bach." He pulled the bill of his baseball cap. "I heard about your partner, Mrs. Whilts. That was some nasty business."

I grimaced. "That's a good word for it."

"I'm sorry."

"Thank you."

"What are you gonna do now? Is the law firm gonna fold?" He pressed his hands together between his knees, as if he were cold.

"Too soon to tell. Tell me, what are you doing up here in the stands, Johnny? Shouldn't you be in uniform, prepping for the game?"

He shrugged.

I waited.

Ted stood. "I'm going to get us something to drink. You want anything, Johnny?"

"Could you bring me a Coke? That'd be great."

Johnny waved his hand. "Nothing for me, thanks."

"Come on. How 'bout a Coke or Dr. Pepper?"

Johnny said, "Yeah, okay. A Coke."

Ted clomped down the stadium steps, whistling.

"Serious now, Johnny? What's really going on?"

The blonde giant rubbed a finger over his nose. "Honestly?"

"Honestly."

He grimaced then leaned toward me, keeping his voice low. "Everyone knew I got arrested for raping Lydia."

"Yeah, but those charges were dismissed."

"Doesn't matter."

Frowning, I asked, "What do you mean?"

"Some folks figure where there's smoke, there's fire. I've been kicked off the football team."

"What? That's ridiculous! Don't they know Lydia's accusations were false?" I searched the stands, wanting to find that wretched girl and strangle her.

"Lydia quit school."

"What?"

He clasped his hands together, chafing them. "She's not here anymore. Nobody believes me when I try to tell them it was all a big lie."

"This is bullshit. Well, if Lydia won't tell the truth, then I will. I'll expl—"

"No, no. Don't do that."

"But I don't understand. You're completely innocent."

The teen didn't say anything, just fiddled with the hole in his jeans over his exposed knee.

"So the coach kicked you off the team?"

"Yeah. Some guys stood up for me—they believed me, but in the end, coach won." He shrugged, as if it wasn't a big deal for his world to fall to shit pieces.

"Aw, man. You didn't deserve that. Just wait'll I find Lydia. Where the hell is she? Jim Hedgmon, the prosecutor, is looking for her, too."

"I don't know."

Ted returned, balancing a tray with three drinks and some nachos. He gave me a questioning look, but I shook my head. This is something else we'd have to talk about later. Maybe I'd hit the tequila sooner than I'd expected.

Johnny took his drink, thanked Ted, and said, "I just saw you here and figured I'm come to say thanks and tell you goodbye."

"Why? Where are you going?"

"Moving to Dallas. Going to live with my aunt. I'll finish my junior and senior years down there."

"That's pretty drastic."

Johnny cut me off. "I want to. This last month showed me who my real friends were and some things can't be taken back. I want to go where I don't have this cloud hanging over me."

"Give it some time. This will pass."

He rubbed the back of his neck then nodded. "Yeah, I hear what you're saying. You're a smart woman, Mrs. Bach, but…"

"You feel betrayed and don't trust folks around here."

He faced me.

In his eyes, I understood his truth. Not able to argue something so fundamental and incontrovertible, I held out my hand.

Johnny shook it, then kissed my cheek. "Goodbye, Mrs. Bach."

"Goodbye, Johnny. Good luck and take care."

He'd already headed down the stadium steps, throwing a wave over his shoulder.

Ted handed me my Coke. "Here," he said, breaking his silence.

"Wow. That's so sad."

Digging a chip into the nachos, Ted said, "I give him credit. The kid's making the best of a bad situation."

"But look at all he's sacrificing! Starting quarterback, most popular guy in school—that's why Lydia picked him. She wanted folks to think a guy like would be interested in somebody like her."

"Let it go. This is for the best."

"No. I don't want to let it go. I want to find Lydia and demand that she clear Johnny's name."

"You're nuts." A faint whiff of surprise interlaced his declaration.

Ignoring him, I rambled, "She can put an ad in the newspaper. No, nobody reads those anymore. She can text the whole damned school, post it on YouTube,

Instagram, Snapchat, Twitter—tell everyone that Johnny is innocent."

"As God as your witness and you'll never go hungry again? You and Tara won't give up and will live to see better days?"

"You think I'm being over-dramatic? Don't you think Lydia should explain this to others?"

"No."

"She drove him out of town," I argued.

"Lydia lied. I get that. Her lies were damaging. I get that, too, but her lies covered up something really horrible that happened to her. Remember she's a victim here, too. With this move, Johnny should recover nicely and eventually, he's going to be fine. But Lydia will be troubled for the rest of her life. Let it go. There are no winners here."

Frowning at Johnny's departing figure, I wasn't sure how to accept this.

"You're a good lawyer, Cooper." Ted nudged me.

I didn't say anything, still internally wondering when the world had turned topsy-turvy.

He nudged me again.

Turning to him, I asked, "Why do you say that?"

Without a hint of humor on her face, he said, "Because you care."

"Anybody would."

"You're wrong. Tanny didn't and Sam probably wouldn't, either."

I searched the horizon. Johnny had disappeared.

"Where could Lydia be?" I wondered again.

Chapter 26

What are Pigs for?

Not surprisingly, the high school team lost without their star quarterback. It wasn't just any loss—it was a rout. I couldn't wipe the smirk off my face as we sauntered out of the stadium.

"Well, I hope the coach gets fired."

"Tanny," Ted tried to scold, but he was chuckling, too.

"Cici!" Somebody bellowed, but I didn't turn around.

"Do you know that guy?" Ted asked, pointing to the hairy man striding for us.

I groaned. "Lordie. That's Ed Abrams, a client. I call him Flotaki because…"

"Oh. I figured 'cause he had a toupee or something."

We exchanged wry looks. "Yeah, that'd have been good, too."

Ted swallowed his laugh as Flotaki approached us.

"Cici! Cici! How you doing?" Like a bull, Flotaki wrestled his way through the crowd, tagging his two kids behind him. A flurry of rat-a-tat-tats heralded the closely-following Louisa.

"Cici?" Ted asked, quirking his eyebrow at me again.

"Flotaki's never gotten my name right." I sighed.

"Hey. Glad to catch up with you," my client said, huffing and puffing to a standstill.

I said, "Hello, Mr. Abrams. Louisa. Some game, eh?"

"Are you kidding me? They got their asses kicked," Flotaki scoffed. "Goddamned sorry about that shooting spree in your office. Can't imagine what Caroline was thinking."

His two kids paled and shuffled closer to each other, huddled apart from Flotaki and Louisa.

Tugging Flotaki's sleeve to draw him away, I whispered, "Let's talk of their earshot."

Ignoring my none-too-subtle hint, he said, "Go ahead and file for the divorce. She'll be in prison the rest of her life, I suppose."

The little girl started crying.

"Here, now, little one." Ted said, pulling a quarter from her ear. "Did you know you had money in you?"

"That's a magic trick," her brother accused.

"Course it is," Ted agreed. "Wanna see how I do it?"

The boy's curiosity overcame his hostility. Wordlessly, he motioned Ted to show him how he'd performed the trick and Ted complied, taking their attention off their father's conversation.

I hissed at Flotaki, "What the hell's wrong with you?"

"What do you mean?"

"Don't talk about their stepmom going to prison. That's painful for them. Shit, where's your empathy? You're their father."

"I wasn't telling the kids, I was telling you. It's the truth, ain't it? Say, I wanna ask if I can hire you to represent Caroline."

"What?"

"In the murder charge," he clarified.

Dumbstruck, I had no response to such a colossally horrible suggestion.

"Hey." He snapped his fingers in front of my face, as if I were the idiot in this scenario. "You're still my lawyer, ain't ya?"

"Tanny was your lawyer, but she's dead now. She's dead because your wife killed her, remember?"

He shook his head, as though trying to rid himself of an annoying gnat. "Yeah, well, that's why I'm asking."

"Do you intend to hire an attorney to defend Caroline?"

"Sure. Louisa says it's the least I can do." He grinned at his ex-wife then waggled his fingers at her.

Bile rose in me. I wanted to puke.

"Well, I wouldn't want the case, and I seriously doubt if Caroline would want me as her defense counsel, anyway." Feeling calmed by that assessment, I ventured further. "By the way, I should probably get out of your case, too."

He waved his hand. "Oh, don't worry about that. Louisa and I are living together now, anyway."

"Of course you are." I smiled without humor. "Caroline's been gone...what? A week?"

"Yeah," he said, missing my sarcasm.

"Fine. Tell Louisa to ask Matt Bearus to withdraw her motion. Then have her ask him for a lawyer referral for Caroline. I'm done here."

As I pivoted away, he stopped me by grabbing my forearm. "Why are you being such a bitch?"

"A bitch?" My voice raised an octave.

Louisa called out, "What's the matter, Ed?"

"Cici's trying to drop me." He expressed his disbelief by thumbing my direction.

"Really?" She asked, amazed. "Why?"

Flotaki answered, "Yeah, and she's being pretty bitchy about it, too."

I stared from him to her then back again. "Are you out of your fucking mind?"

"Cooper," Ted warned.

Shoving my sleeves up to my elbows, I was just starting to warm up. "No. Really. I mean it. Are you out of your goddamned minds? Because you—" I flung an accusing finger at Flotaki. "Were screwing around with her,—" I pointed at Louisa. "Caroline was driven to murder. My boss was murdered. Why the hell would I work for you?"

My angry bellow lingered in the cool night air as Flotaki and Louisa glowered at me, utterly gobsmacked.

Ted's muffled voice penetrated my red haze. "Cooper—"

The little girl was crying again. I slowly came aware of her wails as I glanced in Ted and the children's direction.

Flotaki sneered, "Well, ain't you Miss High and Mighty?"

"Well!" Louisa huffed. "You have no right to treat us that way! No right! How dare you speak to us like that? Who the fuck do you think you are? You were hired by Ed to do a job for him, but there's plenty more attorneys he can hire. Who the fuck are you?"

"Yeah!" Flotaki joined in, his ex-wife/new girl-friend's indignation setting his own aflame. "Who the fuck do you think you are, Princess?"

Forgetting Ted, forgetting the kids, forgetting the public parking lot, I answered. "WHO AM I? WHO AM I? I'll tell you who I am, you low-down, rotten, hairy beast of a boy-child! I am somebody, unlike you and the cheap tart you're with, who can manage to keep my pants zipped! Try it sometime. It's called self-control!" I threw out that last helpful pointer just for the hell of it.

Louisa made a sound then dashed away. Flotaki grabbed each kid by the arm then they followed the tart.

Even as they ran away, I raised my fist and in true Scarlett O'Hara fashion yelled, "IT'S WHAT ADULTS DO!"

"Jesus, Coop." Ted rubbed his forehead.

***

It was my turn to take Luke and Matt out for burgers. I had some spare cash burning a hole in my pocket. Night court was turning the tide for me, financially speaking. Thank God traffic cops wrote speeding tickets.

"So?" I showed them the letter I'd received earlier that day, the reason I'd been freaking out and called the war counsel.

"You fired a client in a high school parking lot?" Luke read Louisa's written allegations, enclosed with the letter from the Disciplinary Administrator's office asking for my side of the story. I had seven days to respond.

Matt read the letter then laughed. "You dropped the f-bomb in front of kids?"

I toyed with my straw. "I just lost it."

They grimaced in unison.

"That bad?"

Luke sighed, placing the letter on the tabletop, away from the ketchup. "Losing your temper with a client isn't unethical. Not smart, but not unethical."

"There's no law that can compel people to behave civilly." Matt lifted his top bun, drizzled ketchup onto his burger then shoved it into his mouth.

"But I have to respond?"

"Of course you do," Luke said.

"Well, what should I say? How should I say it?" I removed my pickles, tossed them onto Luke's plate.

He collected them, nodding his thanks.

"Scrape and bow," Matt said around a mouthful of burger. He wiped his chin. "Explain you're stressed from Tanny's death and carrying the work load of three lawyers. Say you're sorry and that'll be the end of it."

Biting my bottom lip, I reluctantly admitted I meant every word I said.

Matt grinned. "I'm sure you did. Did you really call him a 'fucktard?'"

"No," I said irritably. "That's just something Louisa embellished. I don't want to apologize. Makes me feel like I'm taking it back and I meant every word I said."

"Of course you're taking it back. Your ass is in a sling. Choke a bit on humble pie, if you have to, curse him under your breath and write the damn four-page letter to the Administrator."

The hamburger tasted like sawdust. I gulped some soda, hoping to wash it down my suddenly arid throat.

"I take it you've withdrawn from his case?" Luke asked.

I shook my head.

"That's the first thing you want to do. Don't give a reason for it, just move to withdraw. Set it for hearing, send him a copy."

"'kay."

"What would you have done in my situation?" I asked Luke, the oldest of the three of us.

He wiped his mouth with the paper napkin. "You really want to know?"

I could tell that was my warning shot and whatever followed, I wouldn't like. Sighing, I confessed, "Yeah, I really want to know."

"I'd given him the name of an expensive criminal defense attorney, wished him and his a pleasant evening, gone home, and gotten drunk."

That made me smile. The first smile since I'd received the Disciplinary Administrator's letter. Slitting the envelope, pulling out the sheet of ivory paper and reading below the golden, embossed seal made me feel like I'd swallowed ten thousand nails, one at a time. The only thing comparable to getting a letter like that would be one that started off, "Greetings from your Draft Board."

"Not hungry?" Matt asked, eyeing the rest of my meal.

Shaking my head, I pushed my plate towards him and he scooped up the hamburger and finished it in a couple of bites. I watched, stunned. "God, you're a pig."

Matt tutted, wagging his finger in front of my nose. I slapped it away.

"If this situation with Flotaki and Skank has taught you anything, it should teach you to watch your manners."

I grinned. "Shuddup."

He ate in silence while I forced myself to gather the courage to ask my next question. Looking out the grease-smeared window, I strove for nonchalance. "What's likely to happen once I respond with the scrape and bow routine?"

Matt laughed. "Nothing."

"Nothing? I won't lose my license or get suspended or something?"

"Shit, Coop. It's not like you slept with your clients or stole their money. That'll get your ticket punched for sure. What you did was mouth off to an asshole. The panel isn't going to care about that shit. Hell, we've all wanted to do it at some point in our careers."

I looked towards Luke for reassurance. "Serious?"

"Yeah, you might get an ass-chewing. Your punishment is the groveling letter you're forced to write."

He jabbed his finger on the formica to press his point. "So make sure it's sincere and humble."

"Got it."

"In all fairness, I have to tell you they could lower the boom on you, maybe with a censure or something of that sort, but I doubt it. You weren't lawyering at the time of the incident, which actually works in your favor. Had this happened in your office or, God forbid, Court, we might see a different outcome."

I cringed, "But I called him names in front of his kids."

Matt waved it away. "You think his wife hasn't done that? Hell, his kids probably have heard it all."

Luke stood up then said, "Write a draft. Email it to me and I'll get back to you with any changes."

"Really? Thanks."

He gave a wry smile. "What are buddies for?"

Matt snatched a handful of fries from my plate and shoved them into his mouth. "Do I need to leave a tip?"

Luke held the door open for me and hollered back, "Yeah, you pig."

Chapter 27

Night Visitors

They came to me with their arms open wide. Loving lights shone in their eyes, their smiles warm on brightened faces lit by some other-worldly light. I strained to embrace them, but the tips of my fingers never could quite touch them. My father held his hand out, as if wishing to clasp mine, but an unbridgeable distance prevented it.

Oddly, I didn't feel disappointment. I felt elated by the sight of my dad and sister. My father looked like a young man, his hair showed no signs of graying and there were no wrinkles to his face. He was more youthful than I remembered. Gloria hadn't changed, but she also had never looked so beautiful. Her smile revealed sparkling eyes and gleaming teeth as an invisible breeze lifted the strands of her hair until they flowed.

"Oh, I've missed you both so much!"

Gloria's beatific smile never faltered, but she remained quiet.

"We're so proud of you," Dad said without words.

"Thanks, Dad. I love you."

I felt them return my love then a wondering…

"I'm fine." Startled by the realization, I discovered what I said was true.

Their presence imbued me with a sense of tranquility and the conviction that everything in my world would be all right.

Dad nodded. I could almost hear him say the words, "Of course."

Then he smiled, took my sister's hand and she said—again without words, "You go be happy, Coop."

"Don't leave!"

Hand in hand, Dad and Gloria faced me, surprised by the sudden urgency. They both reassured me. "You'll be fine. Besides, it's not as if we'll go anywhere right away…we're gonna hang around a bit."

"Oh, good," I breathed, but they'd already faded to white mists.

***

Soft murmurings tickled my ear. My sleep-warmed body willingly conformed to the heated planes of Ted's hard body. Strong arms curled about my waist as his mouth passed over my skin and left a trail of sparks. Snuggling deeper into the embrace, sounds of contentment left my throat.

Although I didn't have the courage to say, 'I love you,' my body expressed those sentiments with as much thoroughness as I could muster. Our lovemaking progressed, building slowly with a new element to it, something which was reverent.

"Every time I kiss you," Ted said between nibbles, "It just keeps getting better. Every time we make love, it gets hotter and hotter."

I smiled. After receiving the highest compliment of my life, how was I supposed to respond?

He laid his palm against my cheek, cradling it. "I love you, Cooper Bach."

"You do?" A wave of heat crept into my face until the tips of my ears burned with pleasure.

"Yes, I do."

"When? When did you know?"

He gave me that tilted, wicked grin of his. "The moment you stepped into my bar then scoffed when I said I was a Boy Scout. You were so…"

"Pissy?" I fluttered my lashes.

Recalling his descriptor, he flashed another grin. "Aggravating. Yeah, but when you dashed out without your purse and I stood over you holding that damn umbrella, all I knew was I had to kiss you. I had to."

"I love you, too. I don't know if I can exactly pinpoint the time I fell in love because it seemed so gradual, but I've definitely loved you a while now."

"Forgive me? For leaving?"

"I don't think that's the right word—forgive." I frowned, concentrating on how to express emotions too big for mere words.

Ted drew away, his frown matching mine.

Shaking my head, I explained, "There's nothing to forgive. I understood why you distanced yourself-God knows, I've recalled your words a hundred times. And you were right. I needed some space to get back to me."

"All I want is for you to be happy and well." He leaned against the pillows, pulling me next to his side. Silence passed as I laid my ear against his chest, listening to his heartbeat.

"I am."

"Well, I'm not," he said shortly.

Half-rising on a bended elbow, I gave him a questioning look.

"When are you going to make an honest man of me?"

I snorted with laughter. Cool, Coop.

Ted didn't seem to mind. He flipped over and laid on top of me bracketing my hands above my head and mock-threatened, "You have to marry me. I'll make you an offer you can't resist."

"Wha… what's your offer?"

"Marry me. Make me the happiest of men." His mien was serious, gone was the lackadaisical Ted.

"Sounds tempting." I caught my breath as he lowered his head and attached his mouth to one of my nipples. He drew it deeply into his mouth, so deep I shuddered.

"That's not all," he said, moving his attention to the other breast.

I moaned, "There's more?"

Kneeing my thighs apart, he gave me that slow, devilish grin. "Oh yeah."

With a single plunge, he was deeply sheathed inside me, hissing in relief. My inner muscles worked to take him further as we matched rhythm. He set the tempo and I followed. Unhurried, intense. He penetrated to my core, causing my breath to hitch as we climbed that mountain of passion and hurled off the summit.

I closed my eyes, seeing stars burst on the back of my lids. His eyes squeezed shut when pleasure cascaded over him and then he tumbled after me. The universe shrank to the spot where we joined and we left everything else behind in the ordinary world.

I groaned, a delicious languid feeling weighing my limbs.

Golden brown eyes blazed, silently asking for my answer. In a hoarse voice, he asked, "Was that a yes?"

"Absolutely, yes." Even as I spoke the words of acceptance, an icy fist gripped my gut and twisted. Placing my happiness in someone else hadn't been wise. Was I being foolish now? "Except for—"

"Oh, God. I can already tell you're about to aggravate me again." He rolled off the bed and strolled to the bathroom, not an ounce embarrassed at showing his mighty fine ass.

"I don't mean to be aggravating," I protested.

"Yes. You do."

I sat up in bed, pulling the covers around me, chilled now. Looking at the yellow sheets, I remembered how elated I'd been when I'd found them. Part of the reason I'd rejoiced was because they were so damned cheerful. Was I over-analyzing this marriage proposal? Couldn't I just accept the offer, traipse down the aisle and look forward to happily ever after?

"What are you so afraid of?" He leaned against the door jamb. Obviously, he'd just splashed water on his face, droplets shone in his hair. Ted had draped a towel about his waist. In self-protection?

"I don't really know."

"What? That'll I'll die, too? That we'll divorce? What?"

"Yes. Yes to both. You see, I don't want to lose you, too. I don't think I could stand losing you, whichever way."

Most men would have screamed in frustration, but Ted Danveldt wasn't like most men. That signature smile flashed. His caramel eyes glowed with a warmth that set my anxieties to rest. Kneeling in front of me, he squeezed both my hands. "Listen to me. Know this: I will never leave you. Never."

I started to argue, but he cut me off, smiling and shaking his head. "If the Grim Reaper comes for me, I won't answer, okay? I choose to remain with you. I'm never going to agree to a divorce and I'll never regret marrying you. I choose you. I will *always* choose you. Clear?"

It was exactly what I needed to hear. "Yes."

He held me close and rubbed soothing circles on my back. "You will never be alone again, Cooper. I promise you that. We're going to have beautiful babies and grow old together and make love four times a week."

"Four?"

He chuckled. "All right. Six times a week. Damn, you drive a hard bargain."

I giggled too hard to protest.

Chapter 28

Lord Byron Again

I strolled into work late with a bounce in my step and a grin on my face. A pleasant heat still at my center from Ted's spicy lovemaking of the morning.

Immediately, Melinda knew something was up. A slow smile stretched across her face as her painted eyebrows inched up her forehead. "Uh-oh, I know that look," Melinda teased.

"I hope so."

She waggled her eyebrows. "That good, eh?"

"Ted asked me to marry him."

Like tires at Talladega, Melinda squealed. In the small space of a heartbeat, she'd moved from her chair and hugged me. Laughing at her exuberance, we completely ignored the demands of the office and conversed at length about reception places, wedding colors, and the like. I asked her to be my bridesmaid, which set off another round of squeals.

After a while, we finally decided to get to work and I skipped to my office. Before delving into the cases littering my desk, it struck me that after all those long, long months of mourning, I felt euphoric. As if after swimming in turbulent waters, I'd finally reached the shore and had been welcomed into a meadow filled with fragrant flowers. In a flash of insight, I finally understood why Dad had selected 'Ode of Joy' for Gloria's funeral.

In the afternoon, Melinda and I were scheduled to meet Sam at his house. I'd hoped Sam would tell us he'd be returning soon. Handling all the cases was exhausting. Every Monday morning we fielded several phone calls from divorce clients, accusing their soon-to-be ex of violating custody exchange rules over the weekend. Barraged with whines like, 'He got out of the car and came to the front porch! The front porch!' or 'She was twenty-five minutes late. Do you think she could have called or text? No. The stupid bitch.' or 'He brought his girlfriend to the police station!'

Was I an attorney or a schoolyard monitor? Tattle-tale brats tugging at my skirt for attention—that's the nature of the divorce client. I had to take care not to consider one client the more stupid person on the face of the earth, because sure enough—another would waltz into my office and claim the distinction. I was discovering daily the existence of a newer, lower order.

I couldn't wait to shove some of these cases back onto Sam again.

Sam and Tanny's house stood atop a slight incline, something which almost constituted a hill in the flat lands of Kansas. It was costly and sophisticated, an English Tudor with dark paneling and furniture. Comfort was secondary to formality. In the living room two tapestry settees flanked a marble fireplace, but the footstool was covered in a cross-stitch that disinvited anyone to actually rest the soles of their feet upon it. Original art work hung in gilded frames beneath accent lights made of brass, lending the room all the warmth of a museum. Tanny hadn't made a home; she'd organized a showplace.

Steve led us to the kitchen, surprising me of its modern lines. Apparently, Tanny hadn't cared to be inconvenienced here. The white kitchen with stainless steel appliances and black granite countertops seemed sterile, unfriendly in a different way than the living room, but not a comfortable house by any stretch.

Sam hailed us from the back yard and Steve took us to him. The patio was laid with red brick laid in a herringbone pattern, again in keeping with the formality of the exterior. The cost for constructing this outdoor living area probably exceeded my monthly income by six or seven times. I remembered how he'd chipped in the forty dollars for the funeral bills.

Sam greeted us then poured pink lemonade as Steve's wife served us finger sandwiches and cucumber slices. After the snack was eaten, Steve and his wife cleared the dishes and left.

"This is awkward for me." Sam cleared his voice.

"Take your time," Melinda said.

I remained silent, dreading whatever news he was about to impart. Sam hadn't given me a whole lot of reasons to like him—I didn't think that was going to change after sharing finger sandwiches and cucumber slices.

Sam touched his now-perspiring forehead.

With her well-honed maternal instincts, Melinda squeezed his hand.

Like Slim Pickens riding the bombshell all the way to the crash site, he jumped in with, "I'm closing shop."

Melinda made a sound, which I couldn't interpret, being too dazed.

"What did you say?" My voice sounded distant.

"I'm retiring from the practice of law and closing shop."

"Oh," said Melinda.

"I've been wanting to walk away for a while now, but we couldn't afford it. Now I'm going to take the life insurance money and move away. Start a new life. I don't want to be miserable anymore."

There was a pause.

Melinda recovered first. Gripping his shoulder, she urged him, "You do that, Sam. You're entitled to some happiness."

Not sure I shared that sentiment, I sat there and drank the rest of my pink lemonade.

"I've already talked with Luke Wilson. He'd like to offer you both jobs at his firm," Sam said.

That surprised me.

"Could you remain with me for two more weeks? We need to re-assign cases, move the equipment to the new firm or sell it and give him the proceeds."

"Sure," I said. Two weeks wasn't going to kill me.

Sam told Melinda, "Transfer the insurance policies, malpractice, worker's comp, health—all that." He waved his hand in the air, too distracted to be specific.

"Luke practices real estate law," I said, wondering if I'd be working domestic cases there.

Sam nodded. "Yeah. You should finish your divorce cases, but after that, I think he'll have you handle the normal associate caseload. It's a good crew."

"What about wages?" It felt gauche for asking, but my budget was still tight, despite the night court work I'd picked up.

A red flushed crossed his cheekbones. "He's already told me it'd be negotiated, but it'll be more than what we paid."

Clamping my mouth shut so that I wouldn't spew out, "It'd pretty much have to be," I clenched my fists.

Sam looked straight at me then whispered, "You know. I didn't get it, but now I do."

Realizing he was referring to the mysterious process of grieving that was daily unfolding to him, I nodded. I plunged in with this hard-won advice. "Not today and not tomorrow, but eventually your grief will turn. It's an uphill climb, but your grief will turn."

"Has yours?" Sam asked. For the first time in our acquaintance, his eyes expressed a look of concern. Pain will humble a person, I suppose.

Patting the back of his hand, I replied, "Yes, it has."

"Good for you, Coop."

Out of his back pocket, he withdrew two envelopes, giving one to Melinda and one to me. We took them and by mutual agreement, tucked them away. Melinda said her goodbyes with a few tears shed between them both. She reminded Sam to leave her a forwarding address and asked what he wanted to do with his own health insurance policy.

"Cancel it," he said. "I won't need it where I'm going."

"Where are you going?" I asked.

His face broke into a rare grin. "Rio de Janeiro." Sam closed out our luncheon by giving us fierce hugs and because of what has passed between us, that moment of shared understanding, it didn't feel weird, but totally natural.

Driving back to the office, I mused aloud, 'Fare thee well! And if forever, Still forever, fare thee well.'

"What's that supposed to mean?" Melinda asked.

I shrugged. "I think Sam's gonna—what's the matter?"

Melinda had opened her envelope and gasped. "Oh Lordie, Lordie, Jesus!"

"What? What?"

Her hands fluttered about her chest, but all she managed was, "Oh Lordie!" She flapped the paycheck in front of me. Sam had paid her a ten thousand dollars bonus and in the Memo section he'd written, 'Thank you for your many kindnesses.'

"Oh Lordie!"

I handed it back and grinned. "You deserve it. Every penny."

Mine was substantially less, but that was only fair. Melinda had put up with Psycho and Satan much longer than I had. At any rate, I was tickled that I'd even gotten a bonus. Maybe Sam was letting go of his some of his stinginess. I hoped he'd be happy in Rio de Janeiro. I sincerely hoped so.

Epilogue

"Mrs. Bach?"

"Mrs. Danveldt," I corrected the young college graduate. We shook hands in the lobby of Wilson, Danvelt & Spade.

"You represented my grandmother once, Irene Cuttlebum. Came to her funeral, remember?"

The distant memory of Mrs. Cuttlebum, the old lady with the toilet paper cozy for a hat came to mind. Digging a little deeper, I remembered meeting a gangly teen at Mrs. Cuttlebum's house. He'd been chewing an apple. "Yes! I remember. How are you, Brandon?"

"Fine, fine. Just graduated K-State a few months ago."

"What was your major?"

"Architecture."

I smiled. "You knew even back when I first met you that you wanted to be an architect, didn't you?"

"Yeah."

"Would you like something to drink?"

"Sure. Coke, if you got any," he said.

"Two cokes, Melinda. Say, do you remember Mrs. Cuttlebum? This is her grandson, Brandon."

Melinda greeted him then returned with the two drinks, saying it was nice to see him again.

I led him into my nicely furnished office. Brandon sat on the cream sofa and I took my seat in the leather chair.

He looked a little nervous. Wiping his palms on the top of his thighs, he said, "So you're married now?"

"Yes, to Ted Danveldt. He owns the bar 'Tipping Cows' and the restaurant 'Sheahans.' We've got two boys and a little girl."

"That's great."

"Thank you. So you're an architect?"

"Yeah. I'm on the prelim team for Stinson & Zuckerman," he said, naming a prominent architectural firm from the city.

I nodded, wondering if he had a zoning question or some sort to ask.

He explained, "We're building a three-level shopping mall on Tenth and Maple."

"Oh, good!"

"Yeah," he smiled briefly. "The pylons are pretty tall, you know. So we're setting the footings. I'm on site two days ago to see to the preliminary work—soil testing, trenching—" He waved, indicating there was more. "It's my first day on the job. Anyway, we dug up a body."

"Oh. Wow."

"Yeah. About fifteen feet down."

"What did you do?"

"Called the coroner. She had it picked up within a couple of hours, but now the site's been shut down to investigate. The lead detective told me it looked like it might take another week to ten days."

"That's going to put you behind schedule," I said.

"Yeah," he agreed.

"Have you talked with the coroner today?"

"Yeah. This morning they scanned the dental records of missing persons. Said the victim was a teenage girl named Lydia Sanderson."

Gooseflesh rose on the surface of my arms, a sickening pit swelling in my stomach. "Oh, God. I knew her."

"You did?"

"Oh, man."

Brandon squirmed. "I was hoping you could tell me what has to happen next. The coroner told me to talk with the detective, but he never returns my phone calls. I wondered if I should contact the family?"

"No, no. The coroner will do that. The family will take possession of the body after it's been autopsied."

"I'd like to know how she died—I mean, I know. I just want to know—"

"How do you know how she died, Brandon?"

He grimaced. "There was a huge crack in her skull. Her arm was broken, too. We found it several feet away from the grave. In fact, that's what we found first—her arm."

"Man! You had a lousy first day of a job."

"Yeah." He rubbed the back of his neck. "I just…it's, I guess, curiosity, but—"

"You want to find out who did this to her and why, right?"

"Yeah, it's been bugging me and I wanted some answers. The girl deserves that much."

"Agreed. I can call the DA's office and see if they'll open a case once the findings are back from the coroner's office. That may take a few weeks," I cautioned.

"Sure. Let me know if there are any charges for this."

No way was I going to charge him. It wouldn't take too much effort on my part. As strange as it seemed, I felt honor-bound to see the end of Lydia's saga. From what he'd said, it sounded like murder. From what I remembered about her father's molestation, he was the most likely suspect. Searching through my memory, the timing certainly seemed to square with that conclusion. I remember Jim Hedgmon being furious that the girl had vanished. Even Johnny Eaton had said she'd dropped out of school. Why hadn't we suspected foul play then?

"No charges, Brandon. Thanks for the information. I'll call you as soon as I know more. Take care now."

He shook my hand once again. "Glad I found you. I know you'll do the right thing."

After he left, I stood there a while longer then slowly walked back to my desk and called home.

"Hey," Ted said.

"Hi. Hey, I'm gonna have to work late tonight."

"Okay."

"Yeah, I need to call Jim Hedgmon and take him out for a beer. An old case we worked on years ago has just reared its ugly head. We thought our teen victim had left town, but now her body's been discovered."

"Oh?"

"Yeah. I suspect it may be a homicide, so that's why I gotta meet with him."

"Bring him to the bar. I'll ask Mom and Dad to watch the kids."

"Thanks."

"They love spending time with the rugrats, anyway," he said.

"I know. Oh, and remind them to give Gloria her allergy medicine."

"Got it."

"Ted?"

"Hmm?"

"I love you."

"I love you, too."

Not willing to let him off the marital hook that easily, I pressed. "Ted, if you had it to do all over again, would you still choose me?"

Silence beat before I could sense his crooked grin over the phone.

"Every time, Coop."

"Me, too."

I smiled as I hung up, giving thanks for the blessings in my life.

Made in the USA
Middletown, DE
16 January 2017